Russian Writers on Russian Writers

Russian Writers on Russian Writers

Edited by
Faith Wigzell

BERG
Oxford/Providence USA

First published in 1994 by
Berg Publishers
Editorial offices:
150 Cowley Road, Oxford, OX4 1JJ. UK
221 Waterman Street, Providence, RI 02906, USA

Library of Congress Cataloging-in-Publication Data
A catalogue record for this book is available from the British Library.

British Library Cataloguing in Publication Data
A catalogue record for this book is available from the British Library.

ISBN 0 85496 942 X

Printed in the United Kingdom by Short Run Press, Exeter.

Contents

Notes on Contributors   vii

Writers on Writers: Introductory Essay   ix
Robin Aizlewood and Faith Wigzell

1. Familiar Solidarity and Squabbling: Russia's   1
   Eighteenth-Century Writers   *W. Gareth Jones*

2. Fet on Tiutchev   *Robin Aizlewood*   15

3. Chekhov and Merezhkovskii   *Stephen le Fleming*   27

4. Shestov on Chekhov   *Malcolm Jones*   39

5. Gumilev's Reviews of Viacheslav Ivanov's   51
   Cor Ardens: Criticism as a Tool in the Polemics of Literary
   Succession   *Pamela Davidson*

6. Missing Links: Russian Women Writers as Critics   67
   of Women Writers   *Catriona Kelly*

7. Marina Tsvetaeva as Literary Critic and Critic of   81
   Literary Critics   *Sibelan Forrester*

8. Air. Suffocation. Muteness: Akhmatova, Mandel´shtam,   99
   Pasternak and Tsvetaeva   *Anatoly Naiman*

9. Joseph Brodsky on Marina Tsvetaeva   *Henry Gifford*   117

10. Nabokov and Dostoevskii: Aesthetic Demystification   131
    Nora Buhks

11. The Myth of the Poet and the Poet of the Myth: 139
    Russian Poets on Brodsky   *Valentina Polukhina*

12. Trifonov on Dostoevskii   *David Gillespie*   161

13. Zinov´ev on Chekhov   *Michael Kirkwood*   169

Index   187

Notes on Contributors

Robin Aizlewood is Lecturer in Russian Language and Literature at the School of Slavonic and East European Studies, University of London. He is the author of *Verse Form and Meaning in the Poetry of Vladimir Maiakovskii* (1989) and articles on nineteenth- and twentieth-century Russian literature.

Nora Bukhs teaches at the Sorbonne. She is the author of *Le Journalisme de la Perestroïka: les techniques du renouveau* (1988) and editor of *Les Médias en URSS à l'heure de la glasnost* (*Revue des Études Slaves*, vol. 52, no. 3, 1990) and *Vl. Nabokov et l'Emigration* (*Cahiers de l'émigration russe*, no. 2, 1993). She has written numerous articles on eighteenth- and twentieth-century Russian literature, particularly on Nabokov.

Pamela Davidson is Lecturer in Russian Language and Literature at the School of Slavonic and East European Studies. She is the author of *The Poetic Imagination of Vyacheslav Ivanov* (1989) and the editor of *Posviashchaetsia Akhmatovoi*, an anthology of poems dedicated to Akhmatova (1991). She is currently preparing an annotated bibliography of criticism of Ivanov.

Stephen le Fleming is Lecturer in Russian at Durham University. He is especially interested in the relationship between Chekhov and his contemporary critics.

Sibelan Forrester is Assistant Professor of Russian Literature at Oberlin College, Ohio. She received her Ph.D. from Indiana University in 1990 on the topic of Marina Tsvetaeva's self-definition as a female poet. She has published an article in the *Slavic Review* and given several papers on Tsvetaeva and other women writers and Silver Age topics at Slavists' conferences.

Henry Gifford was formerly Winterstoke Professor of English, University of Bristol. His publications include *The Novel in Russia* (1964), *Tolstoy* (1982) and *Pasternak: A Critical Study* (1977, reissued 1991).

David Gillespie teaches Russian language and literature at Bath University. He has published several articles on post-war Russian literature; his book *Iurii Trifonov: Unity through Time* was published in 1992.

Malcolm Jones has been Professor of Slavonic Studies at the University of Nottingham since 1980 and is best known for his studies of Dostoevskii. He has also written on other issues in the fields of Russian and comparative literature, literary theory and the history of ideas in Russia.

W. Gareth Jones is Reader in Russian at the University of Wales, Bangor. His publications include *Nikolay Novikov: Enlightener of Russia* (1984) as well as numerous articles on eighteenth-century Russian literature.

Catriona Kelly is Lecturer in Russian Language and Literature at the School of Slavonic and East European Studies. She is the author of *A History of Russian Women's Writing, 1820–1992* (1994), editor of *An Anthology of Russian Women's Writing, 1777–1992* (1994) and author of numerous articles on Russian literature and popular culture.

Michael Kirkwood is Professor in Slavonic Languages and Literatures at the University of Glasgow. His main research interests are in applied linguistics (language planning and second-language pedagogy) and the writer Alexander Zinov´ev. He is the editor of *Language Planning in the Soviet Union* (1988) and the author of *Alexander Zinoviev: An Introduction to his Work* (1993).

Anatoly Naiman is a writer and poet living in Moscow. He is the author of *Remembering Akhmatova* (Russian version, 1989, English version, 1991), *Poems of Anatoly Naiman* (1988) and *The Commander's Statue and Other Stories* (1992).

Valentina Polukhina is Reader in Russian at Keele University. She specialises in modern Russian poetry and is the author of several studies of Brodsky, including *Joseph Brodsky: a Poet for Our Time* (1989) and *Brodsky Through the Eyes of His Contemporaries* (1992). She is also co-editor, with Lev Lossev, of *Brodsky's Poetics and Aesthetics* (1990).

Faith Wigzell is Senior Lecturer in Russian Language and Literature at the School of Slavonic and East European Studies. She is co-editor with Jane Grayson of *Nikolai Gogol´: Text and Context* and the author of a study of the fourteenth-century hagiographer Epifanii Premudryi and numerous articles on nineteenth-century literature and popular culture.

Writers on Writers: Introductory Essay

Robin Aizlewood and Faith Wigzell

The title of this collection rests on one of the words commonly used to link writers, the preposition 'on'. Much more typically, however, writers are simply linked by the conjunction 'and', which is all-encompassing in its scope and has generated any number of critical studies, from brief notes through articles up to books. The conjunction is as open in its possible implications in this context as it is in such titles as *Fathers and Sons* and *Sons and Lovers*. One thinks almost immediately of Tolstoi and Dostoevskii; then there is Pushkin and Byron, Turgenev and Henry James, Gumilev and Akhmatova, and so on. The pairings and permutations are endless; they may derive from critical perception and/or be prompted by one or other (or both) of the writers concerned. Moreover, in all cases the order could be reversed. The resulting difference of approach or perception might vary in significance and magnitude, but potentially it would be there: somehow George Steiner's *Tolstoy and Dostoevsky* would not be quite the same with the title the other way round.[1] In general, the approach adopted reflects the preoccupations of the period or individual scholar, critic, or reader, from biographical through comparative and intertextual to questions of influence. The scope of 'and' can extend to a study of writers from different periods and languages. It could even – in fact quite easily – extend to writers who knew nothing of each other. This, however, would not be possible for 'on'. Not only must the first writer know of the second, but also must have expressed an opinion (a recorded opinion) about the other; there is a unilinear directionality about writer 'on' writer which writer 'and' writer does not have. The preposition's scope is contained within that of the conjunction and at first sight seems much more specific: it defines the writer as critic.

While the initial definition implied by 'on' might seem simple and straightforward enough, in a whole number of ways its implications are quite diverse and its demarcation far from discrete. To start with, the

1. George Steiner, *Tolstoy and Dostoevsky,* London, 1959.

writer as critic can be defined, or addressed, as an aspect of the writer as reader, with all that this implies in the context of the widespread orientation towards the reader in modern literary theory. Furthermore, questions concerning the status or indeed definition of writer and critic/reader, and the relation of critic/reader to writer – or of criticism/reading to creativity – may also be engaged. These are very general questions which, however phrased and approached, have long received the attention of critics and writers alike.

More specifically, diversity and problems of demarcation are encountered at the level of genre. The writer may appear in the role of critic in a wide range of guises and genres, from the professional to the informal, both literary and non-literary. At times the definition as reader – or some other role – may supersede that of critic.

At one end of the range the professional guises include: the writer of literary essays, memoirs, or critical articles; reviewer, editor, or publisher; and teacher or lecturer. These, of course, have a historically determined dimension and have emerged (for example, the journal reviewer) or significantly evolved alongside the development of the writing 'profession' over the last two or three centuries. For Russian writers in this century, one of the differences between the experience of emigration as against the Soviet Union lies precisely in this area. More generally, even if the writer as teacher is, perhaps, a timeless role, the concrete forms it takes – which, in the West, currently include creative fellowships and employment in academic faculties – are not.

Towards the other end of the range we move into letters, notebooks, notes in the margin, etc. Then, beyond the written word, there is the realm of the spoken word (already implied in the writer as teacher). This is the location, one imagines, where much of what writers say about each other may be found, and much of that remains unrecorded. Historically, of course, as in salon periods, or more recently in some kinds of radio or television interview, the spoken word may be a far from informal medium. As far as the salon is concerned, in the Russian context one thinks especially of the age of Karamzin and Pushkin,[2] or subsequently of the Silver Age and Viacheslav Ivanov's famous 'tower'. The record of comments made in conversation, however, takes us into autobiography or, more often, into other people's – maybe other writers' – memoirs. Here the genre of writer on writer has diffused into another's writing, and even with a witness such as Nadezhda Mandel'shtam in her memoirs we would not invariably take the record

---

2. Concerning the role of the salon in the age of Pushkin, see William Mills Todd III, *Fiction and Society in the Age of Pushkin: Ideology, Institutions and Narrative*, Cambridge, Mass.–London, 1986, pp. 55–72.

of views Mandel´shtam expressed about other writers as read.[3] At the other end of the range the boundary between 'criticism' and 'literature' may dissolve. The literary essay, for example, may sometimes be approached as a critical text, at other times as a literary one; or as both: Sibelan Forrester's discussion in this volume of Tsvetaeva's apparently improvised but scrupulously finished critical essays is an example of the latter. This feature accords with the general tendency towards dissolution of genre in the twentieth century. Equally, the distinction between criticism and literary reminiscence, intertextuality, two writers' dialogue and so on is not a hard and fast one. On the one hand, a work of literature may contain moments of criticism, as in the case of Nabokov's criticism of Dostoevskii discussed by Nora Buhks: a poem in the form of a parable, written on the fortieth anniversary of Dostoevskii's death, was directed against the assertion that 'beauty will save the world'. On the other hand, one should not exclude the relation of writer *on* writer from the domain of intertextual dialogue. Some aspects of Pushkin's reference to other writers in *Evgenii Onegin* might be described as criticism, others as parody, reminiscence, influence, intertextuality and so on, but without these categories necessarily being exclusive of each other.

The context in which a writer's criticism functions or is received may also vary greatly. Indeed, as already mentioned, historically the way in which one writer may stand in relation to another as critic can function very differently or hardly at all. In the modern period, as a reviewer, editor, or lecturer, a writer may principally be engaged in earning a crust, and this in turn raises questions concerning the role of the writer, the writing profession and the institution of literature and criticism, in a given culture and society. But in earlier periods writers have been placed in a different relation. In Russia the phenomenon of writer commenting on writer does not emerge until the eighteenth century. Prior to this, authorial personality was deemed less important than the question of the adequacy of the text for its intended function; for example, was a piece of hagiographical writing an appropriate depiction (in terms of content, structure and style) of the subject's sanctity? Not surprisingly, where examples of one writer commenting upon another do occur, criticism is always directed at the writer's inability to conform to literary norms. This both takes the form of writer attacking writer, as when Prince Andrei Kurbskii sneers at Ivan the Terrible's crude mixture of styles and convoluted syntax in his epistles, and autocriticism (the Archpriest Avvakum warding off imaginary critics by asserting his right to compose his autobiography in

3. Nadezhda Mandel´shtam, *Vospominaniia*, New York, 1970; *Vtoraia kniga*, Paris, 1972.

the vernacular). In eighteenth-century Russia, polemic among writers, now armed with the tenets of French Classicism, was initially also focussed round the appropriate style for a work. Within a couple of decades the view of writing as a profession serving readers who could choose what to read begins, as Gareth Jones shows, to result in a greater range and complexity in writers' criticism of writers.

We have moved here to a consideration of one writer's criticism of another in a narrower literary context. So when the review becomes part of the literary apparatus in the nineteenth and twentieth centuries, it may be written and perceived as part of the literary polemics of the day. In this volume this is illustrated, though in different ways, by Fet on Tiutchev, Merezhkovskii on Chekhov, or Gumilev on Ivanov. When there are competing factions or movements, or simply when a new writer emerges, the phenomenon of writer on writer may play an important role in defining aesthetic positions. This might either be as antagonist or as proponent/ally/apologist. Moreover, it can often – even quite typically – take place between successive generations, in which case the roles of teacher and follower may come to the fore and lead as often to misrepresentation and misunderstanding as to sympathetic insight. This particular aspect of writer on writer is discussed by Pamela Davidson in her study of Gumilev and Viacheslav Ivanov (Gumilev, of course, not being the only writer to go through this relation to Ivanov). In addition, the generational aspect reminds us that the phenomenon of writer on writer has a specific temporal dimension, since there is a necessary relation of contemporaneity or antecedence between the two writers. The genre of a piece of criticism is also linked to the temporal dimension: a review will as a rule be concerned with the present day, a literary essay can have a wider view.

A writer's criticism of other writers is often only a part, and maybe not the central part, of his/her writings about art. As well, or instead, these may be on more general themes: on culture, literature, poetry, the novel, the creative process, etc. T. S. Eliot explicitly divided his criticism into 'Essays of Generalization' and 'Appreciations of Individual Authors', but this division is not always applied or applicable, and so once again the subject of writer on writer may diffuse into something broader. In Russia criticism by writer on writer frequently forms part of a general consideration of the current state of literature under attack from political authority or (especially recently) by commercial considerations.[4] Moreover, the narrower focus of writer

4. For example *World Literature Today*, vol. 67, no. 1, 1993, is devoted to the state of literature in contemporary Russia. One section contains reflections by Russian writers, including emigrés, on the contribution made by the once-flourishing literary journals, and the prospects for Russian literature.

on writer may vary enormously in significance. The penning of reviews as part of the professional business of being a writer may be treated as so marginal that it hardly figures in the writer's, or others', framework of his/her *oeuvre*. Nabokov's many reviews written in emigration in Germany are but one example, while Yeats at one stage referred to his 'criticisms' in the following way: 'One has to give something of oneself to the devil that one may live.'[5] With certain writers and at certain times reviews have a habit of getting lost; finding and attributing them is certainly of interest, but may still feature under the heading of *marginalia*. Alternatively, however, criticism and editorship can be occupations – almost career occupations – that mark a writer's position in the literature of his/her period. This applies to numerous Russian writers – Pushkin, Nekrasov, Dostoevskii, Briusov and Tvardovskii are some of the names that spring to mind.

Yet the turn to write a particular piece about another writer, perhaps involving a move into an unfamiliar genre or even medium, may be of considerable significance at a given moment in a writer's literary biography. This reminds us of the unsurprising fact that, although the preposition 'on' ostensibly directs us towards the writer being written about, such writing may be to some degree – perhaps a very large degree – autoreflexive; the very choice of writer about whom to write can tell us a great deal. This can range from the simplistic quality of Zinov´ev's initial identification with a Chekhovian character, as discussed by Michael Kirkwood, to Mandel´shtam's *Conversation about Dante*. More generally, the dialogue between certain writers, their self-definition in relation to others, both of which indissolubly involve some element of writer *on* writer, may be a central feature of those writers' art. In the Russian context, for example, one thinks almost inevitably and immediately of Mandel´shtam, Akhmatova, Pasternak, Tsvetaeva, both separately and together. In this volume Anatoly Naiman suggests that for these four poets communication was as much part of the poetic, as of the actual environment in which they lived. If the writers concerned are poets, as is the case with these four, then the question may once again be placed in a wider context: that of a poet's prose, with its ramifications in poetics and epistemology.

But in addition to the question of a poet's prose, the focus on writer as critic raises a number of other larger issues of definition too, a thorough consideration of which goes well beyond the scope of this

5. From a letter to Robert Bridges of 1897, quoted in Vinod Sena, *The Poet as Critic: W. B. Yeats on Poetry, Drama and Tradition*, Delhi, 1980, p. 2. Sena's study starts from the fact that, although the volume of Yeats's 'criticisms', written over fifty years, exceeds that of his 'creative' output, this side of his writing had hitherto been paid scant attention.

introduction. As mentioned earlier, these include questions concerning the status or indeed definition of writer and critic/reader, and the relation of critic/reader to writer, or of criticism/reading to creativity. When a writer turns to criticism, is this a change of identity? Or is the writer different as a critic (or reader) from the critic who is not a writer? Is the writer, for example, a privileged critic? By extension, the writer as critic could be related to the role of the critical faculty in the creative process, and hence to the whole area of inspiration, reason and feeling, the conscious and the unconscious and so on, in art.

There is a familiar opposition of writer and critic, but at the same time this opposition may be disturbed or dissolved. It is well known for writers to assert how creativity and criticism go together. In 'The Function of Criticism' T. S. Eliot emphasises the role of the critical intelligence in creation and then continues:

> If so large a part of creation is really criticism, is not a large part of what is called 'critical writing' really creative? If so, is there not creative criticism in the ordinary sense? The answer seems to be, that there is no equation. I have assumed as axiomatic that a creation, a work of art, is autotelic; and that criticism, by definition, is *about* something other than itself. Hence you cannot fuse creation with criticism as you can fuse criticism with creation. The critical activity finds its highest, its true fulfilment in a kind of union with creation in the labour of the artist.[6]

But criticism has also been perceived in terms of gender identity as a rational, 'male' activity, as Catriona Kelly observes with respect to Russian women writers of the early twentieth century. Those who commented on other women writers tended to fuse criticism with creation through a personal response. In its consideration of 'the other', such criticism is an examination of self even if only of the disincentive kind (what kind of woman writer not to be).

Beyond the question of the identity of writer and critic, there is also the question of the difference or privileged status of the writer as critic. As a practitioner, the writer may seem to be a privileged interpreter 'on art', but is he/she a privileged reader and critic of Dostoevskii? Eliot, for example, at one time held the view that 'the *only* critics worth reading were the critics who practised, and practised well, the art of

6. T. S. Eliot, 'The Function of Criticism', in *Selected Prose of T. S. Eliot*, edited with an introduction by Frank Kermode, London, 1975, pp. 73–4. Eliot's and Matthew Arnold's title has recently been taken up again by Terry Eagleton in his study of the emergence and development of the 'institution' of English criticism, *The Function of Criticism: From* The Spectator *to Post-Structuralism*, London and New York, 1984. Lukács argued that the fusion of writer and critic in the great writers of the past was broken by the specialisation of the two activities under capitalism (Georg Lukács, 'The Writer and the Critic', in *Writer and Critic and Other Essays*, edited and translated by Arthur Kahn, London, 1978, pp. 189–226).

which they wrote', but subsequently retreated somewhat from this position.[7] In accordance with the status of literature and the writer in the Russian tradition, variations of such a position, or approaches to it, are implicit – or explicit – there, as is evident from a number of the studies in this volume. A retreat from the evaluative position, however, still allows for a view of the writer's criticism as distinctive, special. It is in this light – or spirit – that Joseph Brodsky has introduced a volume of critical essays by modern Russian poets,[8] and it is in this light too that Henry Gifford discusses Joseph Brodsky's own criticism here. Historically, however, the thrust of the argument may be reversed, with the critic privileged over the writer. For example, in the great debate over aesthetics in Russia in the late 1850s and 1860s, the radical critic Shelgunov could assert that the writers were only providing the raw material for the critics to work upon.[9]

But the issue can be presented in terms other than that of the status of critic or writer as interpreter of literature, writer or work. It can also be presented in terms of our definitions of writing and writer. In modern literary theory the distinction of writer and critic/reader may be disturbed or dissolved in the opposite direction to that just considered, by starting from the reader: the writer as reader, the reader as writer. Thus, following Barthes, the text may be defined or approached as 'writerly' as opposed to 'readerly'; or in Harold Bloom's conception of influence and misreading, 'the influence-relation governs reading as it governs writing, and reading is therefore a mis-writing just as writing is a misreading. As literary history lengthens, all poetry necessarily becomes verse-criticism, just as all criticism becomes prose-poetry.'[10] In the actual practice of such writers as Barthes, Derrida, Cixous the distinction between creative and critical writing tends to be erased, not just deconstructed in theory. But a sense of the reader or critic as active participant in creation is, of course, not new, even if treated anew in modern thinking. In this volume Sibelan Forrester highlights Tsvetaeva's view of reading as co-creation, referring to the reader's exhaustion as 'sotvorcheskaia ustalost´', while it is interesting to discover from Robin Aizlewood's essay that Fet, for whom the editorial input of Turgenev, Nekrasov *et al.* played a significant role in the creative process, also speaks of the reader's 'sotvorchestvo' in his article on Tiutchev.

7. See 'The Function of Criticism', in *Selected Prose of T. S. Eliot*, ed. Kermode, pp. 74–6.

8. See Joseph Brodsky, 'Preface', in *Modern Russian Poets on Poetry*, edited by Carl R. Proffer, selected and introduced by Joseph Brodsky, Ann Arbor, 1976, pp. 7–9.

9. See Charles A. Moser, *Esthetics as Nightmare: Russian Literary Theory, 1855–1870*, Princeton, 1989, p. 29.

10. Harold Bloom, *A Map of Misreading*, Oxford–New York, 1975, p. 3.

We began this introduction with a consideration of the scope of 'on' in 'writers on writers', and now we have reached the point where it is appropriate to consider the scope of 'writer'. In fact, by starting from writers' writings as critics, rather than from the lyric poem or novel, the scope of 'writer' stands in more problematic, and maybe therefore clearer, focus. It is not readily, or easily, delimited. This accords with the modern disturbance or dissolution of the notion of literature as a discrete entity and the accompanying orientation, or re-orientation, towards discourse(s) and rhetoric advanced by, among others, Todorov, Foucault, de Man and Eagleton.[11] But the scope of 'writer' has always been broader than 'literature'; in the Russian context, and not just recently, it may certainly be approached as open rather than closed. An excellent example would be Rozanov, a critic in a writer, a writer in a critic, a self-conscious dissolver of literature. But if Rozanov is in some ways a special case, he is not the only one, as Malcolm Jones's study of Shestov on Chekhov and S. le Fleming's of Merezhkovskii on Chekhov remind us.

Approaches to the subject of writer on writer have typically taken the form of collections which bring together pieces – reviews, articles, essays, extracts from various writings, poems perhaps, sayings, anecdotes – by a variety of writers about a particular figure. A recent example is Valentina Polukhina's most recent book on Brodsky.[12] Such collections present a prism of varying perceptions and create a picture of cultural context, the reception of the writer concerned, both contemporaneous and continuing. In the Russian tradition this is tied into the tendency towards mythologising of certain figures – for example, Pushkin and Dostoevskii. In the case of Dostoevskii the myth has a number of facets, one of which – Dostoevskii as political prophet – is highlighted by David Gillespie. But such mythologising, as Gareth Jones shows, was already under way in the eighteenth century with Lomonosov, while the most recent candidate is Brodsky, whose progress from man to myth is revealed by Valentina Polukhina.

However, any particular piece by a writer on another writer can be read for what it tells us not about its subject but about its author. Indeed, as was mentioned earlier, autoreflexivity may be the defining feature of such writing. But, even if this is not entirely the case, it is the writer of the piece who will necessarily be the focus of interest in an individual study of one writer on another, for the same directionality applies as in the phenomenon of writer on writer itself. Moreover, the most likely material, as in those studies in this volume which deal with

11. See for example Tzvetan Todorov, 'The Notion of Literature', *Genres in Discourse*, Cambridge–New York, 1990.

12. *Brodsky Through the Eyes of His Contemporaries*, Basingstoke–New York, 1992.

just one writer on another, will be something discrete, such as an essay or article. It is perhaps precisely because of the tendency to diffusion inherent in the phenomenon of writer on writer that it has not often been approached as a subject of study in itself, rather than as part of something broader (be it a collection of the kind specified above or a study of writer *and* writer).

The present volume makes no claims to comprehensiveness, whether in respect of the whole range of comments by one Russian writer upon another/others, or the variety of form such comment can take. Several tomes would have resulted as a consequence of either approach being pursued to its ultimate conclusion. Instead the intention is to illumine the theme of writer and writer in the Russian context, at the same time highlighting many of the ways in which the comment of writer on writer can function. The book is only a beginning: our hope is that it may stimulate further scrutiny of this relatively neglected, yet rich and complex topic.

Familiar Solidarity and Squabbling: Russia's Eighteenth-Century Writers

W. Gareth Jones

From the early days of the development of secular literature in eighteenth-century Russia, writers began to write about writers. Before the century was out, Russia's writers had written about their fellow writers in the many ways in which authors have addressed each other. At the beginning, against the background of a society indifferent to secular letters, and regarding each other as allies in the propagation of Petrine values, they praised and patronised each other. No sooner had literature burgeoned, however, than mutual praise gave way to jealous criticism of each other's efforts, though both mutual praise and mutual criticism were instrumental in raising the profile of writers and establishing their prominence in society. That promotion of their own professional image was necessary before Russia's writers began to consider each other's literary work seriously. The second half of the century saw the beginnings of rudimentary literary criticism; writers contemplated and weighed each other's work as a measure for their own products. And as writers began to be taken seriously by society, to be accepted as a coherent political force, they could be judged for their contribution to the modern Russian state founded by Peter the Great. By the dawn of the nineteenth century writers had written about other writers against this measure as well.

An overriding feature of the interrelationship between Russian writers has been the closeness of their intimacy. This became apparent in the earliest manifestation of a Russian writer responding to another Russian writer. When in 1729 Antioch Kantemir wrote his first satire, an attack on those subverting Peter the Great's reforms, a copy of the supposedly anonymous work found its way to Feofan Prokopovich, an ardent supporter of the Petrine ideology. Feofan responded with fulsome laudatory verses extolling the young Kantemir.

Объемлет тебя Аполлин великий,
Любит всяк, кто есть таинств его зритель;
О тебе поют парнасские лики,
Всем честным сладка твоя добродетель
И будет сладка в будущие веки;
А я и ныне сущий твой любитель;[1]

One of Feofan Prokopovich's supporters in his reform of the Russian Orthodox Church, Feofil Krolik, seconded his mentor's praise of Kantemir, this time in Latin verse.[2]

Kantemir was not shy in exploiting this response by the two prominent dignitaries. In his own commentary to his first satire he drew attention to the encomium bestowed upon him, acknowledging how much Feofan's active promotion of his satire had given confidence to him as a 20-year-old author.[3] The sense of common cause and mutual support was well caught in the suggestive phrase 'Uchenaia Druzhina', or 'Learned Watch' used by Feofan in his laudatory verses to Kantemir, in which the vigilante band of writers in the 'Watch' would use their 'bold pen' as a weapon against the world's vices.[4] In the context of their time, of course, these vices meant a recrudescence of the bigotry of pre-Petrine Russia. The 'Learned Watch', close to the centre of power, had a firm political programme.

This close band of literary brothers would not last long as a pattern for mutual support between writers. It is ironical that a rift would soon appear around the person of Vasilii Trediakovskii, who at first might have seemed a natural recruit to the 'Learned Watch'. Trediakovskii was the subject of an extensive complaint to the Holy Synod subsequent to his enthusiastic reading of Kantemir's first satire on his return from abroad in 1730, and as a consequence he acquired a dubious reputation as a freethinker and atheist.[5] Despite this, for the best part of the next two decades Trediakovskii occupied a leading place in the literary life of Russia, centred on the Academy of Sciences in St Petersburg.

Yet Trediakovskii's treatment by his fellow writers shows that the sense of literary fellowship inherent in the concept of a 'Learned Watch' was not long sustained. The initially friendly and cooperative relations between Trediakovskii and Mikhail Lomonosov, who had returned from

1. Antioch Kantemir, *Sobranie sochinenii*, Leningrad, 1956, pp. 442–3.
2. Ibid., p. 444.
3. Ibid., p. 62.
4. Ibid., p. 442.
5. A. Malein, 'Novye dannye dlia biografii V. K. Trediakovskogo', in *Sbornik statei v chesta´ akad. A.I. Sobolevskogo,* Leningrad, 1928, pp. 430–2.

Germany in 1741, did not outlast that decade. Amicable academic disagreements between the two men developed into bitter personal wranglings. To make matters worse, the conflict was joined by Aleksandr Sumarokov, and the polemics between the three raged through the 1750s and 1760s, only to be silenced by the grave with the death of Lomonosov in 1765 and of Trediakovskii in 1769.[6]

What was the nature of the polemics? To some extent the polemics were based on objective disagreements. Lomonosov's treatise on versification, his *Letter on the Rules of Russian Versification* (1739), for instance, was clearly a critical response to Trediakovskii's pioneering work, *A Novel and Short Method for the Composition of Russian Verses* (1735). Nevertheless Lomonosov referred with approval to his predecessor's work, which had exerted a positive influence on the practice of poetry. Then again, the experimentation with style and vocabulary, where Trediakovskii favoured idiosyncratic heterogeneity, did not accord with the more moderate and measured approach of Lomonosov and Sumarokov. There was sufficient cause for honest dissension.

But the polemics did not remain for long within a polite framework. They soon moved from peevish bickering to take on a vituperative personal aspect. And all three of the major figures, Trediakovskii, Lomonosov and Sumarokov, like a mutually jealous threesome, manœuvred to ostracise one of their number. For example, although relations between Lomonosov and Trediakovskii were strained by 1748, in October of that year Lomonosov could write to Trediakovskii as a colleague regretting Sumarokov's treatment of the latter in his epistles on the Russian language and poetry. 'The gentleman author of these epistles might be advised in a friendly fashion not to hasten their publication and that he should himself look to the need to change things somewhat in his discussion of some persons', wrote Lomonosov,[7] no doubt hinting at Sumarokov's offensive line about Trediakovskii: 'A ty, Shtivelius, vspevaesh´ glasom dikim'.[8] That Lomonosov was not more supportive of Trediakovskii may be explained by the fact that he had been selected by Sumarokov in the same epistle as a model for young men to follow: 'On nashikh stran Malgerb, on Pindaru podoben'.[9] Ten years later the publication of an abusive article by Trediakovskii in Sumarokov's journal, *The Busy Bee* (June, 1759, pp. 353–60), caused

---

6. For a general review of the polemics see P. N. Berkov, *Lomonosov i literaturnaia polemika ego vremeni*, Moscow–Leningrad, 1936. For a selection of the verse polemics see the section 'Stikhotvornaia polemika' in G. P. Makogonenko and I. Z. Serman (eds), *Poety XVIII veka*, 2 vols, Leningrad, 1972, vol. 2, pp. 371–444.

7. M. V. Lomonosov, *Sochineniia*, ed. E. N. Lebedev, Moscow, 1987, pp. 318–19.

8. Ibid., p. 401.

9. Ibid.

Lomonosov in a letter to Ivan Shuvalov to fulminate against a supposed plot engineered by Trediakovskii and Sumarokov to besmirch him. 'In the "Busy" so-called "bee" there has been printed a very despicable piece about mosaics. Its author Tr[ediakovskii] has confounded his coarse ignorance and base spite ... A whole plot may be seen here. Tr[ediakovskii] wrote it, Sumarokov accepted it for the "Bee". ...'[10] The depth of Lomonosov's rancour against Sumarokov was best expressed in his famous letter to Shuvalov, following a vain attempt by the latter to reconcile the two giants of contemporary Russian literature. Shuvalov had clearly miscalculated in his endeavour to restore a united 'Learned Watch' at the beginning of the 1760s. 'Make amends with Sumarokov!' wrote Lomonosov 'that is bring about ridicule and shame, get in touch with a man whom everybody shuns ... Get in touch with that man who cannot say anything without pouring scorn on everybody, praising himself and placing his own sorry versifying above all human knowledge.'[11]

It is true that for Sumarokov the affirmation of his own position as a writer had always been at the expense of belittling rivals. This itch reached its culmination in his fourth satire 'On Bad Rhymesters', which was an occasion to rehearse his disdain for his literary opponents. Apart from Trediakovskii, who had been early identified as an opponent, the 1760s gathered Lomonosov, Vasilii Petrov, Mikhail Chulkov, Vasilii Ruban and others into the enemy camp.

The scorn that writers professed for each other was also expressed in a particularly coarse fashion, with the participants not averse to calling each other animals. Typical of the rage was Trediakovskii's splenetic riposte to Lomonosov's harsh attack on his linguistic views in 1746. A satire by Lomonosov clearly identified Trediakovskii in the following lines:

Языка нашего небесна красота
Не будет никогда попранна от скота.
От яду твоего он сам себя избавит
И, вред сей выплюнув, поверь, тебя заставит
Скончать твой скверный визг стонанием совы
Негодным в русскии стих пропастным увы![12]

Trediakovskii spat back: 'Kogda, po-tvoemu, sova i skot uzh ia,/To sam ty netopyr´ i podlinno svin´ia!'[13] Sumarokov's nervous tic and unpre-

10. Ibid., p. 331.
11. Ibid., p. 334.
12. M. V. Lomonosov, *Polnoe sobranie sochinenii*, 10 vols, Moscow–Leningrad, 1950–9, vol. 8, 1959, p. 542.
13. Makogonenko and Serman, *Poety XVIII veka*, vol. 2, p. 393.

possessing appearance were seized upon as outward signs of his inherent malice: 'Kto ryzh, pleshiv, migun, zaika i kartav/Ne mozhet byti v tom nikak khoroshii nrav'.[14] And Trediakovskii remarked on Lomonosov's notorious drunkenness, inquiring whether he would take a barrel of beer with him to the grave and noting that he need not be pitched into hell with a crook but could be enticed there by a large glass.[15] His drunkenness was also adduced by the anonymous author of *The Epistle from Vodka and Spirit to L[omonosov]* as the reason for the high-flown exaltation of his verse:

Но водка и вино сим вздором говорит,
Что только вы тогда и бредишь лишь стихами
Как хватишь полный штоф нас полными устами.

And he stressed: 'Chto pakhnet vsiakii stikh tvoi vodkoi i vinom'.[16]

Was harm being done to Russian literary life at this early and crucial stage in its development? Is one to regret the disruption of any semblance of a coherent 'Learned Watch', or of the initial cooperation between Trediakovskii, Lomonosov and Sumarokov, despite their honest differences? Is it a matter of regret that so much energy seemed to be expended on personal rancour rather than the literary works themselves? Trediakovskii himself put to the test the possibility that it was his own personal reputation, so damaged by his fellow authors, that set Russia's readers against him rather than his work. In 1756 an ode, *Vneshne teplo* (The Warmth of Spring), was published. While the initials of the title, V. T., encoded the name of its true author, the ode was published under the name of Andrei Nartov, a colleague of Trediakovskii's at the Academy of Sciences. The reaction was heartbreaking for Trediakovskii, who observed that, 'The ode was showered with praise and printed in books. Although I was successful in the substitution of a different author, nevertheless this very success plunged me almost into despair, for I saw that the disdain was really directed only at me and not at my works.'[17]

Behind the personal invective, however, there were positions of principle. The most caustic of satirical poems often had an underlying serious point to make in the literary argument. In 1753, for example, Trediakovskii answered a satire by Lomonosov which continued their serious differences on the nature of literary Russian. If Lomonosov took issue with Trediakovskii for his deliberate use of archaic forms, Trediakovskii's riposte was that Lomonosov used vulgar colloquial

---

14. Quoted by Irina Reyfman, *Vasilii Trediakovskii: the Fool of the 'New' Russian Literature*, Stanford, California, 1990, p. 90.

15. Makogonenko and Serman (eds), *Poety XVIII veka*, vol. 2, p. 399.

16. Ibid., p. 400.

17. Reyfman, *Vasilii Trediakovskii*, p. 47.

words unsuited for the high style required by poetry. There was a positive side to the entertainment afforded by the robustness of the personal clashes, despite the anguish experienced by the participants in it. One need only contrast the entertainment value of the verse polemics of the 1750s and 1760s with the more restrained and moderate polemics of the next two decades to realise its effectiveness in delineating the differing profiles of literary schools and groups. This demerging, or spacing out of groups with various tendencies, was salutary at a time when new traditions were being founded in Russian literary life.[18] In his *Epistles* of 1747, Sumarokov was intent on marking off his own work from the heritage, not only of the influential pioneers, Feofan and Kantemir, but also such contemporaries as Trediakovskii.[19] It has been argued that one of the underlying reasons for the gulf between the two was that Trediakovskii was indelibly marked by his education at the Moscow Academy, while Sumarokov reflected the formation he had received in the Cadet Corps School.[20] For Trediakovskii literature was a social duty, for Sumarokov it was a social accomplishment. If Trediakovskii found Sumarokov's delight in the lighter genres frivolous, Sumarokov in turn was happy to put a distance between himself and the former's moral earnestness and quest for the high genres. Not content with distancing himself from other viewpoints, he set himself up successfully as the representative of a distinct literary coterie.

The affirmation of a literary position by attacking others in personal terms was not perhaps only the result of the touchiness of the awkward personalities involved or the underdeveloped literary manners of the age. The French classical writers of the seventeenth century were the canonical models for the Russian authors of the mid-eighteenth century. The latter took delight in being called the Russian Malherbe, the Russian Racine, the Russian Boileau.[21] Not only the works of these French exemplars were worthy of imitation, but also their behaviour, particularly their enjoyment of literary polemics. If such a paragon as Molière could excite the malice of the public by portraying on his stage two writers on whom he wished to wreak vengeance, should not

18. Iu. V. Stennik, *Russkaia satira XVIII veka,* Leningrad, 1985, p. 93.

19. Ibid.

20. Karen Rosenberg, 'Between Ancients and Moderns: V. K. Trediakovskij on the Theory of Language and Literature', unpublished PhD Dissertation, Yale University, 1980, pp. 240–1.

21. See 'Stikhi k "Opytu istoricheskogo slovaria o rossiiskikh pisateliakh"' by Ivan Rudakov, the senior compositor at the Academy of Sciences Press, in N. I. Novikov, *Izbrannye sochineniia,* ed. G. P. Makogonenko, Moscow–Leningrad, 1954, p. 346. Rudakov claimed that since Petrine times Russia had acquired her own Pindar, Homer, Cicero, Ovid, Anacreon, Milton, Plato, Scarron, Boileau, Malherbe, Racine, Quinault, Molière, La Fontaine, De la Suze and even Sappho: 'In Russia there is a Sappho, and Sappho is not alone.'

Russia's playwrights follow his example? In *Les Femmes savantes* Molière's contemporaries saw Ménage and Cotin – who had not only done Molière an ill service with the Duc de Montaurier and the King, but were enemies of Boileau – mocked for their pedantry under the masks of Vadius and Trissotin.[22] Trissotin was reincarnated in *Tresotinius*, Sumarokov's first comedy, which drew heavily on *Les Femmes savantes* for its plot and characters.[23] It also recreated a contemporary Russian version of the personal *ad hominem* satire of the original, for the original pair of Trissotin and Vadius (Cotin and Ménage) were recast as Tresotinus and Bobembius, who corresponded to Trediakovskii and Lomonosov. Tresotinus and Bobembius fall out, as had Molière's Trissotin and Vadius, but the subject of their quarrel is significantly different. Tresotinus and Bobembius' pedantic dispute is about whether the Russian letter T should have one or three legs;[24] as so often the personal invective covered fundamental differences – in this case the long-standing linguistic disputes between Trediakovskii and Lomonosov.

It could be argued that the quarrels between Russian authors in the mid-eighteenth century stemmed from too great an awareness of the practice of Europe's foremost practitioners.[25] Almost all Boileau's satires, for example, bore the marks of caustic criticisms of authors of whom he disapproved; Pelletier, Scudéry, Cotin, Quinault and Chapelain were all writers who came under his lash. At that stage in the development of French literature, literary criticism was being created by writers themselves and, in Boileau's second satire dedicated to Molière, we see praise of Molière accompanied by probing criticism by Boileau of his own work. What was now happening in mid-eighteenth century Russia was a reprise of this process which had taken place in France. Russians were not only taking on board the genres established by the French neo-classicists but were seconding their behaviour. Russian writers, in creating Russia's new literature, had perforce to create criticism as well. The apparently chaotic exchange of personal insults was a reflection of that peculiar process in which authors followed the example set by Boileau.

Proof of this could be the key role played in the polemics of the 1750s by Ivan Elagin's *Epistle from Mr Elagin to Mr Sumarokov*, known at the time as *A Satire on a Fop and Coquettes*. It was this work

---

22. *Oeuvres de Molière*, ed. Jacques Copeau, Paris, 10 vols, 1926–30, vol. 8, 1930, pp. 52–3. 'Il y a dans l'accent de ces diatribes de gens de lettres quelque chose d'aussi dur que dans les anathèmes des dévots.'

23. Reyfman, *Vasilii Trediakovskii*, p. 84.

24. Ibid., p. 85.

25. Stennik, *Russkaia satira XVIII veka*, pp. 62–3.

that sparked off a further series of wide-ranging polemics between Lomonosov, Sumarokov and Trediakovskii, their supporters and opponents.[26] Elagin's *Epistle to Mr Sumarokov* was clearly derived from Boileau's second satire addressed to Molière, and, while following Boileau in belittling the literary opposition now represented by Lomonosov, he also followed his model in expressing his admiration for his mentor:

> Наперсник Боалов, российский наш Расин,
> Защитник истины, гонитель злых пороков,
> Благий учитель мой, скажи, о Сумароков
> Где рифмы ты берешь?[27]

Important consequences ensued when the next generation of Russian writers – which included Sumarokov's followers – abandoned unconditional reliance on the classical patterns of France which had presented their forerunners not only with strict legislation on genre and language, but also the practice of harsh personal satire directed against those who failed to play the literary game within the established rules. Not one of the three main Russian protagonists, of course, had won during their lifetime the unchallenged prestige of such as Racine, Molière and Boileau. Would any one of them posthumously be honoured with the mantle of their great French models? In her recent book *Vasilii Trediakovskii: The Fool of the 'New' Russian Literature*, Irina Reyfman shows how from the 1770s onwards it was the anecdotes, the legends, the rumours, the gossip from the personal satire that served as the evidence for ranking these authors.[28] But more important was the need to create a mythical hero for Russian literature. It was Lomonosov who was elevated to this role, with even the negative characteristics with which he had been castigated in the literary infighting being turned to his positive advantage.[29] His drunkenness, for example, which had been blamed for the bombast of his verse and which had been cause for much mocking, was transformed into one of the legendary qualities befitting a folk hero.[30] To balance the mythical hero, a mythical anti-hero had to be nominated, and Irina Reyfman has shown how this role of fool was created – however unjustly – for Trediakovskii.[31] Despite his real accomplishments, his contribution to the establishment of modern Russian

26. Makogonenko and Serman, *Poety XVIII veka*, vol. 2, p. 530.
27. Ibid., p. 372.
28. Reyfman, *Vasilii Trediakovskii*, pp. 42–6.
29. Ibid., p. 99.
30. Ibid., p. 101.
31. Ibid., *passim*.

versification, to literary theory and the development of the Russian literary language, Trediakovskii was characterised as a barren pedant, the scribbler of verses cast in ridiculous language and metre. As early as 1789 the pejorative coining 'trediakovshchina' was used to reinforce criticism of a Kapnist poem by Nikolai L´vov.[32] Another sign of the quick rooting of the myth was that Lomonosov soon usurped the praise of those who had previously belonged to Sumarokov's *pléiade* and had in the 1750s joined Sumarokov in casting barbs against Lomonosov. Before the century was out even Elagin, whose *Epistle from Mr Elagin to Mr Sumarokov*, as we have seen, disparaged Lomonosov, had joined in the general praise for him.[33] More remarkably, Sumarokov was assigned the role of being Lomonosov's apprentice merely on the grounds that he was his junior in years. Thus M. M. Kheraskov in his *Discourse on Russian Poetry* as early as 1772 gave precedence to Lomonosov: 'At that time when this great man was charting the path leading to the abode of the Muses, and was laying the cornerstone of our Parnassus, Mr Sumarokov began to flourish.'[34]

The reason for this mythologising of Lomonosov and Trediakovskii by the writers of the generation that succeeded them is ascribed by Reyfman to the mythological spirit of the time.[35] Russians had come to see the Petrine reforms in terms of a distinct break with the past, a national renewal. The father of the renewed nation was Peter the Great. The new nation had to have a new literature, and the writers who consciously set about creating that literature unconsciously sought a figure who would provide for literature what Peter had provided for the State. It was Lomonosov who assumed the mythical position of father and begetter of the 'new' Russian literature.

That mythological spirit may not have been the only cause for the projection of Lomonosov as a towering personality and for the compensatory belittling of Trediakovskii. From the 1770s onwards, the personality of the creative author began to be seen as the most important factor in literature.[36] Giftedness and talent became values that displaced the learning and observance of rules that had hitherto been of paramount importance. It is noticeable that in indicating Lomonosov's precedence over Sumarokov, Kheraskov, in his *Discourse on Russian Poetry*, had

---

32. Ibid., p. 104.

33. Ibid., pp. 8–9.

34. M. M. Kheraskov, 'Rassuzhdenie o rossiiskom stikhotvorstve', *Russkaia literaturnaia kritika XVIII veka: sbornik tekstov*, ed. V. I. Kuleshov, Moscow, 1978, p. 279. This was written in French to acquaint foreigners with the condition of Russian literature, and was intended as an introduction to a French translation of his poem *Battle of Chesme*.

35. Reyfman, *Vasilii Trediakovskii*, pp. 2–3, 18–19, 251–3.

36. W. Gareth Jones, 'The Image of the Eighteenth-Century Author', *Russia in the Age of the Enlightenment*, ed. Roger Bartlett and Janet M. Hartley, London, 1990, pp. 65–6.

praised Lomonosov as a literary engineer who, following his blueprints, 'charts a path' and 'lays a cornerstone'. In the same paragraph he went on to praise Sumarokov for 'having no guide other than his natural gifts'.[37] And these gifts enabled him in his tragedies to have 'touched our hearts and extracted our tears'.[38]

An early indication of this shift of attention away from the correct regulation of literature to its creative author was apparent in the first essay in Novikov's weekly *The Painter* in 1772, 'The Author to Himself'.[39] The self-musing of the author revealed a vulnerable, anxious human being, replete with vanity and self-deception. This essay proposed a new understanding of the author's role: the image of the vulnerable, human writer becomes an integral part of a literary work. This new conception was succinctly formulated by Karamzin in his essay *What is Necessary for an Author?* 'You take up a pen and wish to be an author: ask yourself, all alone, without witnesses, sincerely: *what sort of man am I?* for you wish to write the portrait of your own heart and soul.'[40] In the conclusion to his study of Karamzin, Iurii Lotman wrote that Karamzin 'created for Russian culture models of Writer and Man, which entered the consciousness of a generation, forming the personalities and biographies of other writers'.[41] This boosting of the creative persona of the author was applied retrospectively as well. It was not only the mythological spirit abroad that made Lomonosov pre-eminent as hero and Trediakovskii spurned as a fool. There was also the urge to construct the individual creative personality of these writers, and again the material for their construction would be mainly the stuff of the rumours, legends and anecdotes thrown up by the polemics.

But this material would not be the only source. There was an attempt also to form a psychological portrait of them. When Karamzin differentiated between Trediakovskii, Lomonosov and Sumarokov in his *Pantheon of Russian Writers* (1802) it was the question of their natural giftedness that separated them. Although Trediakovskii in Karamzin's eyes was no fool, but was in fact lauded for his erudition and pioneering

37. Kheraskov, 'Rassuzhdenie', p. 279. It should be noted that Kheraskov's conception of 'natural gifts' differed from Lomonosov's. The latter had indicated 'natural gifts' as the first essential for eloquence in his *Brief Guide to Eloquence*. See M. V. Lomonosov, *Sochineniia*, Moscow–Leningrad, 1961, p. 277. However, Lomonosov defines natural gifts as 'mental', that is 'wit and memory', and 'physical', that is 'a loud and pleasant voice, sustained breath and a strong chest'. For Kheraskov 'natural gifts' are less objective and more akin to inspiration.

38. Ibid., p. 279.

39. *Satiricheskie zhurnaly N. I. Novikova*, ed. P. N. Berkov, Moscow–Leningrad, 1951, pp. 284–8.

40. N. M. Karamzin, *Izbrannye proizvedeniia*, 2 vols, Moscow–Leningrad, 1964, vol. 2, p. 121.

41. Iu. M. Lotman, *Sotvorenie Karamzina*, Moscow, 1987, p. 316.

endeavours, it was his lack of 'giftedness' ('darovanie') that lowered him in the critic's estimation. Although Kheraskov in 1772 might not have credited Lomonosov with the natural giftedness that for him illumined Sumarokov's work, thirty years later the *Pantheon of Russian Writers* was obliged to ascribe the same essential quality to Lomonosov.[42]

The gifted personality that Lomonosov had acquired by the close of the century might well have been promoted by the treatment he had received in Novikov's *Essay at an Historical Dictionary of Russian Writers* (1772), which had been a model for Karamzin's *Pantheon of Russian Writers*. The entries in Novikov's *Dictionary* follow a distinct pattern: there is an account of the writers' careers and a list of their intellectual and literary accomplishments, with a short, generally favourable, appraisal. Occasionally, however, a character description is given which, significantly, precedes the account of their productions. Kantemir is portrayed in these terms:

> At first sight he seemed ungracious; but this imperceptibly disappeared the more he came across people whose intercourse was pleasing to him. His melancholy temper was the cause of long illnesses; however, he not only made merry with his friends, but took pleasure in occasioning them real services. He often said that there was nothing more pleasing than using one's eminence and power to be charitable to one's neighbour. He was able to embellish his conversation, which had more substance than liveliness, with pleasant jokes.[43]

If one looks at the entries for Sumarokov, Trediakovskii and Lomonosov to see how far this pattern is followed, then the great variation in their treatment is surprising. Sumarokov's entry, although positively effusive, is comparatively short, with no room at all for a personal characterisation.[44] The reason for this omission may well have been the fact that he was still alive, and Novikov was loath to analyse the personality of any of his living contemporaries. But the leaving out of a pen-portrait for him might well have contributed to Sumarokov's going down to posterity as a somewhat faceless writer, remembered only for the tics and mannerisms highlighted in the satirical thrusts against him. Although Trediakovskii fared a little better, his posthumous psychological profile was minimal. Novikov was unsparing in his praise of Trediakovskii: he was the first in Russia to establish literary science, the first poet, the first professor of eloquence, the first translator. But the two personal qualities mentioned in his case could not bring him to life. In declaring him 'highly intelligent' and 'exceptionally diligent',

42. Karamzin, *Izbrannye proizvedeniia*, vol. 2, pp. 165–6, 168–70.
43. Novikov, *Izbrannye sochineniia*, vol. 2, pp. 306–10.
44. Ibid., pp. 350–1.

Novikov merely compounded the general picture of the pedant.[45] Lomonosov's treatment is very different. It is true that there is brief mention of those biographical details identified by Irina Reyfman as mythic: Lomonosov's boyhood as a fisherman, his fleeing a forced marriage and the parental home to seek education in Moscow.[46] But much more space is given to his personal characteristics: his high intelligence, his courage and perseverance, his fortitude in overcoming obstacles to learning, the sprightliness and firmness of spirit, his enterprise. 'He had a merry disposition, was succinct and witty in speech and liked to make pointed jokes in conversation; he was loyal to his fatherland and friends, was a patron to those practising the literary arts and encouraged them; in company he was mainly gentle, and generous to those who sought his favour ...'. This picture that might have seemed too idealised ended, however, with a humanising touch, 'but, for all that, he was hot-headed and irascible'.[47] Such a character portrait fitted Karamzin's idea of what an author should be. Such a powerful personality with all his natural gifts of character allied with literary talent would make a powerful writer. And so Lomonosov appeared as a gifted genius, both 'Writer' and 'Man', in the *Pantheon of Russian Writers*: 'His genius sought counsel only with itself, divined, sometimes erred; but in all its works it left the indelible seal of great gifts.'[48] It was a natural endowment of this kind that Trediakovskii lacked. The personal characteristics cited by Novikov of intelligence and diligence were no substitute, as Karamzin made plain. 'If desire and diligence could replace giftedness, whom would Trediakovskii not have surpassed in poetry and eloquence? ... Not only natural endowment, but taste itself is not acquired; and taste itself is an endowment. Learning trains, but does not produce an author.'[49]

There is something paradoxical in Karamzin's putting this stress on the individual differentiation of fellow authors in a work whose very title of *Pantheon* was an image of a temple of collective deities. Presenting a united front of Russian writers had also been the aim of Novikov's collection. It followed an earlier attempt to refute the calumny against Russian culture perpetrated by Chappe d'Auteroche in his notorious *Voyage en Sibérie* (1761).[50] Novikov acknowledged in his introduction that the publication of an article, 'Nachricht von einigen

45. Ibid., p. 354.
46. Ibid., pp. 319–20.
47. Ibid., p. 323.
48. Karamzin, *Izbrannye proizvedeniia*, pp. 168–9.
49. Ibid., p. 165.
50. I. F. Martynov, "'Opyt istoricheskogo slovaria o rossiiskikh pisateliakh" N. I. Novikova i literaturnaia polemika 60-70-kh godov XVIII veka', *Russkaia literatura*, vol. 3, 1968, pp. 184–91.

russischen Schriftstellern', in a Leipzig journal towards the end of 1768 was the impulse behind his own publication. He wished to improve on that article, which he considered to be too short and unbalanced.[51] However, the purpose would be the same; it would be to defend the whole body of Russian literature from any outside misrepresentation. Within the family of Russian writers squabbling might be permissible, and even within the biographical dictionary there are hints of the polemics that had surfaced in Novikov's journals. There is more than a tinge of coolness, for example, in the entries for Vladimir Lukin and Vasilii Petrov. But on the whole there is an effort to present the 317 authors as a brotherhood, a kind of historical 'Learned Watch', vigilant to ward off any more attempts to question the existence of a Russian literary culture. Not surprisingly, the well-known responses from Feofan Prokopovich and Feofil Krolik, quoted at the beginning of this chapter, were used effectively in the article on Antiokh Kantemir,[52] as was Kantemir's returned compliment to Feofan in the contribution on the latter.[53] The mutual support of Russian writers, of which this was an illustration, was conveyed by many more of these appreciations by Russian writers of each other. Significantly, the rifts between Sumarokov and Lomonosov were cancelled by the use of the positive quotation from Sumarokov's *Epistle* of 1747: 'Il´s Lomonosovym glas gromkii voznesi:/On nashikh stran Malgerb, on Pindaru podoben.'[54] Sumarokov, who had been used a touchstone of literary taste in Novikov's journals, was now enlisted to put his seal of approval on a number of writers, Ivan Elagin, Georgii Kozitskii and Elizaveta Kheraskova. The article on Fedor Volkov, one of the founders of the modern Russian theatre and producer of Sumarokov's tragedies, contained Sumarokov's *Elegy to Mr Dmitrevskii on the Death of Mr Volkov*.[55] Trediakovskii's appreciation of Buslaev is repeated.[56] Fedor Kozlovskii is praised in verse by Maikov and Kheraskov.[57] It was the round of interlocking mutual admiration with any polemical differences muted that created this impression of a collective body that easily translated into Karamzin *Pantheon*.

Towards the end of the eighteenth century, therefore, Russian writers, by addressing each other, by appreciating and criticising each other's endeavours, had established a certain tradition of close interrelationship. This intimacy would remain a feature of Russian literary life.

51. Novikov, *Izbrannye sochineniia*, pp. 277–8.
52. Ibid., p. 310.
53. Ibid., p. 340.
54. Ibid., p. 323.
55. Ibid., p. 293.
56. Ibid., p. 287.
57. Ibid., pp. 314–15.

The eighteenth century had shown how writers could close their ranks against threats, either internal, as during the post-Petrine reaction, or external, as happened during Catherine the Great's reign. But the close intimacy could lead to bickering and unpleasant backbiting as writers strove to prove that they alone possessed the key to a correct understanding of literature. That too was to remain a particular feature of Russian literary life. There is little doubt that there was a positive side to the polemics of the 1750s and 1760s, in that Russian writers through their disagreements worked out their positions, and sought out in robust fashion the best paths along which their literature might develop. The writers alone in this period – for writers probably constituted a large proportion of the reading public – selected those of their colleagues who were to be leaders of their profession. The mythological spirit of the age undoubtedly persuaded writers to choose particular heroes and anti-heroes, and the selection may not always have been objectively fair or equitable. But just as important in establishing the figures worthy of emulation was the growing conviction, towards the close of the century, that individual talent was paramount, that authors were inspired not by the indulgent rays of Apollo from above but by an inner spark and inherent fire. Above all, in their wrangling with each other Russian writers had become aware that the importance of an author came not from his membership of a collective union, however learned, nor from adherence to set programmes, however hallowed, but from the strength and sincerity of his individual voice.

Fet on Tiutchev

Robin Aizlewood

Fet's article 'On the poetry of F. Tiutchev' was published in 1859 in the February issue of *Russkoe slovo*, at the height of the great debate about aesthetics that broke out in the second half of the 1850s and continued well into the following decade;[1] the most famous work of radical criticism, Dobroliubov's 'What is Oblomovism?', was published in the May issue of *Sovremennik* that year.

The start of the debate had been marked by the publication of Chernyshevskii's *The Aesthetic Relations of Art to Reality* in 1855, while the same year also saw the appearance of Annenkov's six-volume edition of Pushkin, the first approach to a complete collection of his works: Pushkin was very much an emblem of art's eternal value for the various opponents of the radical position. By the end of the decade the debate had polarised and differences were becoming irreconcilable. A number of writers and critics formerly associated with *Sovremennik* had broken their links with it or would soon do so. Among them was Fet, whose last poem published there appeared in the same issue (no. 6, 1859) as a scathing attack on his art that mockingly used the following sentence from his article on Tiutchev as its epigraph: 'Anyone who is not prepared to throw himself head first from a top-floor window, certain in the belief that he will melt into the air on the way down, is not a lyric poet.'[2]

Both in the debate and in art itself, Fet was readily placed at the other pole from the radicals. His article was perceived and attacked as a par-

---

1. For a full and detailed study of this debate, see Charles A. Moser, *Esthetics as nightmare: Russian literary theory, 1855–1870*, Princeton, 1989.

2. A. A. Fet, 'O stikhotvoreniiakh F. Tiutcheva', in *Sochineniia v dvukh tomakh*, ed. A. E. Tarkhov, Moscow, 1982, vol. 2, p. 156; further references to the article in this edition will be given in the text, citing page numbers only. The guiding hand behind the attack on Fet, 'Shekspir v perevode g. Feta', was Dobroliubov, though it was written by the translator D. M. Mikhalovskii under the pseudonym M. Lavrenskii (see B. Ia. Bukhsthtab, *A. A. Fet. Ocherk zhizni i tvorchestva*, Leningrad, 1974, pp. 40–1).

ticularly forthright statement of the 'aesthetic' position, and his art, with its musical orientation and denial of discursive reason, was increasingly dismissed and ridiculed too (Pisarev later suggested that the only useful-ness his poetry could possibly have would be if the paper it was printed on was used to cover walls or wrap tallow candles).[3] In the article Fet asserts that the artist is only concerned with one aspect of reality, beau-ty, and makes no bones about his opinion of the radical position: 'ques-tions concerning poetry's right to citizenship alongside other human activities, its moral significance, contemporary relevance, etc., I consid-er to be nightmares which I have done with long ago and for good' (p. 146).

The combative, polemical side of Fet's character may have provoked his entry at the height of the debate, but his article also comes at a turn-ing-point in his life, career and literary evolution. Although he had brought out a book of verse as early as 1840 and had subsequently been published in journals, his active participation in professional literary life relates to the 1850s. The appearance of his first major collection in 1850 was soon followed by his association with the circle of writers and crit-ics (Nekrasov, Turgenev, Botkin, Druzhinin, Annenkov and others) who had gathered at that time at *Sovremennik*. Another collection was pub-lished in 1856. This collection, which was edited by Turgenev, received critical acclaim: Fet's finest achievement was generally reckoned to be his 'anthological' verse, but he was also presented – sometimes with a certain ambivalence – as the poet of 'feeling' (as for 'thought', howev-er, even as sympathetic a critic as Botkin asserted that Fet totally lacked depth).[4] Fet could now consider the career of professional writer. In addition, in 1857 he married Botkin's sister, Mariia, and in 1858 he resigned from the army, in which he had served since 1845, finally giv-ing up hope of acquiring through promotion the gentry status he craved, but which was denied him because of his illegitimate birth.

If Fet was to be a professional writer, then penning reviews and arti-cles on other writers or the literary scene would be a useful, even neces-sary, supplement to his poetry. But, if anything, the article on Tiutchev, his first proper attempt in this direction, merely served to hasten his departure from literary life, what with the ensuing attack on him in *Sovremennik* and the upper hand gained by the radicals in the debate and

3. D. I. Pisarev, *Literaturnaia kritika v trekh tomakh*, ed. Iu. S. Sorokin, Leningrad, 1981, vol. I, p. 284.
4. V. P. Botkin, 'Stikhotvoreniia A. A. Feta', in his *Literaturnaia kritika. Publitsistika. Pis'ma*, ed. B. F. Egorov, Moscow, 1984, pp. 209–10, 212; this review article was one of the last pieces of 'aesthetic' criticism to be published in *Sovremennik* (no. 1, 1857), though, somewhat anomalously, original works by Fet and others continued to be pub-lished there until the end of the decade.

in control of journals. Convinced that he could not support himself through literary activity, in 1860 Fet bought a property in the Mtsensk area and proceeded to turn himself into a successful farmer.[5] Although another collection of his verse did come out in 1863 (still not sold out when he died), he receded from the literary scene and his creative work came more or less to a halt through the 1860s and into the first half of the 1870s. When his creativity returned, his poetry had undergone a certain transition to acquire a clearer expression of thought, with a philosophical base in Schopenhauer, whom Fet translated into Russian. Therefore, besides the article's role in his career, writing about Tiutchev, a 'poet of thought', would seem to bear an obvious relation to the future direction of Fet's art.

As a piece by a writer on a writer, 'On the poetry of F. Tiutchev' engages with one of the underlying issues of the aesthetic debate: namely, the respective roles of critic and writer;[6] in addition, the relationship between critic – or writer as critic – and writer is a central one in Fet's art itself. From the radical perspective the key figure was not the writer but the critic. Shelgunov, looking back on the period, characterised the relationship between the two as follows:

> All our artists would wander off along various paths, because it is only the critic-journalists who show them the way. Who guided our novelists – Turgenev, Dostoevskii, Goncharov, Pisemskii and all the other writers of more recent years? They were guided by Belinskii, Dobroliubov, Pisarev. Novelists merely collect the firewood and stoke the engine of life, but the critic-journalist is the driver.[7]

Such a view, however contentious, undoubtedly had a powerful and pervasive influence. Goncharov, for example, gives a lot of ground to the critics in his article 'Better late than never' (1879) and happily concedes that the artist may need 'the assistance of a subtle critical interpreter like Belinskii or Dobroliubov' in order to understand the meaning of his work.[8] Fet, on the other hand, invokes the authority of the great artists, not the critics. His article, meanwhile, stands as a fine piece of criticism.

5. In a letter to Turgenev of 12 October 1861, Fet's close friend I. Borisov put this all down to the attack on him in *Sovremennik* (*Turgenevskii sbornik*, vol. 3, 1967, p. 352). But it is also interesting that the turn to prose was fruitful, only the line that Fet subsequently developed with success (at least in terms of output) related to his life, not art, in addition, of course, to his translations of Schopenhauer. In the 1860s he published periodical pieces on country life, including a series called 'Iz derevni' which eventually extended to over a thousand pages, and in the 1880s he produced voluminous memoirs.

6. See Moser, *Esthetics as nightmare*, pp. 28–9.

7. Quoted ibid., p. 29.

8. I. A. Goncharov, 'Luchshe pozdno, chem nikogda. (Kriticheskie zametki)', in his *Sobranie sochinenii*, ed. A. G. Tseitlin, 8 vols, Moscow, 1952–5, vol. 8, pp. 139–40.

This is a significant merit, for Fet had been presented by Botkin (speaking, one can assume, for the whole of the old *Sovremennik* circle) as short on critical acumen in relation to his own work: 'Fet has little critical tact and is too soft on his own works; as an improviser, he generally leaves them to their own fate.'[9] This 'fate', as it happens, leads directly to the question of the part played by others' criticism in Fet's poetry. For at least from the time of his association with the *Sovremennik* circle, the criticism of other writers/critics played a prominent editorial role in his work, one that in some ways is not so far removed from that claimed by Shelgunov. The most authoritative study of this role in the fate of Fet's literary heritage was made by Bukhshtab over fifty years ago.[10] In the first instance Fet looked to his mentors for a judgement of whether his poems were good or bad. For example, in a letter to Nekrasov in June 1854 he wrote: 'I have sent Avdot´ia Iakovlevna a poem, but, as with all the other poems written at the coast, I need Turgenev to tell me what's good and what's rubbish.'[11] But Turgenev, Nekrasov and others went further than passing judgement on quality, they sought to correct what they saw as a lack of clarity and comprehensibility: they objected to his subjectivity, musicality and what Turgenev called his 'philozophy' ('filozofiia'), and wanted to turn him into an objective, contemplative, 'anthological' poet. As Fet responded to what was rejected by producing new variants (sometimes a whole series of them), his critics became involved in the very process of producing his 'finished' poems. The most remarkable product of this process was the 1856 collection of Fet's poetry, edited by Turgenev. It was based on the 1850 collection, but almost half of the 182 poems from there were excluded, including some that are quintessential Fet. Of the ninety-five carried forward, only twenty-seven stayed in the same form. The changes Turgenev insisted upon affected not just words or lines, but also whole stanzas, most often the last. Given Fet's orientation towards melody and intonational composition, this could affect a poem drastically, as when Turgenev – amazingly – struck out the last stanza of 'Ia prishel k tebe s privetom'; individual lines were also altered to reduce the 'musicality' of sound effects.[12]

In the light of this genesis of his most acclaimed collection one can see that, in reversing roles and himself writing about another writer, Fet is indirectly – or inversely – engaged with a vital, and seemingly

9. Botkin, 'Stikhotvoreniia A. A. Feta', p. 218.
10. B. Ia. Bukhshtab, 'Sud´ba literaturnogo nasledstva A. A. Feta', *Literaturnoe nasledstvo*, vols 22–4, 1935, pp. 561–602.
11. Quoted ibid., p. 573.
12. See ibid., pp. 564–74; for the poet's own rather terse account of this editing, see A. Fet, *Moi vospominaniia. 1848–1889*, Moscow, 1890, vol. I, pp. 40, 104–5.

fraught, issue of his own art, and indeed the article contains many echoes of his dialogue with his critics. Much later, in his *Reminiscences*, Fet called the 1856 collection a 'mutilated edition';[13] but the experience was also a positive one, for he allowed most of Turgenev's alterations to stay in later collections. More importantly, such editing became an integral part of his later practice, when he used trusted writers/critics – especially Strakhov, Polonskii, Solov'ev, Tolstoi and Grand Prince Konstantin Romanov – to act as critics for him in the creative process.[14]

Thus in 'On the poetry of F. Tiutchev' Fet is participating in more than the public debate about aesthetics, he is engaged in a private dialogue as well – at a crucial point in his life and literary biography – about the very nature, process and direction of his art. Accordingly, the article not only has a wider and narrower audience in mind, but also, within this, explores the creative interrelations between writer and critic/reader. In this respect, it is significant that it is addressed in a subtitle to Apollon Grigor'ev, who is himself a most unusual, genuine combination of critic and poet. Grigor'ev represents a special combination of public and private audience too. The two poets' friendship dated back to their student days, when Fet lodged with Grigor'ev's family and they wrote and read poetry together. In the 1850s Grigor'ev was a leading figure in the public debate; but he had not been part of the *Sovremennik* circle, and now took an independent stance, separate from the aesthetic camp (at this time he was associated with *Russkoe slovo*, where 'On the poetry of F. Tiutchev' was published). Moreover, although he too had criticised Fet for a lack of clarity, he had a subtle and high appreciation of the distinctive character of his poetry.[15]

The presence of two audiences is given in the very first paragraph, where Fet contrasts the 'narrow circles' who so appreciated Tiutchev's collection of 1854 with the 'mass of the reading public' (p. 145) who have yet to do so. This opening paragraph already establishes the parameters of Fet's polemic with the reading public's heroes, the radical

13. Ibid., p. 105.
14. See Bukhshtab, 'Sud'ba literaturnogo nasledstva', pp. 574–9; in a recent study of one of Fet's late poems Venclova links this whole phenomenon to the nature of Fet's art itself, with its orientation towards marginal psychic states, the subconscious, stream of consciousness, etc. (Tomas Venclova, 'A. A. Fet. "Moego tot bezumstva zhelal..."', *Russian Literature*, vol. 17, 1985, p. 92.
15. Grigor'ev's appreciation of Fet had a strong influence on subsequent critics. He published a positive review of Fet's 1850 collection in *Otechestvennye zapiski*, no. 2, 1850, and devoted a number of pages to his poetry in 'Russkaia iziashchnaia literatura v 1852 godu' of 1853: Grigor'ev distinguishes two sides in Fet, the 'anthological' and the 'subjective', and, though he recognises weaknesses in the latter, is clearly drawn to the side which he sees as 'original' ('samobytnyi') – Fet as the poet of the undefined, unspoken, vague feelings (Apollon Grigor'ev, *Literaturnaia kritika*, ed. B. F. Egorov, Moscow, 1967, pp. 86–7, 98–102).

critics who insisted on the contemporary social relevance of art. His opposition is apparent from the very first words: 'For a long time now I have been meaning to say something about the little book of Tiutchev's poems which appeared in 1854' (p. 145). The point is not just that 1854 was part of a different epoch in social and political terms (a fact which Fet, dilatory enough as a reviewer, seems not to notice), but more generally that the length of time does not matter. ... Art is not contemporary but eternal.

Having set up his alternative audiences, Fet now begins to explore the relationship between critic/reader and writer in terms of their understanding of art. In the second paragraph the audience narrows to Grigor´ev, whom Fet is pleased to address directly (in the familiar 'you' form) because their common convictions about art spare him the need to spell everything out. The next paragraph then returns to the 'mass of the reading public', who look for 'theory', a favourite word of the radicals. Against this Fet opposes the authority of 'poet-thinkers', such as Schiller, Goethe and Pushkin (pp. 145–6). This dual definition is extremely significant in the context of the article as a whole and its role in the evolution of Fet's art. At this stage, however, it works polemically, by stealing another of the radicals' words ('thinker'), while at the same extending the 'narrow circle' in space, time and stature: the understanding of art, as well as art itself, is not local and contemporary.[16]

In giving his definition of the nature of poetry, Fet contrasts the artist with 'us': the artist only becomes such when his vision enables him to see beauty where 'we cannot see it, or can sense it only vaguely' (p. 146). But he also contrasts those who are able to see art with those who cannot; quoting a line from Chénier, he says that someone 'who cannot see the triumph of art' in it 'should not hold forth about poetry: it is a closed book to him' (p. 147). As Fet's discussion of art proceeds, there comes a point where the artist objectivised as 'he' is found in the same context as 'I' and 'we', a context that is clearly auto-reflexive:

> I am certainly not advocating grammatical carelessness, but in talking about poetic vision I even forget that the pen exists [i.e. the skill of writing]. Give us vision in a poet above all else, vision in respect of beauty, and all the rest is secondary. The more this vision is detached and objective (more powerful), even given its very subjectivity, the greater the poet and the more eternal his creations. No matter if personal impressions are the subject of his song (p. 148).

16. Fet ranges far and wide in time and space in his references to art and artists, from ancient Greece and China to Rembrandt and Beethoven. The name of Heine, however, is notable for its absence, although in the perception of writers/critics of the time Fet was persistently associated with him as a poet of 'feeling'. This omission might well be related to the reorientation of Fet's art that is adumbrated in the article.

'Grammatical carelessness', 'subjectivity', 'personal impressions' can all refer to Fet and the criticisms made of his poetry. Moreover, the notion of 'forgetting' when inspired immediately recalls his art too (compare 'Ne znaiu sam, chtó budu/ Pet´ – no tol´ko pesnia zreet').[17] Here, however, it is not poetic inspiration but the inspiration of the poet-critic, so in a curious way this passage demonstrates what it states, as Fet, inspired in his criticism, objectifies his own subjective experience as a poet. The culmination of this exploration of the creative interrelations of the artist and the perceiver of art comes during the transition from the more general opening pages to the discussion of Tiutchev. Fet concludes that image and thought in poetry 'invite the soul of the perceiver to fill in what is left unsaid, eliciting a new act of creation, and in this way work in harmony to make him a co-participant in the pleasure of art' (p. 151). This assertion of the creative relationship between poet and reader has a resonance far beyond the context of both the public and private debates conducted in the article, but it can also be read within that context. While Fet's formulation is at one remove from his experience with Turgenev and others, the notion of creative co-participation recalls their role and could be considered to carry an implicit recognition, at least in general, of their contribution to his creative process.

As Fet moves on to a critical appraisal of Tiutchev ('our poet'), initially through a comparison with Pushkin ('our Pushkin'), he continues to play on the opposition of 'you' and 'us'. But in so doing he seeks to bring 'you' over to 'us', not only by analysis of his chosen poets but also by appealing to the aesthetic sense which 'fills in what is left unsaid'. To this end he gives both a detailed comparison of Pushkin's 'Sozhzhennoe pis´mo' and Tiutchev's 'Kak nad goriacheiu zoloiu' (pp. 152–4), and a string of examples that, for him, go beyond words (p. 158). So, at the end of the essay, having dismissed poetry on topical themes as something that poets have had to suffer over the ages, Fet is able to call for readers to rise to the demands of Tiutchev's poetry – to rise to the creative participation he outlined earlier – in implied opposition to all that the radical critics seek from art.

Fet has no common ground with the radical critics in the public debate conducted in the article; but the narrower debate within that, the private dialogue with the old *Sovremennik* group, with Grigor´ev, even with himself, is an open and substantial one. In fact, the scope of 'wide' and 'narrow' should be inverted, for the private dialogue takes in the public one and goes far beyond it. Fet is discussing issues – the criticism

17. A. A. Fet, *Polnoe sobranie stikhotvorenii*, ed. B. Ia. Bukhshtab, (Biblioteka poeta, Bol´shaia seriia), 2nd edn, Leningrad, 1959, p. 254; these lines, from the last stanza of 'Ia prishel k tebe s privetom', offended Turgenev and were excluded by him from the 1856 collection.

of his poetry, the need for clarity, the relationship between thought and feeling, and so on – which are central to his art and which adumbrate the transition to his later work.

An intermediate figure between the public and private debates is Nekrasov, who, as the public debate became polarised, alone remained with Chernyshevskii and Dobroliubov at *Sovremennik*. Nekrasov had sent Fet his 'Poet i grazhdanin' prior to its publication in a collection in 1856, and Fet's article contains obvious echoes of this poem. First Fet dismisses the question of poetry's 'rights of citizenship' as a 'nightmare' (p. 146), and then he reworks the famous lines 'Poetom mozhesh´ ty ne byt´,/ No grazhdaninom byt´ obiazan':[18] 'You can possess all the other qualities of some well-known poet and yet lack his vision, his perception, and as a consequence not be a poet' (p. 147). More subtly, and positively, Fet invites Nekrasov back to the side of true art when he says that the smooth verse of a 'rhymer who is no poet' ('stikhotvorets-nepoet') bears no comparison to the 'at first sight clumsy verse of the true poet' (p. 157), which is a reference to Nekrasov's own description of his verse as 'stern' and 'clumsy' ('Moi surovyi, neukliuzhii stikh').[19]

Besides such individual references, the whole article draws on Nekrasov's survey 'Russian poets on the second rank', published in *Sovremennik* in 1850. Nekrasov was seeking to account for the eclipse of poetry in Russian letters and to raise its profile once more. He begins as follows: 'There is no poetry about. Only a few people regret this fact, many more are glad, while the great majority spare it no thought at all.'[20] After a survey of some other poets, including Turgenev, the second half of the article turns to Tiutchev (identified by his initials) and bemoans the absence of his verse for ten years. Nekrasov even ends by stating that Tiutchev is a 'first-class' poet; but it is still his title that stays in the mind. Tiutchev is presented as primarily a nature poet, and in addition, by implication secondarily, a poet of thought. Indeed, in his nature poems Nekrasov hails him as a master of that poetry in which 'there is apparently no content or thought whatsoever'.[21] Nekrasov does not offer any proper analysis of Tiutchev's poetry, his purpose being mainly to present and enthuse. Yet although his judgement is for the most part positive, even ecstatic, he makes some less favourable comment too, and unfortunately contrives to include 'Son na more' in a list of Tiutchev's 'comparatively weakest poems'.[22]

18. N. A. Nekrasov, *Polnoe sobranie stikhotvorenii v trekh tomakh*, ed. K. I. Chukovskii, (Biblioteka poeta, Bol´shaia seriia), 2nd edn, Leningrad, 1967, vol. 1, p. 235.

19. Nekrasov, *Polnoe sobranie stikhotvorenii*, p. 187.

20. N. A. Nekrasov, 'Russkie vtorostepennye poety' in his *Polnoe sobranie sochinenii i pisem*, ed. K. I. Chukovskii *et al.*, 12 vols, Moscow, 1948–53, vol. 9, p. 190.

21. Ibid., p. 205.

22. Ibid., p. 221.

Nekrasov actually quotes from Fet alongside Tiutchev, comparing the former's 'Vesna' with the latter's 'Vesennie vody'. He praises Fet's poem in parts, but 'regrets that it is spoilt by a number of unsuccessful lines', adding that 'this is quite a common failing in Fet'.[23] Quite apart from Nekrasov's association of the two poets, the issues he raises are close to those which are raised by Fet and which refer to himself as much as to Tiutchev. An interesting example is the question of poems that appear to lack content: Fet's 'lack of content' was rarely treated without condescension, while Nekrasov hails Tiutchev as a master of the art. Most importantly, whereas Nekrasov presents Tiutchev as primarily a nature poet (compare the attempts to present Fet in a particular mould), Fet sees him clearly as a poet of thought. All in all, Fet advances considerably on Nekrasov and ends, pointedly, by quoting the whole of 'Son na more' with the question: 'Who could dispute that these images are the product of a gigantic inspiration, a really powerful art?' (p. 163).

Fet's dialogue with Nekrasov extends into his debate with the old *Sovremennik* circle and beyond. He addresses their criticism, much of which had already been incorporated into his poetry, but in some respects seeks to modify and deflect it; and in writing auto-reflexively about Tiutchev, he also looks beyond the limitations they had both perceived in, and imposed on, his art. In this way the article can be seen to look forward as well as back, since it carries Fet's answer to his creative/critical experience of the preceding years.

Fet asserts, for example, the need for a balance between subjectivity and objectivity in art, in recognition of the criticism of Turgenev and others. The objectivity he has in mind, however, relates to the poet's ability to distance himself from his subjective input, his thoughts and feelings, and not at all to the objective, external input to art which the radicals might demand. He also addresses the question of content, its richness or poverty. Here he deflects the criticism (largely, but not exclusively, from the radicals) and then turns it on its head. First he rejects the equation of content with thought, understood in its everyday or philosophical sense; instead of 'your quasi elevated thought' (pp. 147–8), he once again champions a poet's vision. Subsequently, in his comparison of Pushkin and Tiutchev, he seeks to show how either feeling or thought may be in the foreground of a poem. But not both – if this occurs, then there is what Fet provocatively calls an 'excess of content' (p. 157).

Fet takes up the question of 'clarity' too, which was one of the main causes for Turgenev to call for new variants. But from the start he allies 'clarity' ('iasnost˝') with 'subtlety'/'fineness' ('tonkost˝'). The first

23. Ibid., p. 209.

authorities he invokes, Schiller, Goethe and Pushkin, are described as 'having a clear and subtle understanding of the significance and essence of their craft' (p. 146). Shortly afterwards, he shifts these qualities on to beauty itself, with its 'clear, yet delicately sounding, forms' (ibid.), a definition which reminds one of the musical orientation of Fet's poetry. Later on the emphasis has shifted further: 'in some works of art the thought is so subtle and is fused with the feeling to such an extent that, even if one writes reams, it is difficult to express it clearly; this, however, is not in the least detrimental to the richness of the content and the worth of the whole' (p. 152). By the end of the article, while reasserting his recognition of the need for clarity, Fet feels able to add the rider that 'there is more than one kind of clarity' (p. 163).

In addition, Turgenev had criticised and corrected what he called 'blemishes' ('piatna' – literally 'spots'/'stains') in Fet's poetry; Fet, on the other hand, says that there are 'blemishes' in Tiutchev's poetry, but adds that 'when you think of the sun, you forget about the spots' (p. 149). Further criticism and corrections made by Turgenev concerned archaisms and rhythmical irregularities. Again Fet notices the same, but in this case he simply says 'no matter' (p. 160), and his later poetry continued to use some of the very words that Turgenev had deleted.[24]

Finally, an interesting echo of Turgenev's practice of removing final stanzas can be seen in the suggestion that the last two stanzas of 'Ital´ianskaia villa' spoil the poem. Fet considers that Tiutchev's subjective propensity to reflection, poetic thought, gets the better of him in a poem where the first five stanzas embody the feeling inspired by Italy, so that the switch to reflection creates that 'excess of content' (p. 160) he had mentioned earlier. Rather than dismissing the final two stanzas, however, he suggests they might serve to make another poem.

The question of content, poetic thought and the relationship of thought and feeling in poetry has run throughout the article, starting with the original dual definition of 'poet-thinkers' applied to Schiller, Goethe and Pushkin. As we have seen, this recurrent question and much else besides, not least the very role of writer on writer, engages with fundamental issues concerning Fet's own art and its future direction. By turning to critical prose and objectivising these issues in his discussion of Tiutchev's poetry, Fet, consciously or unconsciously, is mapping his possible future direction in a more Tiutchevan perspective.[25] The process which leads to his later poetry, in which Fet becomes a poet of thought as well as of feeling, may already be under way.

24. See Bukhshtab, 'Sud´ba literaturnogo nasledstva', p. 572.
25. In addition to the general orientation towards expression of thought, Fet's later poetry also shows more specific parallels with Tiutchev (see Bukhshtab, *Ocherk zhizni i tvorchestva*, pp. 114–15).

In his introduction to a selection of essays by modern Russian poets on poetry Joseph Brodsky has written about the phenomenon of a poet turning to prose:

> A poet turning to prose (something usually dictated by economic considerations, 'dry spells', or more rarely, by polemical necessity) is like the shift from gallop to trot, a time-exposure photograph of a monument, or Apollo's one year's service as shepherd for the flocks of King Admetus.
>
> In other words, a poet's turning to prose is the tribute of dynamism to the stasis which preceded it; only the latter gains anything from such a switch...[26]

Fet's article on Tiutchev is dictated, at least to some extent, by all the factors that Brodsky mentions. But in Fet's case the gain is in some way not only that of prose. At any rate, his turn to prose in 'On the poetry of F. Tiutchev' should be seen as a significant moment in the dynamics of the evolution of his art.

26. Joseph Brodsky, Preface to *Modern Russian Poets on Poetry*, ed. Carl R. Proffer, Ann Arbor, 1976, pp. 8–9.

–3–

Chekhov and Merezhkovskii

Stephen le Fleming

In any relationship there is repulsion as well as attraction, and upset equilibrium as much as stability. Contact between Chekhov and Merezhkovskii was sporadic, but interesting for the reactions which followed their mutual enthusiasm.

In 1888 Chekhov wrote his first stories for a 'thick journal', *Severnyi vestnik*, and the first serious criticism of his work, as opposed to a short review, was published: Merezhkovskii's article 'An old question apropos of a new talent',[1] was ostensibly a review of the fourth and fifth published collections of Chekhov's stories, *In the Twilight* of 1887 and *Stories* of 1888. It was printed with reservations by *Severnyi vestnik* in 1888: an editor's footnote suggested that the author's views on art differed 'only in detail' from those of the journal's regular contributors, but at least two of them were upset, and one, M. A. Protopopov, never wrote for the journal again. On 2 October 1888 the journal's literary editor, A. N. Pleshcheev, wrote to Chekhov:

> Yesterday evening Merezhkovskii came to see me and read a little piece he had written about you. Honestly, it is better than anything the reviewers have said about you. I think you will like the article. It is fresh, young and extremely pleasant. He raves about you, of course, and analyses most of your stories ... The question is: whether 'non-tendentious' writers have any use. The answer, naturally, is positive.[2]

Chekhov replied on 4 October, interested to know what Merezhkovskii had written about him, and, prompted perhaps by Pleshcheev's reference to him as 'non-tendentious', concerned to state his literary *credo*:

1. D. S. Merezhkovskii, 'Staryi vopros po povodu novogo talanta. *V sumerkakh* An. Chekhova. Spb. 1887g. *Rasskazy* An. Chekhova. Spb. 1887g.', *Severnyi vestnik*, no. 11, 1888, pp. 77–99.
2. *Literaturnoe nasledstvo*, Moscow, vol. 68, 1960, p. 332.

I am frightened of those who look for a tendency between the lines and who like to see me as a liberal or as a conservative. I am neither a liberal, nor a conservative, nor a gradualist, nor a monk, nor an indifferentist. I would like to be a free artist, nothing else, and I regret that God has not given me the strength to be it. I hate deceit and violence in all their forms and I dislike consistory clerks as much as I dislike Notovich and Gradovskii. Pharisaism, obtuseness and arbitrary rule do not prevail only in merchants' houses and jails; I see them in science and literature, and among young people. That is why I have no particular affection for gendarmes, butchers, scientists, writers or young people. A trademark or label is to me a prejudice. My holy of holies is the human body, health, intelligence, talent, inspiration, love and absolute freedom, freedom from force and deceit in whatever way they might be manifest. This is the programme I would hold to if I were a great artist.[3]

Judging from this letter, written before he had seen Merezhkovskii's piece, Chekhov's intention was to write serious literature that was not committed to the social themes demanded by the critics who had dominated minor Russian writers since the 1840s. Realism had required the writer to address a contemporary issue and suggest, in as much as censorship permitted, a way out of the particular moral or political quandary which he had chosen to explore. By the 1880s the giants of Russian literature had completed their exploration of contemporary reality, and the younger generation was turning to new subjects and new genres.

Merezhkovskii began his review by noting the general decline in aesthetic appreciation and the rise in the popularity of the short prose form. Modern writers like Chekhov were attracted to the form 'because these small graceful novellas seemed created intentionally to convey the microscopic details and transitory, musical shades of feeling which are so dear to modern art'.[4] Reviewers and commentators – 'there being no literary critics as such' – had been restrained, Merezhkovskii thought. Though generally favourably disposed, they judged a writer not for the qualities he possessed, but for those they considered he lacked. It was much easier to roll out abstract formulae and theoretical demands than to analyse the work itself, easier to mock than to explain. Unless a work exhibited a blatant social tendentiousness giving the 'critics' something to argue about, it left them in helpless bewilderment; they either denied that such a work was possible or else, if they saw that the public liked it, they gave it restrained and insincere praise. This was why reviewers had paid Chekhov's stories less attention than they deserved.

3. A. P. Chekhov, *Polnoe sobranie sochinenii i pisem v tridtsati tomakh*, Moscow, 1974–83, *Pis'ma*, vol. 3, 1976, p. 11. O. K. Notovich was the proprietor and editor of the St Petersburg daily *Novosti* (News); G. K. Gradovskii was a political journalist.
4. Merezhkovskii, 'Staryi vopros', p. 78.

Merezhkovskii's swipe at the reviewers was echoed many times by Chekhov himself. While it was true that reviewers like Mikhailovskii, Skabichevskii and Protopopov did scan literature single-mindedly for ideological substance rather than aesthetic qualities, Merezhkovskii was himself not entirely innocent of a similar appropriation of Chekhov to advocate his cause. In 'The Steppe', for instance, he found an idea suspiciously reminiscent of his own religious pinings: 'In the depths of nature the poet senses a mystery: the aesthetic enjoyment experienced on superficial contemplation gives way to more profound mystical feeling, almost terror, which is nonetheless not without a vague, but alluring fascination.'[5]

As a rule, Merezhkovskii found, Chekhov's most successful character was a type of dreamer and loser, a passionate idealist and poet, almost always meek in a feminine way, mild and gentle, but devoid of will-power and any sense of direction. And while there was no actual tendentiousness in Chekhov, it was possible to trace a favourite dramatic conflict: 'the poet likes to juxtapose two psychological elements – consciousness, destructive analysis and reflection on one side and the unconscious, indestructible force of instinct, feeling, passion and the heart on the other'.[6]

Merezhkovskii then leapt smartly into the saddle of a nearby hobbyhorse and proceeded to argue the case for the social usefulness of even untendentious art generally: if pure science is beneficial in expanding the boundaries of human consciousness and sensibility, then on the same basis artists, even untendentious ones, 'increase the overall sum of aesthetic pleasure accessible to humanity in general ... any poem by Fet or poetic novella by such writers as Chekhov must be considered useful, valuable and totally justified from the point of view of scientific utilitarian morality'.[7] Merezhkovskii concluded with some general comments on the validity of tendentiousness if it was organic to the writer's temperament.

Chekhov was excited by this thoughtful and original response. After the lukewarm, grudging, repetitive notices that his stories had so far evoked, this appeared to be original and unprejudiced criticism. It showed that a provincial, petty-bourgeois medical student lacking an aesthetically cultured background could develop into a writer whom critics would take seriously. Small matter that the author was still a student, six years younger than he was himself. The article had been published in a major journal of the day and would be widely read. It argued for the kind of freedom that Russian literature had not enjoyed since

5. Ibid., p. 80.
6. Ibid., pp. 92–3.
7. Ibid., p. 97.

Lermontov, freedom from 'tendentiousness' (political and moral bias) and freedom to exploit the poetic, evocative, allusive registers of language, to insinuate dissatisfaction, rather than to specify solutions to social problems.

Chekhov gave his response, as so often, in a letter to Suvorin: on 3 November 1888 he wrote that the poet Merezhkovskii, who he thought must be a science student, had published a long article on him, and deduced that:

> anyone who has assimilated the wisdom of the scientific method and can therefore think scientifically experiences many delightful temptations. Archimedes wanted to overturn the world, and today's hot-heads want to embrace what is scientifically indefinable, they want to find the physical laws of artistic creation, to pin down the common law and the formulae by which the artist who senses them instinctively creates pieces of music, landscapes, novels, etc. These formulae probably exist in nature. We know that in nature there exist a, b, c, d, do, re, mi, fa, sol, there is the curve, the straight line, the circle, the square, the colour green, red, blue ..., we know that all this in certain combinations makes a tune or a poem or a picture, just as simple chemicals in certain combinations make a tree or a stone or the sea. But we only know that the combination exists; the sequence of the combination is hidden from us. Anyone who understands the scientific method senses in his heart that a piece of music and a tree have something in common, that both were created according to identically true, simple laws. Hence the question: what are these laws? Hence the temptation to write a physiology of art (Boborykin) or, in the younger and more timid, to make references to science and the laws of nature (Merezhkovskii).[8]

Chekhov went on to warn that if critics adopted a scientific approach they would waste years producing 'ballast' and confusing the issue further, while scientists argued about the cells or nerve-centres which governed the creative faculty. For those who wished to employ the scientific method the answer, he half-seriously suggested, was to develop the philosophy of art by isolating from the great works of art of all ages what was common to all of them. He then turned back to Merezhkovskii, reproving him for his timidity and seeing this as an indication that he had not yet clarified his ideas.

Merezhkovskii's review also attracted the attention of rival critics: Venevich (V. K. Stukalich), writing in a Moscow daily, objected to Merezhkovskii's attempt to exculpate Chekhov from the charge of lacking a sense of civic duty and felt that he had not made the distinction between premeditated tendentiousness and 'civic sense, social and moral ideas which it is necessary for everyone to keep in store, most of

8. Chekhov, *Polnoe sobranie, Pis'ma*, vol. 3, p. 53.

all for a writer'.[9] The objection was invalid, since Merezhkovskii had been at pains to distinguish between an artificially imposed tendentiousness which was ruinous to art and 'organic' tendentiousness which was a source of poetic inspiration for some artists. Another critic, hiding his identity behind a cryptic pseudonym, objected to the use of language in Merezhkovskii's article, even finding fault with the phrase 'human world'. Rather mysteriously he concluded that 'even Mr Merezhkovskii admits in the end that Mr Chekhov's works are sometimes not devoid of tendentiousness'.[10]

V. V. Kuz´min, the regular reviewer of the daily *Novosti dnia*, thought it right for Merezhkovskii to praise Chekhov for the many excellent pages and well-drawn types in his works, but wondered if it was entirely proper for a critic to praise a colleague on the same journal: the issue of *Severnyi vestnik* in which Merezhkovskii's article appeared also carried Chekhov's latest story 'The Name-Day Party', as well as a poem by Merezhkovskii. He found the article, with its name-dropping and use of unusual critical terms, such as 'architectural beauty of the artistic plan' and 'the soul of an object', too dazzling, and was amused by the editor's 'tactlessness' in printing an article with which his other contributors disagreed, albeit not too profoundly.[11] Merezhkovskii had already found himself at cross purposes with the journal's major critic, N. K. Mikhailovskii, earlier in the year: the March issue, as Burenin noted with glee, had contained both Mikhailovskii's articles attacking modern poetry and several of Merezhkovskii's poems.[12]

Pleshcheev had reported Merezhkovskii's intention of visiting Chekhov while in Moscow to see *The Wood Demon*; but it was a year before they met. In his letter to Suvorin of 5 January 1891 Chekhov mentioned that 'the poet Merezhkovskii has twice been to see me. A very intelligent man.'[13] Pleshcheev saw a different side of the picture in his letter to Chekhov of 12 January: 'Merezhkovskii told me that he had been to see you, but I could not get anything substantial out of him about you. I suppose he kept talking to you about aesthetics and God, whom he is now engaged in a search for (making far too much noise, some say).'[14]

Merezhkovskii had indeed undergone a profound reorientation of his ideas since his first essay on Chekhov. He had, according to his auto-

9. *Russkii kur´er*, no. 319, 18 November 1888.
10. B-i-ch-, 'Iz literatury i zhizni', *Den´*, no. 189, 25 November 1888.
11. Chitatel´ [V.V. Kuz´min], 'Zametki chitatelia. VI', *Novosti dnia*, no. 1944, 2 December 1888.
12. V. Burenin, 'Kriticheskie ocherki', *Novoe vremia*, no. 4316, 4 March 1888.
13. Chekhov, *Polnoe sobranie, Pis´ma*, vol. 4, p. 157.
14. *Literaturnoe nasledstvo*, vol. 68, pp. 361–2.

biography, been an enthusiastic 'positivist' as a student, though this did not satisfy his religious nature. He had then been influenced by the leading Populists: 'Mikhailovskii and Uspenskii were my first teachers', he wrote,[15] recalling that Gleb Uspenskii had encouraged him to look for a religious meaning in the philosophy of life of the common people. A hand-copied edition of Tolstoi's *Confession* had also affected him strongly and he had realised that 'positive populism' was not the whole truth for him.[16]

Almost at the same time he fell under the influence of Dostoevskii and foreign writers, Baudelaire and Poe in particular, beginning his interest in Symbolism.[17] In 1892 he published an edition of poems under the title *Symbols* and sent Chekhov a copy with an inscription recalling their meeting in Venice in March 1891. Chekhov left a notebook entry for 24 March 1891 that they had talked about death when Merezhkovskii and his wife Zinaida Gippius visited the hotel where he and Suvorin were staying:[18] *Death* is the title of the first of the three long poems that made up the edition. They express religious and romantic longings, and in the last of the three, *Vera*, Merezhkovskii muses on the historical role of the poet in arousing consciousness. There is a poignancy which persistently contradicts the positivistic certainties which Merezhkovskii had earlier espoused, and which echoes the awful realisation of emptiness in Nikolai Stepanich, the dying professor in Chekhov's 'A Dreary Story' of 1889, what Mikhailovskii called in his review of it 'toska po obshchei idee' (a longing for a meaning to it all):[19]

> Великий век открытий и чудес!
> А между тем нам как то скучно ... Стоны
> Разврат и голод ... Жар любви исчез ...
> Вселенную мы знаньем победили,
> А в сердце ... в седрце мрачно, как в могиле.[20]

Chekhov and Merezhkovskii both saw their characters' awareness of the need for a meaning to life which would transcend death, but from this point their thinking would lead them away from each other. They met occasionally, for example at the joint name-day parties which Chekhov and Ivan Leont´ev (Shcheglov) held in St Petersburg in

15. D. S. Merezhkovskii, 'Avtobiograficheskaia zametka', *Polnoe sobranie sochinenii*, 24 vols, St Petersburg, 1914, vol. 24, p. 112.

16. Ibid., p. 113.

17. Ibid.

18. Chekhov, *Polnoe sobranie, Sochinenia*, vol. 17, p. 250.

19. N. K. Mikhailovskii, 'Pis´ma o raznykh raznostiakh', *Russkie vedomosti*, no. 104, 18 April 1890.

20. D. S. Merezhkovskii, *Vera, Polnoe sobranie*, vol. 23, p. 93.

January 1892 and 1893. But the difference in their mentalities was now to be revealed. Chekhov, brought up in a warm family atmosphere partly overshadowed by a strict, almost fanatically religious father, had spent years freeing himself from conformist servility.[21] His medical training in Moscow had replaced the discipline of unquestioning religious obedience with the demands of materialistic rationalism. He was sceptical of Merezhkovskii's belief in the possibility of discovering answers to practical social problems through religious experience.

Merezhkovskii, in contrast, escaped from a cold, lonely boyhood in the family of an august official to a humanities course at St Petersburg University and marriage to the poet Zinaida Gippius, who supported his mystical aspirations.

On 25 December 1891 Chekhov wrote to Pleshcheev: 'Merezhkovskii is sitting at home just as mixed up in ultra-high-flown soul-searching as always, but is just as lovable as always.'[22] On 1 March 1892 he wrote to Suvorin that 'the exalted and pure-in-heart Merezhkovskii would do well to swop his quasi-Goethian way of life, his spouse and "the truth" for a bottle of good wine, a shotgun and a pretty woman'.[23]

That year Merezhkovskii gave a series of lectures in St Petersburg which he then published as a book, *On the Reasons for Decline and on New Trends in Contemporary Russian Literature*.[24] Chekhov was mentioned in the chapter devoted to the contemporary generation of Russian writers, though in a letter to Suvorin on 17 December 1892 he deplored the lectures as tactless.[25]

The book began with a reminder of Turgenev's deathbed appeal to Tolstoi to return to literature. Turgenev, he felt, had been prophetic in seeing the decline of Russian literature, and hence of the language, the very embodiment of the national spirit, as a disaster no less terrible than war, disease and famine.

Merezhkovskii deduced several social, cultural and historical reasons for the decline of literature, devoting much space to the critics. By the time he came to examine the contemporary literary scene, he had established that the highest moral significance of a work of art lay not in its touching moral tendentiousness, but in the artist's disinterested veracity, integrity and sincerity. The essence of art could not be reduced to beau-

---

21. Chekhov's famous letter to Suvorin of 7 January 1889 describes a young writer with a background like Chekhov's 'squeezing the serf's blood out of himself drop by drop and waking up one fine morning to feel that real blood ran in his veins, not serf's', *Polnoe sobranie, Pis'ma*, vol. 3, p. 133.

22. Chekhov, ibid., vol. 4, p. 336.

23. Ibid., p. 8.

24. D. S. Merezhkovskii, *O prichinakh upadka i o novykh techeniakh sovremennoi russkoi literatury*, St Petersburg, 1893.

25. Chekhov, *Polnoe sobranie, Pis'ma*, vol. 5, pp. 143–4.

ty or justice, but went back to the source from which both derived and which united them, making justice beautiful and beauty right. The nineteenth century had seen a clear division established between the known and the unknown world. For Merezhkovskii the age was defined by extreme materialism on the one hand and passionate upsurges of idealism on the other. Science and religion, which had previously crossed each other's borders, were now defined by them, constituting a tragic contradiction, a struggle which could not but be reflected in literature.

Popular taste demanded realism, an artistic materialism corresponding to scientific and moral materialism. But idealism in art was not a recent fashion; it was a return to ancient tradition. What shone through the beauty of the poetic symbol acted more strongly on the emotions than was defined by the words.

In the final chapter of his article Merezhkovskii surveyed the work of some of the contemporary literary generation, noting those qualities which for him suggested a break with the past. In Garshin's first story 'Four Days', for example, the nameless Russian soldier's experience becomes profoundly significant, so that the naturalism engenders a series of poetic symbols and the realist story becomes a lyrical *poema*.

Not long before he killed himself, Garshin had read Chekhov's 'Steppe' with a real sense of excitement at Chekhov's feeling for nature and health and his quiet love of life, claiming that the story had allowed him to forget his own sufferings for a time. He might have appreciated Chekhov so deeply because he himself was so different. While for Chekhov, whose origins lay in the depths of Russia, nature meant strength and health, Garshin was a poet of Petersburg; he almost always depicted one very modern type – a personality morbidly torn between two courses. Chekhov, on the other hand, was best at describing simple people, unthinking but capable of deep feelings. In fact, according to Merezhkovskii, Chekhov was, if anything, too healthy: it made him rather indifferent and unreceptive to many contemporary issues.

Like Garshin, however, Chekhov discarded everything superfluous, reviving the laconic simplicity which made prose as compact as poetry. He was turning away from the ponderous ethnographic accounts and 'official paperwork' of the positivist novel to a form of ideal art: not Garshin's subjective lyricism, but the small epic poem in prose. Chekhov's thirst for new experience was restrained by a dispassionate mind, but redeemed by an artistic sensitivity which allowed him to see the imperceptible. He reacted to every little flicker of life, and his impressionability made him notice fresh nuances in the most familiar everyday reality. He affected people like a burst of music flowing unexpectedly from some grim apartment block, leaving an impression of freshness. Chekhov's pursuit of beauty linked him to the modern generation of artists; but while Garshin acted through symbols, Chekhov followed Turgenev on the path to a new idealism in being an impressionist.

Merezhkovskii's concern for the essentially poetic qualities of Garshin and Chekhov led naturally to a consideration of two contemporary poets, Fofanov and Minskii. He found Minskii's confessional account of his abandonment of civic motifs profoundly sincere and significant. It expressed the same passionate demand for a new idealism as was found in Garshin, Fofanov and Chekhov.

Merezhkovskii included critics in his survey, approving particularly of S. A. Andreevskii whose graceful and original studies were compact poems in prose, like Chekhov's and Garshin's, but poems of criticism. Though Andreevskii had no strict analytical method, he was inspired by love, which was the only way to a poet's soul. This new criticism stood free of literary allegiances and was more interested in eternal questions, such as the writer's attitude to God, death, love and nature than the propagandist critics had been.

Merezhkovskii concluded by recalling that nineteenth-century Russian literature had, despite the ostensible realism of the novel, expressed insatiable mystical yearnings, most significantly in Dostoevskii's psychological profundity and Tolstoi's searching for a new truth and a new faith. The revival of idealist art had been clouded only temporarily in Russia by pedantic utilitarian criticism, and in Europe by the crude materialism of the experimental novel. The modern generation was now faced with the difficult task of making the transition from a spontaneous creative period of art to a critically conscious, cultured period. It was possible, he thought, that consciously embodying free divine idealism in literature would prove too great a task for them. But at least they would be lucky enough to sense the first stirrings of the new life.

In 1892 there had evidently been some talk of Chekhov editing a literary journal to be published by Merezhkovskii, but in his letter to Suvorin on 22 November 1892 Chekhov wrote that he had heard nothing;[26] Merezhkovskii had probably agreed with him that he was unsuitable as an editor, though he would willingly contribute. Nothing more was heard of this project for ten years.

In 1901 Merezhkovskii instituted meetings of what was to be known as the Religious–Philosophical Society, gatherings of prominent intellectuals with the aim of adapting Christianity to the modern world. This did not prevent Chekhov proposing him, together with Mikhailovskii, P. I. Veinberg and V. D. Spasovich as honorary members of the Russian Academy for 1902 in a letter to the Chairman of its Russian Language

26. Ibid., p. 131.

and Literature Section on 5 December 1901.[27] Yet on 17 December he was quite scornful to V. S. Miroliubov, the editor of *Zhurnal dlia vsekh*, who had been named as one of its organisers.[28] And he was unimpressed when he wrote to Diagilev on 30 December 1902 that he thought the intelligentsia was playing at religion, mainly because it had nothing better to do: 'It could be said that the educated part of our society has abandoned religion and is distancing itself further and further from it whatever they might say and whatever philosophico-religious societies might meet.'[29] For Chekhov culture did not depend on religion:

> Contemporary culture is the start of a labour in the name of a grand future, a labour that may continue for tens of thousands of years before mankind discovers, albeit in the distant future, the truth of the real God, that is, does not guess, nor look for him in Dostoevskii, but knows him clearly, as it knows that twice two is four.[30]

Neither was Diagilev impressed by Merezhkovskii's mystical searchings; but a merger between Merezhkovskii's journal *Novy put'* and Diagilev's *Mir iskusstva* was proposed as a commercial move. Chekhov was offered the literary editorship, while Merezhkovskii was to have run the critical section. Chekhov declined regretfully on 12 July 1903 on the grounds that he was unable to live in Petersburg and a journal could not be edited from a distance. Furthermore he could not have worked under the same roof as Merezhkovskii:

> who has a definite, didactic faith, while I lost my faith a long time ago and can only look with bewilderment at any member of the intelligentsia who believes. I respect D. S. [Merezhkovskii] and value him as a man as a literary figure, but if we were to be harnessed to the same cart we would be pulling in opposite directions.[31]

Merezhkovskii met Chekhov occasionally from 1892 onwards, but, from the publication of *On the reasons for decline* in 1893, appears to have ignored him in his writing until after Chekhov's death. A year later he published a short commemorative piece in the Moscow daily *Russkoe slovo*,[32] expanding on it in his essay 'Chekhov and Gor'kii' which formed the second article in his collection *The Approaching Vandal* of 1906.[33]

27. Ibid., vol. 10, p. 131.
28. Ibid., pp. 141–2.
29. Ibid., vol. 11, p. 106.
30. Ibid.
31. Ibid., p. 234.
32. 'Svirel' Antona Bednogo' (Anton the Poor's Reed Pipe), *Russkoe slovo*, 24 July 1905.
33. D. S. Merezhkovskii, 'Chekhov i Gor'kii', *Griadushchii kham*, St Petersburg, 1906, pp. 43–101.

In this piece he saw Chekhov and Gor´kii as representing for the average member of the Russian intelligentsia promoters of 'humane ideas' – belief in the triumph of progress, science and reason. And the *intelligent* would have considered it an insult to the writers and to himself if Merezhkovskii had tried to point out that both writers' work had proved the impossibility of his belief. Chekhov and Gor´kii were the first conscious proponents of the 'religion of mankind', a religion without God, which had always been the religion of the Russian intelligentsia. Mankind without God is mankind against God, mankind as God, Man as God, I as God – such was the metaphysical ladder Merezhkovskii saw the Russian intelligentsia dimly contemplating. Chekhov's *intelligent* was still on the lowest rung; Gor´kii's vagabond was already at the top. Thus Chekhov's characters had no life; their only passion, and it was a passion for them, was despondency ('unynie'), in which they indulged in their cities, their decaying estates, in factories, monasteries and professorial studies. Despondency, the leitmotif of Chekhov's music, was epitomised in the old shepherd Luka Bednyi's five or six notes which he kept trying to connect into a tune in *The Reed Pipe* (1897). In *Three Sisters*, however, the storm, which will mark the end of mere existence and the beginning of events, is seen as imminent, and, whatever the horror of the end, we will never forget Anton Bednyi's pervasively despondent reed-pipe which prophesied this end.

What is evident from this relationship is that Chekhov rejected any kind of subjective mystical dimension to existence, and any accommodation with those like Merezhkovskii who, however sincerely, believed in its possibility. In 1897 he had written in his diary: 'between "there is God" and "there is no God" lies a whole huge field which a genuinely wise man crosses with great difficulty. The Russian knows either one of these two extremes and is not interested in the area between them; and so he usually knows nothing, or very little.'[34] Chekhov and Merezhkovskii saw each other standing at opposite extremes and, without hostility, dug in.

---

34. Chekhov, *Polnoe sobranie, Sochinenia*, vol. 17, p. 224.

– 4 –

Shestov on Chekhov

Malcolm Jones

I

N. Baranova-Shestova tells us in her biography of her grandfather that Shestov first contemplated an article on Chekhov in the early years (1901–2) of the twentieth century. On Shestov's behalf, Diagilev wrote twice to Chekhov, asking for precise details of the dates of composition and publication of his stories and other works, to assist Shestov in writing an article which Diagilev was determined to publish. Shestov, Diagilev reported, had read several of Chekhov's works in Kiev, had seen *The Seagull* and *Uncle Vania* in Moscow, and had come to the conclusion that their author would be an exceptionally interesting subject for an article.

On 20 December 1901 Chekhov replied, enclosing a note in his own hand of the chronological arrangement of his works in the Marks edition.[1]

Shestov almost met Chekhov personally in Moscow in 1902, but his quarry had already departed for Yalta. It appears that in 1903 he sketched a book entitled *Turgenev and Chekhov*. Only the first half appears to have been written and it was never published.[2]

An article written in 1904 appeared in *Voprosy zhizni* in March 1905. To his sister Shestov wrote that everything that he had written in *The Apotheosis of Groundlessness* (also 1905) was stated more clearly and coherently in the Chekhov article.[3]

This remark may be taken as a warning that what Shestov had penned was not just a straightforward literary critical essay but, like his other works on great Russian writers, a development and application of his own existentialist philosophy.

1. N. Baranova-Shestova, *Zhizn´ L´va Shestova*, 2 vols, Paris, 1983, vol. 1, p. 53.
2. Ibid., vol. 1, p. 64.
3. Ibid., vol. 1, p. 80.

II

'Chekhov is dead; now it is possible to speak freely about him.'[4] Shestov hardly allows a decent interval to elapse before making his attack. 'Speaking freely', it turns out in this case, means 'denouncing'.

Shestov makes us choose: we cannot be both pro-Shestov and pro-Chekhov. Nor can we be indifferent. There is no third way. Chekhov has committed crimes against humanity: 'You must either reject Chekhov or become his accomplice.'[5]

> To define his tendency briefly, I would say that Chekhov was the poet of hopelessness. Stubbornly, despondently, monotonously, during his entire period of literary activity, for about twenty-five years, Chekhov did one thing only: in one way or another Chekhov killed human hopes. In my opinion this is the essence of his creative activity ... what Chekhov did is called crime in ordinary language, and it is subject to the severest possible punishment ... And Chekhov himself faded, withered and died before our eyes. The only thing about him that did not die was his amazing art of killing by a single touch, by even a breath or a glance, everything by which men live and of which they are proud. Moreover he was always perfecting himself in this art, and he attained a virtuosity superior to that of any of his rivals in European literature.[6]

Despite Shestov's stern injunctions, most critics, not sharing Shestov's value system, have found a third way. Forced to choose, it is small wonder that they have turned the tables, preferring to reject and ignore Shestov than to become his accomplice.

'Pathological', 'abnormal', the two magic words which, Shestov suggested, might allow us to reject Chekhov and his work painlessly, have more frequently been applied to Shestov himself.[7]

More surprisingly, some have set his views alongside those of other critics and juxtaposed them as though they were all engaging in the same sort of intellectual exercise and simply reaching different conclusions. Such, by the very nature of the work, is what happens in Charles Meister's recent compendium of Chekhov criticism from 1880 to 1986. All the same, Meister realises that there is something eccentric about Shestov's approach: 'Unlike nearly every other critic, Shestov found that Chekhov's deep pessimism led him to a wilful desire to destroy his characters.'[8]

4. Lev Shestov, 'Tvorchestvo iz nichego', *Nachala i kontsy*, St Petersburg, 1908 (reprinted Ann Arbor, 1978), p. 1.

5. Ibid., p. 8.

6. Ibid., pp. 3–6.

7. Ibid., p. 8.

8. Charles W. Meister, *Chekhov Criticism, 1880 through 1986*, North Carolina and London, 1988, p. 7.

According to Shestov, Meister tells us, it is cruel of Chekhov to have Van´ka misaddress the envelope. Chekhov's heroes are faced with the prodigious task of trying to create something out of nothing, a meaningful philosophy out of an absence of conviction. Why should anyone be interested in the professor from 'A Dreary Story'? Chekhov becomes interested in Katia only when she has become weak and despondent. For Shestov, 'The Duel' is another example of Chekhov's gloomy philosophy. 'Ward No. 6' shows how futile it is for a Chekhov character to try to create a meaningful life out of a void. In 'The Black Monk' Chekhov displays his tendency to choose for the subject of his stories abnormal people who philosophise unconvincingly. *Ivanov* shows Chekhov to be a poet of hopelessness. And so on through the major plays, climaxing with the news that Shestov is among those who consider that Sonia's final opinion in *Uncle Vania* should not be taken literally.

Only Robert Jackson seems seriously to have thought it worth challenging Shestov head-on. Here is the expert witness for the defence. Meister tells us that Jackson 'disputes' Shestov's charge of Chekhov's pessimism, pointing to the early comic stories, faith in mankind's future and a lifetime of humanitarian works; that he 'disagrees' with Shestov on whether *Ivanov* illustrates Chekhov's destructive tendencies and with Shestov's assessment of Chekhov as a poet of despair, pointing out that Chekhov cannot be equated with his characters, for in describing them he maintains an aesthetic distance from them.

In the face of Shestov's passionate accusations none of this sounds enough to secure a reduction in Chekhov's sentence, let alone lead to his acquittal and vindication.

For Shestov does not deny the brilliance of the early comic works or the humanitarian disposition. Moreover he is well aware of the artistic genius of the mature works and of the importance of Chekhov's innovations. Shestov's charge is that, notwithstanding all this, Chekhov is guilty of a lifetime of the most heinous crimes. His charges are moral: in Chekhov's works we see the author, unremittingly, time and again, in the dreary characters he thrusts into the foreground of his works, and in the even drearier fate he mercilessly and with consummate artistry devises for them.

To be fair to Jackson,[9] his defence of Chekhov is more persuasive and coherent and certainly more balanced than would appear from the fragments of his argument distributed in Meister's book.

To begin with, Jackson grants that Shestov is perhaps the most impressive exponent of the view of Chekhov as a melancholy and

---

9. Robert L. Jackson, 'Introduction, perspectives on Chekhov', *Chekhov, a collection of critical essays*, Englewood Cliffs, NJ, 1967, pp. 8–10.

destructive writer in his 'remarkably provocative though one-sided essay'. But he regards the fact that Shestov limits himself to a close analysis of only three or four of Chekhov's works as 'unsettling', finds it difficult to accept Shestov's view of a 'cheerful and joyful' early Chekhov whom, like Chizhevskii, he finds more melancholy than Shestov does, and points out that in the decade and a half following 'A Dreary Story' and *Ivanov* (the key works in Shestov's scenario, which he regards as 'strongly autobiographical in character'), affirmative notes may be heard. In such works as 'The Duel', 'The Lady with the Pet Dog', 'The Betrothed', and especially in *The Seagull*, man's interaction with reality seems to contain a creative potential.

Yet Jackson concludes that, although Shestov dramatically overstates his case (wherein lies its special appeal), he indirectly calls attention to a decisive feature in Chekhov's developing world view when he notes that 'the Chekhovian hero is left to himself':

> Shestov, then, touches on something central to Chekhov's world view: man must create everything himself, must seek out – in the words of the professor in 'A Boring story' – the 'general idea or god of a living man'. This may be a bleak, even tragic perspective, but it is the path of the free man.[10]

Jackson tries, as every good scholar should, to sift the valid criticism from the exaggerated denunciation, the objective truth from the subjective value judgements of a thinker best known for his espousal of existential paradox, to remove Shestov from Shestov's writing and to see what the residue has to tell us about Chekhov that we cannot glean from other sources. Jackson ends up in a kind of dialogue of equals with Shestov and with Chekhov.

But, of course, that was not how it was in Shestov's mind. Shestov wants not a civilised debate, but rather to dispose of Chekhov once and for all; and the more aware he is that he is also taking on public opinion and unusual artistic talent, the less room for manœuvre he is inclined to allow his adversary. Shklovskii said of Tolstoi that in seeking historical sources for *War and Peace* he needed not reliable witnesses but those he could most easily dispute.[11] So it is with Shestov. He does not focus on texts which will allow Chekhov to make his own case, but on those which best demonstrate his guilt. It is not for nothing that Shestov started life as a lawyer.

Most critics have been less accommodating to Shestov than Jackson is. The anger to which his article gives voice does not necessarily evoke

10. Ibid., p. 10.
11. V. Shklovskii, *Material i stil´ v romane L´va Tolstogo 'Voina i mir'*, (Slavistic Printings and Reprintings), The Hague–Paris, 1970, p. 44.

calm responses. Those who do not agree with him find it more satisfying and easier simply to ignore him or to take bits of his article out of context.

III

It is indeed tempting, in the light of all this, to cast Shestov aside as a Chekhov critic and to read his article merely as an expression of his evolving philosophy, discreetly sparing Chekhov the unpleasantness of having to answer the charges laid against him by such an embarrassing foe.

Yet Shestov, if taken seriously, does force Chekhov to answer a serious charge. And we first of all need to understand the position from which Shestov approaches his task.

Shestov's is not the sort of charge which sophisticated Western critics are nowadays accustomed to entertain.

By modern Western standards, Shestov commits various critical solecisms. He sees Chekhov's œuvre as autobiography, and holds him personally responsible for its social effect. In pursuit of this objective he identifies a handful of works as particularly telling autobiographical exposés and assimilates all the others to these, regarding any contradictory features as secondary and inauthentic. He regards artistry too, even brilliant artistry, as secondary to moral value. He does not deny the presence of great artistry in Chekhov, or Chekhov's attempts to disguise his crime (and deceive himself) by the introduction of 'positive' elements. For Shestov these are not mitigating factors: they make matters worse. One trembles to think what charges he might have levelled against his Norwegian contemporary, Edvard Munch.

Under the influence of Nietzsche and Dostoevskii, Shestov had already established himself as a passionate opponent of philosophical idealism, of vague moral idealism and of philosophical positivism. It is important to appreciate this when evaluating his rejection of the 'positive values' in Chekhov. His two most important works before the Chekhov essay were *The Good in the Teaching of Tolstoi and Nietzsche: Philosophy and Preaching* (1900) and *Dostoevskii and Nietzsche: the Philosophy of Tragedy* (1903). What impressed him about all three thinkers was their constant, unremitting struggle to understand the suffering, evil, tragedy and paradoxical nature of human experience. What he rejected in each of them was their yielding to the temptation to find refuge in the 'far easier and consoling task of preaching' simple 'truths'[12] and moral rules and thus find a tranquillity which

12. Bernard Martin, 'Introduction', Lev Shestov, *Dostoevsky, Tolstoy and Nietzsche*, Ohio, 1969, pp. x–xi.

eluded them in real life. Tolstoi found his escape in preaching the broth-erhood of man and a God whom he (unbiblically) equated with the Good. Nietzsche, having cast off science, the 'Good', love and compas-sion, eventually took refuge in the concept of the *Übermensch*; Dostoevskii, in the platitudinous morality which threatens to mar his great work as early as *Crime and Punishment*. Nevertheless, Shestov retained the utmost respect for the spiritual wrestling of each of these thinkers. So far as Dostoevskii is concerned it is in *Notes from Underground* that the writer's awakening occurred. For Shestov *Notes from Underground,* with its protest and struggle against positivism and idealism and against the idea that twice two equals four, was a *locus classicus* in modern thought.[13]

Shestov's is a monologic voice in Bakhtin's sense.[14] He does not brook contradiction. His objective is to put Chekhov in his place in rela-tion to his own evolving philosophy and if possible to use him to exem-plify some aspect of it.

IV

Thus it is that Shestov proceeds to analyse Chekhov's œuvre, now com-plete. We may summarise as follows. There is not a single one of humanity's hopes, in the past or the present, that Chekhov does not dash: art, science, love, inspiration, ideals, the future. Chekhov has only to touch them and they wither. The only thing not to wither was the amazing artistry with which he achieved this. Even Maupassant lags behind him.

There are two works in particular, written in 1888–9, which express this tendency perfectly: 'A Dreary Story' and *Ivanov*. They mark a spir-itual revolution in Chekhov's life and work, a putting behind him of the gay, carefree, youthful writer who published in the humorous journals. These are the most autobiographical of all his works. The hero of *Ivanov* calls himself a worker who has overstrained himself.[15] The theme of the two works is the same.

This overstraining poisons Chekhov's view of the world and is a kind of sickness. The realisation of this may be sufficient to make us forget about him. But if for some reason we do not wish to forget about him we have to take a moral stand, either with him or against.

As a matter of historical fact Chekhov could never have written his stories without the example of Tolstoi's 'Death of Ivan Il´ich'. And Tolstoi could never have got away with this tale of 'a donkey become

13. L. Shestov, *Dostoevskii i Nitshche. Filosofiia tragedii*, St Petersburg, 1903.
14. M. M. Bakhtin, *Problemy poetiki Dostoevskogo*, 3rd edn, Moscow, 1972, pp. 132 ff.
15. Shestov, 'Tvorchestvo iz nichego', p. 7. In tracing Shestov's argument in his arti-cle on Chekhov, I hereafter give references only to key passages.

tragic hero' if he had not already had behind him *War and Peace* and *Anna Karenina,* and the·reputation of a first-class artist. But even Tolstoi, with all his scepticism about world-views, does not show Chekhov's revulsion when confronted by ideas. *Ivanov* exemplifies the principle of arbitrary chance which throws down the gauntlet to philosophies of life of all kinds. It is perhaps Chekhov's most original insight. But it is also the source of his greatest torment, since it leads to a sense of impotence in the face of deeds already committed. There is nothing to be done except fall on the ground, scream and beat one's head on the floor. This is the fate of all Chekhov's heroes. The decent thing to do is to avert one's gaze. But Chekhov, on the contrary, shows us every detail of their torment and evokes sympathy in the audience. So long as a person has a task or a future, Chekhov loses interest. He is interested solely in death, disintegration, dissolution and hopelessness. It is impossible to find in his heroes any general idea, any ideal of a living person, and this fact characterises all his later work from 'A Dreary Story' onwards. In this work the idea persecutes Chekhov; from *Ivanov* the reverse is the case, and Chekhov persecutes the idea. He frees himself from his previous prejudices, but can find nowhere to go. He prefers to have nowhere to go than to yield to traditional answers. His heroes are therefore confronted with the task of creating out of nothing. They end up in a position of hopelessness with no way out and convinced of the absolute impossibility of whatever they are undertaking.

The good has never feared the daylight. Good people have always sought the company of others, while the evil have lived in isolation. Chekhov's people fear the daylight and live solitary lives. Perhaps they are going somewhere. But they never call on others to follow. They have nothing to teach. Their instinct tells them that each new philosophy is merely a new way of assembling the old bricks and stones. Even youth and ideas cannot overcome destruction and death. It is Ivanov, not L´vov or Sasha, who sets the tone. There is no ideal in Chekhov, not even an ideal of the everyday. At the end of 'A Dreary Story' the hero has no advice to give in response to Katia's desperate pleas. All he can say is 'I don't know.'

The same philosophy is evident in 'The Teacher of Literature'. But in 'Ward No. 6' it is clear that Chekhov has understood his own problem. He has sensed that the state of hopelessness is intolerable. He begins to preach an ideal. But not for long. The conclusion to 'The Duel' is only apparently idealistic. Von Koren is of the same type as Goncharov's Stolz. But whereas Oblomov is depicted as not entirely without hope, this is not the case with Chekhov's Laevskii. Von Koren, who is always apparently right, is a representative of that positivist-materialist philosophy which Chekhov often softens with a hint of idealism. He is merciless towards idealism of any kind, preferring crude materialism. Von Koren's materialism clearly demonstrates our dependence on nature. Every time he speaks he hits out not at Laevskii but at Chekhov himself. Why does Chekhov do this to himself? Perhaps because he secretly believes that salvation lies in self-torment. Perhaps he does not dare to offend that positivistic idealism which was then fashionable. At the end of the story Laevskii is reformed. Normal readers are not usually astute psychologists: astute psychologists are more likely to sense that morality is being mocked.

It remains true, however, that positivist (scientific) materialism is the only philosophy that Chekhov takes seriously: he senses the terrible dependence of the living human being on unseen, but powerful and soulless natural laws. The past can be countered only by forgetting and submitting. The last of Chekhov's plays to portray any protest is *Uncle Vania*. Like the old professor, like Ivanov, Uncle Vania creates a terrible fuss about his ruined life. He has recourse to every imaginable absurdity, gratuitously insulting his own mother and shooting at the pathetic father of poor Sonia, because there is no rational course of action for him to take. As usual with Chekhov it is impossible to be reconciled to reality, impossible not to be reconciled, and therefore the only thing left is to beat one's head against the wall. Science, however far one pursues it, will not provide the elixir of life. Sonia and Astrov, meanwhile, build around themselves a wall of fine words to protect them from the curiosity of others.

In 'The Black Monk' Chekhov shows that every abnormality leads via an absurd life to an absurd death. Perhaps he does not want to believe this; perhaps he hopes for something from abnormality but fails to find a way out of the labyrinth.

The Seagull is Chekhov's most characteristic drama. All the characters are either blind, fearing to step outside the house lest they should be unable to find their way home, or half mad, threshing out in all directions, not knowing where they are going or why. To this pattern are assimilated 'My Life', 'Ionich' and 'Three Years'. In the end, Chekhov's characters expend all their inner strength to no avail; they achieve nothing. Nobody believes that by altering the conditions of human life it is possible to alter its destiny. Everywhere there reigns an unspoken conviction that the will should be harnessed to goals totally unrelated to the organisation of the human race. The only possible concluding words for an article on Chekhov are: 'résigne-toi, mon coeur, dors ton sommeil de brute'.

V

Shestov refers in his article to several Russian writers. He cites Mikhailovskii in order to explain why the astute critic who so accurately pinpointed Dostoevskii's Achilles' heel fails unaccountably to perceive the danger Chekhov presents. He refers to Tolstoi chiefly to account for the fact that Chekhov was able to succeed against the odds with his depressing portrait of the human condition. He compares Chekhov's Laevskii and Von Koren with Goncharov's Oblomov and Stolz.

But the sensitive reader will notice that the spirit which animates Shestov's attack on Chekhov is that of Dostoevskii's man from underground, or, more exactly, the man from underground as Shestov sees him.[16] It is this spirit we see in the attack on hopelessness and degeneration, of despair born of philosophical nihilism, and also in the attack on positivistic materialism, whether of the idealistic kind (as Shestov explicitly says, that of the 1860s) or of the more recent scientific kind.

But Shestov not only sees in Chekhov the foes against whom the underground man rails; he also perceives and rails against the frailties of the underground man. Like the underground man, Chekhov understands that idealism can be countered only by mockery, and materialism only by beating one's head against the wall. Chekhov's heroes, like Dostoevskii's hero, do both. What we discover therefore is that Shestov on Chekhov is the ghost of Dostoevskii in Chekhov, the difference being that Chekhov is the quietest of Russian writers, his characters passive. In other words, Chekhov develops the impotence of the man from underground rather than his protest: his anger is turned inward not outward.

The article on Chekhov also, Shestov explained, stated more clearly and coherently what he had written in *The Apotheosis of Groundlessness*. As D. H. Lawrence observed in his introduction to his English translation (which he called *All Things are Possible*) Shestov rejects the whole tradition of Western philosophy. To speak anachronistically, he deconstructs it, from metaphysics to materialistic positivism.[17] But here he is less harsh on Chekhov, and the idea of creation from nothingness is seen not as a crime but as our common lot. The title of the essay on Chekhov may therefore mislead the reader, as it seems to have misled Meister, into thinking that the attempt to create from noth-

16. For a persuasive analysis of Shestov's debt to Dostoevskii's *Notes from Underground*, see James S. Wernham, *Two Russian Thinkers*, Toronto, 1968, pp. 57–65. To judge from the infrequency with which it is cited, this excellent book would seem to have been unjustly neglected.

17. Lev Shestov, *All Things are Possible*, London, 1920, introduction by D. H. Lawrence.

ing was, in Shestov's view, the root of Chekhov's inadequacy. Perhaps Shestov has subtly shifted his ground in the process of clarification. For why should he otherwise have chosen 'creation out of nothing' as the title of his onslaught? But the nub of the problem is not in fact that Chekhov creates out of nothing. It is that out of nothing he is capable of creating only hopelessness and despair. For he has overstrained himself. It is thanks to Dostoevskii that Shestov is able to clarify his earlier work.

VI

If Chekhov's art is as morally obnoxious as Shestov makes out, why, one wants to ask, does not Shestov do the decent thing and simply avert his gaze, as he says Chekhov ought to have done with the world he depicts? The answer seems to be that he thinks Chekhov is dangerous and that someone must speak out and tell the world.

Shestov's reading of Chekhov is of course in its own way vastly appealing. It is appealing because of its style, its consistency, its clarity, its passion, its simplicity and, it must be said, its plausibility. It takes a strong moral stance which challenges head-on the atmosphere of weary *fin de siècle*. It does not hesitate to declare the moral and practical bankruptcy of the world Chekhov depicts and of Chekhov's complicity in it. An audience living in another era may feel that this world-weariness is part of its charm. Shestov, living in the society it depicts, is driven (like Dostoevskii's man from underground) to channel all his energies into exposing and denouncing an art which can get no further than reflect its degeneracy and moral exhaustion, and infect its audience with the same *malaise*. And, of course, Shestov's fluent, direct literary style has its own appeal.

At the end of the day it is possible to feel that Shestov is unjust, is selective in his evidence, wrong to apply moral judgements to great art, wrong to confuse the real author with the text, wrong to try rhetorically to persuade us that no more complex judgement is possible and yet, at the same time, to feel that it is impossible to reject what he says entirely. And, more importantly perhaps, that the kind of case he is making, that literature should not be immune to moral judgements, and that writers should be held responsible for the effect of their work, is not one that should be dismissed out of hand. That is not because it is self-evidently true. The history of political and moral censorship (even self-censorship) is enough to convince of the damage which this attitude may cause. Rather it is because the reverse attitude, that all works of genius are entitled to be circulated, irrespective of their damaging social effects, is no less questionable. The period in which Shestov lived contains sufficient evidence of both to require no further comment.

Of course Shestov's rhetoric echoes Kierkegaard and the New Testament when he tells us we have to choose: either we are for Chekhov or against, there is no third way. It is clearly possible to find a third way, and many more ways still. But this is not simply rhetoric. The challenge is justifiable if we accept his premises about life and philosophy. If we accept that it is a crime against humanity to create a literature of 'overstrainedness' in which characters are condemned to the sisyphean task of creating out of nothing, then, if we discover that this is what Chekhov does, Shestov's position is logical. We may accept his view and find Chekhov not guilty. We may accept his reading and not consider that Chekhov is guilty of a crime (or think it a lesser offence). Or we may accept that he has committed a crime but consider that he has expiated it by what he has given humanity. Or, of course, we may reject both Shestov's view and his reading of Chekhov.

Most present-day Western readers will probably reject Shestov's premisses. They are likely, moreover, to find his reading one-sided. But as with Tolstoi's philosophy of history, they may find that it contains enough truth to make them think again, specifically about the debate concerning Chekhov's pessimism and optimism. Some will moreover welcome the contribution it makes to the dialectic of Russian culture at the turn of the century, and particularly to the clash of the secular scientific spirit with a passionate religious voice, not long before those revolutionary events which smothered the religious renaissance and deified social engineering. Certainly the richness and variety of Russian culture in the first quarter of the twentieth century cannot fairly be reduced to such simple terms; but in the event political categories suggest themselves as the most useful because, as Christopher Read reminds us, art was increasingly politicised after the Russo-Japanese war of 1905.[18] In the early years of the century there was a relatively clear divide between Symbolists and Realists. When the Vekhi group published its papers in 1909 the political lines were fairly sharply drawn.

Although there was much blurring of categories and interaction between various groups in the years that followed, Shestov did not participate in it. Eschewing compromise, he continued to affirm an unrelenting religious existentialism which led him into exile, where he eventually left his mark on French existentialist thought, most notably on Albert Camus.

18. Christopher Read, *Culture and Power in Revolutionary Russia*, London, 1990, pp. 21 ff.

But this is what Shestov's article is: the antithesis in a dialectic of which we are presumed to know the thesis. We are perfectly entitled to try to define a superior synthesis ourselves, Shestov's antagonism towards Hegel notwithstanding. But not, if we accept the rules of dialectic, to smooth the opposition over or avert our gaze.

5

Gumilev's Reviews of Viacheslav Ivanov's *Cor Ardens*: Criticism as a Tool in the Polemics of Literary Succession

Pamela Davidson

The title of this volume, *Russian Writers on Russian Writers*, suggests an interesting question. Is there a generally valid distinction to be drawn between the literary criticism of writers and that of critics, and, if so, what are the main factors which inform this difference?

The critic's judgement is usually rooted in the current climate of literary opinion and often tends towards a conservative approach; it may well be linked to a particular critical method, sometimes imposed upon the writer under consideration. In the Russian tradition, for example, criticism has frequently been dominated by ideological or social concerns.

The well-spring of a writer's response to another writer is somewhat different. It is to be found in the dynamics of the writer's own creative process and development. The act of criticism may be a form of self-definition, a way of underlining a creative affinity, emphasising a difference or marking a new point of departure.

When one is dealing with relations between contemporaries, there is a further important area of difference. The critic delivers his verdict upon a writer who does not usually respond directly or openly. By contrast, the writer who comments on another writer is potentially engaging in a two-way dialogue – of which criticism may only form a small part.

Finally, while the critic may not aspire to be a writer, the writer-critic competes with his fellow-writer on a professional level – their critical exchange is much more likely to be coloured by elements of personal rivalry or even hostility. This tendency can be exacerbated in cases where there is a substantial age difference between two contemporary writers, and criticism may become a tool in the hands of younger writers seeking to take over from the older generation.

These distinctive features peculiar to a writer's criticism are all very much in evidence in Gumilev's reviews of Viacheslav Ivanov's collection of verse, *Cor Ardens*, published in two parts in 1911 and 1912. Although Gumilev has often been described as a dispassionate literary critic, a close reading of his reviews reveals that they were far from being objective pieces of literary criticism;[1] rather they constituted a form of preliminary and covert literary manifesto and served as an important tool in his struggle to sort out his own complex and somewhat confused relationship to his Symbolist heritage and to establish an independent literary platform.

I

Before looking at the texts themselves, a brief outline of Gumilev's relationship with Ivanov will help to set them in context.

The first point concerns the younger poet's almost pathological craving for a teacher figure, accompanied by a strongly ambitious urge towards complete mastery of his craft and independence. This tendency comes across strongly in his early letters to Briusov, the first poet to fulfil this role in his life.[2] Around 1909, however, Gumilev's allegiance seems to have shifted at least in part to Ivanov. This change may to some extent have resulted from his growing sense of crisis over two aspects of his poetry – his knowledge of versification and what he terms 'ideological content' ('ideinost'), the sophistication of his ideas and of their expression in his verse.[3]

1. In his introduction to N. S. Gumilev, *Pis'ma o russkoi poezii*, compiled and edited by G. M. Fridlender and R. D. Timenchik, Moscow, 1990, Fridlender argues that Gumilev's criticism was not affected by differences of opinion or literary groupings, and that he paid full tribute to Ivanov despite their polemical disagreements over questions of aesthetics. He concludes that 'Gumilev stremitsia byt' v svoikh otsenkakh maksimal'no bespristrastnym' (p. 23). The present chapter seeks to show precisely the opposite – how strongly Gumilev's assessment of Ivanov as a poet was affected by the desire to escape the dominant influence of his personality and ideas.

2. See in particular Gumilev's letters to Briusov of 24 March 1907, 15 August 1907, 6 April 1908, 15 June 1908 in N. S. Gumilev, *Neizdannye stikhi i pis'ma*, Paris, 1980, pp. 13, 19, 44, 48. Gumilev constantly addresses Briusov as *maitre, uchitel'* or *pokrovitel'*, begs him to continue guiding him, and reminds him that the development of his talent lies entirely in his hands.

3. It is interesting to note that as early as 1906 Gumilev was making a special study of Ivanov's verse, following Briusov's advice, in order to improve his understanding of certain aspects of versification. See Gumilev's letter to Briusov of 30 October [1906] in Nikolai Gumilev, *Neizdannoe i nesobrannoe*, compiled and edited with commentaries by Michael Basker and Sheelagh Duffin Graham, Paris, 1986, p. 96. The worry over his lack of knowledge of the technical aspects of versification persists throughout his early letters to Briusov. See his letter of 24 March 1907 for example 'Odno menia muchaet i sil'no – eto moe nesovershenstvo v tekhnike stikha' (Gumilev, *Neizdannye stikhi*, p. 13). Concern over the *ideinost'* of his verse becomes a prevalent theme from the summer of 1908. On 14 July 1908, for example, Gumilev wrote to Briusov expressing the worry that the philosophical development of the themes of his work may be childish. On 20 August

Ivanov was ideally equipped to guide him in both these fields – versification and *ideinost'*. Gumilev's first visit to the older poet's celebrated salon at the tower took place in November 1908.[4] At first his attitude to Ivanov was tempered with irony – he refers to him as the 'Queen of Sheba', for example, in a letter to Briusov of 26 February 1909.[5] But later in the same year he informs Briusov that it is only now, after attending Ivanov's lectures on poetry, that he is beginning to understand what verse is all about.[6]

In August and September 1909 the two poets met with particular frequency, and Ivanov exerted a considerable ideological influence on Gumilev around this time, initiating him into his ideas on the theurgic role of art, mysticism and theosophy.[7] The extent of their closeness at

---

1908 he wrote again that his views on art had undergone a complete change ('perelom vo vzgliade na tvorchestvo'). He is aware of the inadequacy of the thought content of his verse ('v moikh obrazakh net ideinogo osnovaniia') and resolves to remain silent until he matures. See Gumilev, *Neizdannye stikhi*, pp. 51–3.

4. In his letter to Briusov of 30 November 1908 Gumilev mentioned the meeting, but was quick to reassure Briusov that the latter's role as his teacher remained unchallenged ('Viacheslav Ivanovich vchera mne skazal mnogo novogo i interesnogo, no uchitel' moi Vy i mne ne nado drugogo'). See Gumilev, *Neizdannye stikhi*, p. 56. The hasty reassurance would seem to suggest that Gumilev was already wavering in his loyalties. According to Akhmatova, Briusov tried to prevent Gumilev from meeting Ivanov, wishing to retain him under his own influence (Lidiia Chukovskaia, *Zapiski ob Anne Akhmatovoi*, vol. 1, *1938–1941*, Paris, 1976, p. 46).

5. The phrase was originally Briusov's, as Gumilev notes in his letter; he is anxious to reassure Briusov that he has not fallen prey to the 'Dionysian heresy'. See Gumilev, *Neizdannye stikhi*, p. 60.

6. 'I mne kazhetsia, chto tol'ko teper' ia nachinaiu ponimat', chto takoe stikh'; undated letter, ibid., p. 61. Ivanov's lectures for young poets on the theory of verse were held at the Poetic Academy at the tower in 1909. Further evidence of Gumilev's appreciation of Ivanov's poetic technique around this time can be found in a letter to M. Kuzmin of early May 1909: 'Viacheslav Ivanovich chital svoi "Venok sonetov" – udivitel'no khorosh', (Gumilev, *Neizdannye stikhi*, p. 120).

7. See Gumilev's six letters (1909–12) to Viacheslav Ivanov in Gumilev, *Neizdannoe*, pp. 122–5 and the detailed accompanying notes on pp. 253–61. Four of these letters and one additional letter from Gumilev to Vera Shvarsalon were also published with extensive notes in R. D. Timenchik, 'Neizvestnye pis'ma N. S. Gumileva', *Izvestiia Akademii nauk SSSR, Seriia literatury i iazyka*, vol. 46, 1987, no. 1, pp. 62–9.

Ivanov's diary of 1909 gives details of his frequent meetings with Gumilev in the course of August and September 1909. See Viacheslav Ivanov, *Sobranie sochinenii*, edited by D. V. Ivanov and O. Deschartes, 4 vols (to date), Brussels, 1971–87, vol. 2, 1974, pp. 782–4, 791, 795–6, 799. Although the diary contains no specific references to discussions of mystical matters, this was the period of Ivanov's maximum absorption in theosophy and occultism, following the death of his second wife, Lidiia Zinov'eva-Annibal, in October 1907 and the growth of his nascent feelings for her daughter, Vera Shvarsalon, soon to become his third wife.

In this context one can understand Gumilev's reference to theosophy in his letter to Ivanov from Africa of 5 January 1910: 'Peredaite, pozhaluista, Vere Konstantinovne, chto ia vse vremia pomniu o teosofii'. Timenchik notes that Gumilev, Kuzmin and Vera Shvarsalon were considering a plan for a theosophical society in November 1909 (Timenchik, 'Neizvestnye pis'ma', p. 63).

this point can further be gauged from the fact that Ivanov very nearly accompanied Gumilev on his trip to Africa in November 1909.[8]

While Gumilev could absorb Ivanov's lessons on poetry on a technical level without relinquishing his independence, his relationship to Ivanov as a 'thinker' was more complex. Here one senses that Gumilev was both very susceptible to Ivanov's influence – particularly in view of his own self-confessed weakness in this area – and also, as a result, extremely anxious to assert his independence.

This tension underlies Gumilev's reaction to the review which Ivanov wrote of his third collection, *Pearls*, published in *Apollon* in April 1910.[9] Ivanov wrote that Gumilev had now reached the end of his romantic, dreamy phase, marked by the influence of his teacher, Briusov, and was ready to embark on a new independent stage of poetic development, 'when the true experience of his soul, acquired through suffering and love, would tear apart the veils ('razorvet zavesy') still shrouding the essential reality of the world from the poet's gaze ('pered vzorom poeta')' – the implication was that Gumilev should shed his youthful romanticism and come to adopt a more Ivanovian type of poetics, characterised by a combination of real experience and belief in a higher transcendent reality, rather than by the subjective world of fantasy and dreams. With typical astuteness Ivanov had divined Gumilev's weak spot – his immaturity and excessive dependence on a teacher figure – and was trying to exploit this weakness in order to bring the younger poet more closely within the sphere of his own influence. Gumilev strongly resented the prescriptive tone of this review and appealed to Briusov for guidance in helping him to resist its message.[10]

When Gumilev came to write his review of the first part of *Cor Ardens* in the following year, he had a slightly clearer but still rather vague idea of his poetic aims, now defined in a further letter to Briusov

8. On 3 January 1910 Ivanov wrote to Briusov: 'Chut´-chut´ bylo ne uekhal s Gumilevym v Afriku ... no byl bolen, otseplen delami i – beden, ochen´ beden den´gami.' See *Literaturnoe nasledstvo*, vol. 89, Moscow, 1976, pp. 523–4.

9. *Apollon*, no. 7 (April), 1910, pp. 38–41, second pagination. The same issue contained Gumilev's much more flattering assessment of Ivanov's verse in his essay 'Zhizn´ stikha', discussed below. It is significant that Gumilev had originally asked Briusov to review *Pearls* (dedicated to him, as his teacher), but Briusov declined the invitation (for their exchange of letters, see Gumilev, *Neizdannye stikhi*, pp. 64–5 and *Neizdannoe*, p. 136).

10. Gumilev wrote to Briusov about this review shortly before his wedding to Akhmatova, which took place on 25 April 1910. His extreme indignation can be sensed from the fact that he devotes most of his letter to the review, after only a brief opening reference to his impending marriage. He is aware that Ivanov is trying to channel his poetic development in a particular direction, and resists this, but indecisively ('teper´ ia ves´ ustremlen k inomy, novomy. Kakoe budet eto novoe, mne poka ne iasno, no mne kazhetsia, chto eto ne tot put´, po kotoromu menia posylaet Viacheslav Ivanov'). See Gumilev, *Neizdannye stikhi*, pp. 65–6.

as the attempt to widen and 'render concrete' ('konkretizirovat´') the range of his images.[11] The desire to break free from Ivanov's pervasive influence, coupled with uncertainty as to exactly how to achieve this, seems to have informed the rather ambivalent attitude to the poet which can be sensed in his writing of this period. In June 1911, for example, he wrote to Ivanov, asking him in an excessively deferential manner to approve the publication in *Apollon* of certain poems enclosed with the letter as a proof that he has not yet disowned his 'always doubtful but always devoted pupil'.[12]

II

A similar ambivalence is reflected in Gumilev's two reviews of *Cor Ardens*. The general tone of the first review appears to be fairly positive, with just a few reservations.[13] However, a closer reading reveals evidence that Gumilev is already preparing the ground for the much fuller rejection of Ivanov which takes place in the review of the second part of *Cor Ardens* published a year later.

The first review adopts a dual approach to Ivanov's collection, interestingly enough corresponding to the two main areas of the poet's influence on Gumilev: his use of poetic form and ideas. On the one hand Gumilev makes a series of apparently objective and fairly positive observations about the technical side of Ivanov's poetry and his use of language. In each case, however, he then proceeds to relate these observations about poetic form to some aspect of the poet's ideas, and in so doing endows them with a negative value.

Gumilev starts by raising a question, effectively concerned with the relationship of poetry to ideas and with the status of religious or philosophical poetry – are writers who deal with personal mystic experience to be regarded as poets? He cites the examples of Confucius, Mohammed, Socrates and Nietzsche – significantly, all better known as religious thinkers or philosophers than as poets. If these writers can be regarded as poets, so, he concludes, may Ivanov.

Through this rhetorical opening Gumilev scores a number of points. Ivanov's status as a poet is not only implicitly queried, it is also relegat-

11. See ibid., pp. 67–8.

12. 'Etim vy dokazhete, chto Vy ... eshche ne otreklis´ ot vsegda somnevaiush-chegosia, no vsegda predannogo Vam uchenika.' See Timenchik, 'Neizvestnye pis'ma' and Timenchik's accompanying note (pp. 64, 67). The same letter is partly quoted and given an interesting interpretation by Timenchik in 'Zametki ob akmeizme III', *Russian literature*, no. 9, 1981, p. 175.

13. Review of *Cor Ardens: Chast´ pervaia*, *Apollon*, no. 7, 1911, pp. 75–6. This review and the second one were both reprinted in N. S. Gumilev, *Pis´ma o russkoi poezii*, Petrograd, 1923, pp. 117–20 and 147–9, and in the recent annotated edition, Gumilev, *Pis´ma*, pp. 124–5 and 147–8.

ed to a special category which, according to the examples given, is not normally associated with poetry, and is alien to the Russian tradition.

Gumilev then continues to underline the abyss which separates Ivanov from those whom he defines as the poets of 'lines and colours'. Ivanov's verse is characterised by the image of the sky reflected in a lake ('nebo, otrazhennoe v ozere'), while the poetry of the others is described as a lake reflecting the sky ('ozero, otrazhaiushchee v sebe nebo'). Already these two images imply a certain unspoken scale of values – the sky reflected in a lake hints at compression and artificial reduction, whereas the lake reflecting the sky suggests wider vision and extra dimension.

To the second category, to the poets of lines and colours, belong Pushkin and Briusov, Lermontov[14] and Blok. By assigning Ivanov to the first category, Gumilev effectively removes him from this mainstream tradition, making him a poet of the other world, divorced from this world.

This distinction is illustrated by two contrasting pairs of examples. Lermontov's Demon comes down to earth to kiss Tamara, whereas the hero of Ivanov's long poem 'The Dream of Melampus' retires into an abyss of abstractions. A Pushkin landscape is contrasted with one by Ivanov: the first is concrete, the second very abstract.[15]

The point may appear to have been 'proven' in this way, and undoubtedly there is, as in every persuasive distortion, more than a grain of truth in it. However, the examples have been selected from a very varied body of poetry to prove one particular point. Gumilev has chosen one of the most abstruse poems of *Cor Ardens*, 'The Dream of Melampus' (so obscure that Ivanov was compelled to provide notes for it, fearful that his readers would otherwise miss the point), and one of his most abstract, unrealistic landscapes. He could equally well have

14. For evidence of Gumilev's strong personal identification with Lermontov's fate and poetry, see Irina Odoevtseva, *Na beregakh Nevy*, Washington, 1967, pp. 160–73. The statement that Gumilev named Lermontov as his favourite poet (*Lermontovskaia entsiklopediia*, Moscow, 1981, p. 123, repeated by Fridlender in Gumilev, *Pis'ma*, p. 6) refers to this source, but derives from a faulty attribution of words spoken by Odoevtseva to Gumilev.

15. Gumilev's choice of poems is quite deliberate. From Pushkin's 'Otryvki iz puteshestviia Onegina' he chooses the stanza beginning 'Inye nuzhny mne kartiny', which portrays a humble, simple Russian landscape, purposefully evoked to contrast with the preceding highly romantic description of the Crimean landscape (full of phrases which one might well encounter in Ivanov's poetry such as 'brega Tavridy', 'pri svete utrennei Kipridy', 'v bleske brachnom', 'na nebe sinem i prozrachnom'). Gumilev's example from Ivanov, the first verse of 'Sirena', is in fact not a 'landscape' poem at all, but a poem about the forces of memory and fate, conjured up through the evocation of a dream-like and unrealistic setting (the poem comes from 'Eros', the third book of *Cor Ardens: Chast' pervaia*, reprinted in Ivanov, *Sobranie sochinenii*, vol. 2, p. 367).

selected one of Ivanov's less symbolic, more naturalistic landscapes,[16] or an example of his heavily erotic mystic verse, or one of his more playful philosophical poems – any one of which could have been cited in support of a quite different argument.

The review then continues with a series of comments on three aspects of Ivanov's poetic craft, his use of images, language and verse. In each case what starts out as simple description or even praise rapidly becomes tinged with reservation and subtly turns the reader's mind in another direction. A close look reveals the way in which Gumilev's positive evaluation of Ivanov's poetic technique is constantly overshadowed by his desire to escape the influence of his ideas.

To describe Ivanov's images, Gumilev chooses the key term of 'illusoriness' ('prizrachnost´'). Here he is quite deliberately playing on Ivanov's own terminology. Ivanov placed great stock on the concept of 'transparency' ('prozrachnost´'), by which he intended the power of the artistic image to serve as a pure and transparent reflection of the transcendent world. The artist should be endowed with penetrating or transparent vision – he has the ability 'to see through', 'to perceive' ('prozret´'), his visions are *prozreniia* ('insights', 'perceptions') – and his art, the medium of expression, should be correspondingly *prozrachnyi* ('transparent') to allow his vision to shine through.[17]

Prozrachnost´ (Transparency) was the title of Ivanov's second collection of verse, and Gumilev was very much aware of the full resonance of the term. When he gave Ivanov a copy of his second collection of verse, *Romantic flowers* (1908), he inscribed it with the following dedication 'To Viacheslav Ivanov as a token of deep respect for his insights' ('prozreniia').[18] In his third collection, *Pearls* (1910), he chose as an epigraph to one section two lines of a poem from Ivanov's

16. Although Ivanov's landscapes are always imbued with an awareness of the higher reality which they reflect, they are often – in his best poems – densely textured and richly evocative of natural beauty in a manner somewhat reminiscent of the English religious poet Gerald Manley Hopkins. From the first part of *Cor Ardens* one could cite as examples the poems 'Zagor´e', 'Nevedomoe', 'Ulov', 'Vesenniaia ottepel´', 'Liven´', or 'Osen´' (Ivanov, *Sobranie sochinenii*, vol. 2, pp. 278, 280–1, 310–11).

17. For a fuller discussion of the concept of transparency see Pamela Davidson, *The Poetic Imagination of Vyacheslav Ivanov: A Russian Symbolist's Perception of Dante*, Cambridge, 1989, pp. 165–7.

18. This copy of *Romantic Flowers* is held in the Lenin Library, Moscow (GBL). See the note to the reprint of Gumilev's review of *Tender Mystery* in A. V. Lavrov and R. D. Timenchik, '"Ne pokoriaias´ magii imen": N. Gumilev – kritik. Novye stranitsy', *Literaturnoe obozrenie*, no. 7, 1987, p. 108.

Transparency which allude to the same concept: '– Chto tvoi znak? – "Prozren´e glaza,/ Dal´nost´ slukha, okrylen´e nog"' ('– What is your sign? – "In sight of the eye,/Long-range hearing, winged feet"').[19]

Transparency, in Ivanov's view, did not involve a lessening of the reality of an object – on the contrary, it allowed it to retain its own natural appearance, while at the same time enabling it to be 'transparent', to reveal a vision of its inner spiritual essence or deeper reality.

Gumilev, in his review, has made one small but highly significant change. By changing *prozrachnost´* into *prizrachnost´*; by the semantic shift of one prefix, he has transmuted Ivanov's transparency into its very opposite, into something shadowy, illusory and possibly deluding – thus undermining the ontological foundation of Ivanov's poetics.

This transformation is achieved by degrees. The first time Gumilev uses the term *prizrachnost´* in his review, he simply establishes it as the main characteristic of Ivanov's images, and contrasts it with the 'life-like' ('zhiznennyi') imagery of poets of the mainstream tradition (thus implying a certain lack of life in Ivanov's imagery).

On the second occasion the term *prizrachnyi* is used to argue that Ivanov's images are so full and bright that they prevent the reader from grasping the overall sense of the verse and induce a feeling of frustration. By the time Gumilev came to write his review of the second part of *Cor Ardens* a year later, the term had undergone a further 'negative' transformation and turned into a 'deceptive illusion' ('obmanchivyi prizrak'), as we shall see below.

It should be added that the accusation of lifelessness which Gumilev levelled at Ivanov's poetry in 1911 is in sharp contrast with his assessment in the previous year of the poet's verse as a prime example of 'living' poetry.[20] Gumilev was most probably mounting a counter-attack in defence against Ivanov's earlier comment in his review of *Pearls* that the younger poet's verse was lifeless because of its dreamy romanticism

19. The lines are taken from the final verse of Ivanov's poem 'Prishlets' from *Transparency* (reprinted in Ivanov, *Sobranie sochinenii*, vol. 1, p. 753). The question 'Chto tvoi znak' is addressed to Dionysus, who replies by describing his attributes in the last quatrain of the poem, quoted from above. In the first edition of *Pearls* (Moscow, 1910), Ivanov's lines were appended to the section entitled 'Zhemchug rozovyi' and were immediately followed by the poem 'Rytsar´ s tsep´iu' (1908), in which a knight describes the renewal of his spirit of adventure. Gumilev's positioning of the epigraph from Ivanov thus has the effect of linking the spirit of adventure expressed in his poem to Ivanov's Dionysian intuitions. In the later 1918 edition of *Pearls* Gumilev did away with the division into sections and, significantly, removed the epigraph from Ivanov.

20. In this essay, Gumilev specifically made the point that the 'lifelike' quality of a poem does not depend on its relation to real life, but on its intrinsic quality. He singled out Ivanov's poem 'Geliady' from *Transparency* as one of only four examples of what he terms '"zhivye" stikhotvoreniia' in this sense. See 'Zhizn´ stikha', *Apollon*, 1910, no. 7 (April), pp. 9–11, first pagination.

and lack of relation to the transcendent mystic dimension.[21] Gumilev was now attempting to turn the tables on his teacher by claiming precisely the opposite, that the transcendent dimension in poetry – and in Ivanov's verse in particular – renders it lifeless.[22]

As far as language is concerned, here also there is a move towards negative characterisation, again as a result of reading the poetry in terms of the ideas which it is seen to reflect. In earlier essays Gumilev had praised the richness and inventiveness of Ivanov's language.[23] These same qualities are now a matter of debate. It turns out that Ivanov is more of a philologist in his approach to language than a poet. Gumilev asserts that for Ivanov all words are equal, and that his use of them is eclectic and shows no respect for their origins and individual weight: 'for him [words], just like images, are only the clothing of ideas'.

Ivanov was undoubtedly a superb philologist, fluent in several languages, and well aware of the historical weight of words. His verbal inventiveness was a great source of inspiration to poets fairly far removed from him in other respects – as in the case of Khlebnikov, for example.[24] The claim that he disregards the age or origins of words seems to miss the point of what the poet is trying to achieve through his eclectic use of language, deliberately cultivated as a means of synthesising opposites and of conveying the sense of culture as living memory.

21. See, for example, the following features singled out by Ivanov in his characterisation of *Pearls*: 'otsutstvie bystroty, neposredstvennosti, *zhivoi* podvizhnosti, *zhivoi* reaktsii na mnogoobrazie *zhivoi zhizni*'. Ivanov's review ended with the prognosis that if Gumilev were to break through the veils shrouding his gaze from a vision of the 'sushchaia real´nost´ mira' . . . 'togda vpervye budet on prinadlezhat´ zhizni' (ibid., p. 41).

22. Gumilev chooses to ignore the fact that *Cor Ardens* is unique in Russian poetry for its intimate connection with the poet's life; Ivanov himself referred to his wish to 'napisat´ svoiu zhizn´' in connection with his book (diary entry for 27 Aug. 1909, *Sobranie sochinenii*, vol. 2, p. 796). At the end of his first review of *Cor Ardens* Gumilev promises to write about this aspect of the book in his next review ('O samom glavnom v poezii Viacheslava Ivanova, o toi zolotoi lestnitse, po kotoroi on vedet ocharovannogo chitatelia, o soderzhanii, ia budu govorit´, kogda viydet vtoroi tom *Cor Ardens'a*'); the intention was never carried out, however.

23. He commented specifically on the depth and beauty of Ivanov's adjectives and on the principle of 'sploshnaia revoliutsiia' in his poetic art. See Gumilev, *Pis´ma*, pp. 105, 110.

24. For an account of Khlebnikov's early debt to Ivanov, see Aleksandr Parnis, 'Novoe iz Khlebnikova', *Daugava*, no. 7, 1986, pp. 106–7.

However, Gumilev does not, at this stage, take this too far – he recognises (as do Briusov and Kuzmin in their reviews of the same book)[25] that Ivanov's language is always closely tied to the expression of an exact thought and is astonishingly varied and unique in this respect.

On the question of verse, Gumilev acknowledges that Ivanov is an accomplished master of poetic form. But here again, he somehow manages to turn this to Ivanov's disadvantage – apparently, versification is only a 'means' for Ivanov, not an intrinsic source of joy or inspiration: 'for him [verse] is not a helper, not a source of pure joy, but also only a means'.

The general trend of this review is therefore a curious blend of the positive and the negative. Ivanov's uniqueness as a poet of mystic experience is underlined, but this is then turned against him as a way of removing him from the mainstream Russian tradition. His originality and mastery of his craft are recognised on one level, but at the same time the relationship between the poet and his craft is somehow seen to be at fault. In each case Ivanov's considerable technical achievements as a poet are undermined by an implied attack on his ideas, often presented in a subtly distorted form.

III

The year that elapsed between the writing of the first review and the second one was a decisive one in post-Symbolist poetics and in Gumilev's attempts to establish his own independent literary platform. A series of articles in *Trudy i dni* were devoted to this debate, and Gumilev's second review, published in the sixth issue of *Apollon*, can be read as a challenge to Ivanov's attempts to reestablish the supremacy of Symbolism.[26]

25. See Valerii Briusov, 'Novye sborniki stikhov', *Russkaia mysl'*, no. 7, 1911, pp. 20–4, and Mikhail Kuzmin, 'Cor Ardens Viacheslava Ivanova', *Trudy i dni*, no. 1, 1912, p. 50). For a comparative study of contemporary responses to *Cor Ardens* (reviews by Briusov, Kuzmin, Chulkov, Khodasevich, Gumilev and Gorodetskii) in relation to the issue of Ivanov's difficulty as a poet, see Pamela Davidson, 'The Legacy of Difficulty in the Russian Poetic Tradition: Contemporary Critical Responses to Ivanov's *Cor Ardens*', *Cahiers du Monde russe* 35 (1–2, 1994, pp. 249–67).

26. The second part of *Cor Ardens* appeared after some delay in April 1912; Gumilev's review followed in *Apollon*, no. 6, 1912, pp. 52–3.

Earlier in the same year, the first issue of *Trudy i dni* had opened with the seminal essays by Ivanov ('Mysli o simvolizme') and Belyi ('O simvolizme'), claiming the continuing supremacy of Symbolism (*Trudy i dni*, no. 1, 1912, pp. 3–24). The same issue also included Kuzmin's positive review of the first part of *Cor Ardens*, thus presenting Ivanov's collection within the framework of the journal's pro-Symbolist programme.

A discussion of the talks on which Ivanov's and Belyi's essays were based took place at the third meeting of the Society of Lovers of the Artistic Word in St Petersburg on 18

Many of the traits which were identified by Gumilev in his first review as simply characteristic of Ivanov's poetry are taken up in the second review and developed in a more explicitly negative manner.

For example, towards the end of the first review Gumilev wrote that Ivanov's 'intense mode of thought' ('napriazhennoe myshlenie') creates an astonishingly varied language. Early in the second review, the same intellectuality has become 'monotonous intensity' ('odnoobraznaia napriazhennost''), giving a purely intellectual pleasure, and ruling out the 'unexpected joy' of poetic discovery.

Furthermore, the link between Ivanov's intellectual thought and complex language, still recognised and respected in the first review, is now broken. Ivanov's language is here qualified as archaic and barbarian, his syntax is seen as 'painstakingly obscuring the general sense' – obscuring rather than revealing meaning.

Most significantly, however, as noted above, the line of thought already introduced in the first review through the transmutation of *prozrachnyi* into *prizrachnyi*, of transparency into illusoriness, is given a further and much more negative development in the second review. Gumilev asserts that for Ivanov all earthly realities, ideas and names are nothing but a 'deceptive illusion' ('obmanchivyi prizrak') and shadows.

Here he is making an unspoken transition from the recognition of the reality of the spiritual world to the implication that the material, physical world therefore has no reality. Although Ivanov used terms like transparency and even *Maya* (illusion), he did not regard the phenomena of this world as illusory in themselves, only as such if one failed to see what lay beyond them. The poem which Gumilev alludes to in his review as an illustration of Ivanov's illusory symbolism, 'Ad rosam', is in fact devoted to a discussion of the need to rediscover the lost link between the spiritual world and earthly reality, and favours a sort of creative, dynamic symbolism of transformation, not one of negation or

---

February 1912 and was reported in the following issue of the journal in an article by N. V. Nedobrovo, 'Obshchestvo revnitelei khudozhestvennogo slova v Peterburge', *Trudy i dni*, no. 2, 1912, pp. 26–7). Nedobrovo recorded the negative reactions of Gumilev and Gorodetskii, who had declared at the meeting their refutation of the principles of Symbolism and withdrawal from the Symbolist camp.

For helpful reviews of this debate, see the notes introducing Gumilev's letters to Ivanov in Gumilev, *Neizdannoe*, pp. 253–6 and Timenchik, 'Neizvestnye pis´ma', pp. 66–7.

denial.[27] Gumilev's underlying polemical intentions are given away in this section of the review by his use of the word 'symbols' – he is trying to discredit Symbolism by implying that it is based on a view of the material world as illusory.[28]

These specific attacks on Ivanov are inserted into a rather poorly constructed overall argument. Gumilev first sets up a fairly stereotyped image of the Slav soul, composed of conflicting Eastern and Western elements. After promoting the idea of organic synthesis as superior to either of these elements, he argues that Ivanov represents the Eastern extreme.

Gumilev may here have been alluding to Ivanov's interest in theosophy and occultism, which he had witnessed in 1909, or to his experiments in *Cor Ardens* with Eastern verse forms such as the *ghazal*; however, his claim that Ivanov represents a purely Eastern extreme seems quite unjustified in the light of the poet's far greater familiarity and affinity with classical antiquity, medieval Christian Europe and German romanticism.

The final stage of Gumilev's argument is to assert that an extreme is a dead end – and yet surely the course of poetic development has shown again and again that what may appear to be an extreme or dead end can be an unexpected source of renewal or inspiration for the next generation?

Why, therefore, the emphasis on this rather shaky argument (at the expense, one might add, of any serious discussion of the poetry itself)? It appears to stem from the desire, already implicit in the first review, to define Ivanov in such a way that he falls outside the mainstream of the Russian poetic tradition. In the first review, Gumilev had deprived

27. 'Ad Rosam' is the opening poem of the fifth and final book of *Cor Ardens*, 'Rosarium' (Ivanov, *Sobranie sochinenii*, vol. 2, pp. 449–50). For a fuller discussion of its meaning, see Davidson, *The Poetic Imagination*, pp. 208–18. It is interesting to note that another less partisan contemporary reviewer of the second part of *Cor Ardens* singled out the same poem for discussion in his review but described it as typical of Ivanov's poetics of transformation of the earthly. See Pavel Medvedev, Review of *Cor Ardens: Chast' vtoraia*, *Novaia studiia*, no. 13, 1912, pp. 4–5.

28. A later article by Chulkov refutes these contentions. He spotted the way in which the Acmeists used the word *prizrachnyi* to imply – incorrectly in his view – that the Symbolists made the world unreal. 'Chto kasaetsia akmeisticheskoi kritiki simvolizma, to ona svoditsia k odnomu sushchestvennomu upreku. Simvolizm obestsenil etot vneshnii mir, sdelal ego prizrachnym i stalo byt, – zakliuchaiut akmeisty, – pustym'. He argues that the tendency towards 'illusionism' exists as a heresy within Symbolism, but that in true Symbolism 'zemlia real'na i zhiva'. Significantly, he takes the example of the rose to prove his point: 'Roza, kotoruiu budto-by tak grubo rastoptali simovolisty, vovse ne pogibla. Naprotiv, v glazakh simvolista, ona stala bezmerno blagoukhannee i chudesnee ... lish' v simvolizme my nakhodim glubokuiu liubov' k ploti, k zemle, k cheloveku.' See Georgii Chulkov, 'Opravdanie simvolizma', in his *Nashi sputniki: 1912–1922*, Moscow, 1922, pp. 112–13.

Ivanov of his poetic lineage by setting him apart from the Pushkin and Lermontov line of poets; in the second review, he takes this further and denies him his future or poetic posterity.

After a passing bow in the direction of Ivanov as 'an important and original individual', he maintains that to follow him would be a perilous, risky adventure, spelling death: 'for others, not possessing his characteristics, to follow him would mean embarking on a risky, very likely even fatal adventure'. It is rather as if Gumilev is hurrying his reader past a section in the garden of Russian poetry reserved for exotic curiosities from abroad, something worthy of passing comment, but essentially foreign and not designed to flourish on Russian soil. Ivanov, in his view, illustrates one extreme of the Slav soul, and perhaps has a certain curiosity value as such – but cannot represent a path forward for the future.[29]

The review concludes with the following words: 'He is dear to us as an example of one of the extremes to be found within the Slav soul. But, in defence of the integrity of the Russian idea, we must, while loving this extreme, firmly say "no" to it, and remember that it is not by chance that the heart of Russia is simple Moscow and not magnificent Samarkand.'

IV

At the beginning of this essay, I raised a question about the nature of the difference between the criticism of writers and of critics. Gumilev's reviews of Ivanov have provided a telling example of the form that this difference can take, and illustrate the intimate link between a writer's creative development and his criticism.

The fact that Gumilev was not able to assimilate the legacy of Ivanov more smoothly and had recourse to a certain measure of distortion in his reviews is an indication of just how susceptible he was to the powerful influence of Ivanov at this stage of his literary development. His reviews reflect the fluctuations and inconsistencies caused by his conflicting urges towards discipleship and independence.

29. Later Khodasevich was to take a similar view of Ivanov's legacy to future generations. Comparing *Cor Ardens* to San Marco he wrote: 'tvorchestvo Viacheslava Ivanova neizbezhno voidet v istoriiu, no esli i vyzovet naivnye podrazhaniia, to ne budet imet′ prodolzhatelei' (Vladislav Khodasevich, 'Russkaia poeziia: Obzor', in *Alt′siona: Kniga pervaia*, Moscow, 1914, p. 197).

The tone of Gorodetskii's review of *Cor Ardens* was considerably more restrained. However, in a sentence which was later deleted from the printed version, he made a similar point; he wrote that the book reflected 'nachalo, apogei i uklon togo poeticheskogo mirosozertsaniia, kotoroe stroit na pochve simvolizma Viach. Ivanov'. See Roman Timenchik, 'Zametki na poliakh: No. 1', *Giperborei*, no. 1, 1912, facsimile reprint, Leningrad, 1990, [p. 33].

In a note on the history of Acmeism Akhmatova wrote that as a boy Gumilev had believed in Symbolism rather as one might believe in God, and that his subsequent disillusionment had affected his attitude towards Ivanov. In an autobiographical fragment of great interest she goes so far as to attribute the beginning of Gumilev's break with Ivanov specifically to his review of the first part of *Cor Ardens*, recognizing that it had contained elements which had unnerved Ivanov.[30]

The difficulty which Gumilev experienced in disengaging himself from Ivanov's influence was partly due to his own relative immaturity at the time, but was also further compounded by certain aspects of Ivanov's own character. According to the portrait which Berdiaev draws in his memoirs, Ivanov's unique role as a teacher of poetry derived from his considerable talent for friendship and from the exceptional attentiveness which he displayed towards younger poets; however, these qualities went hand in hand with a rather despotic nature and desire for influence over others.[31]

This seems to be confirmed by a very perceptive comment made by Blok in a diary entry for April 1912 about the state of mind which informed Gumilev's response to Ivanov. He wrote that although Gumilev's anti-Symbolist pronouncement 'a word should signify only that which it signifies' might appear stupid if taken literally, it is quite understandable from a psychological point of view 'as a rebellion

---

30. 'Vsego nuzhnee poniat´ kharakter Gumileva i samoe glavnoe v etom kharaktere: mal´chikom on poveril v simvolizm, kak liudi veriat v Boga. Eto byla sviatynia neprikosnovennaia, no po mere priblizheniia k simvolistam, v chastnosti, k "Bashne" (V. Ivanov), vera ego drognula, emu stalo kazat´sia, chto v nem porugano chto-to' (Akhmatova's note, 'K istorii akmeizma' in her 'Avtobiograficheskaia proza' edited by R. D. Timenchik, *Literaturnoe obozrenie*, no. 5, 1989, p. 7). The second (untitled) fragment includes the following statement: 'Akmeizm voznik v kontse 1911 g[oda]. V desiatom godu Gumilev byl eshche pravovernym simvolistom. Razryv s "bashnei" nachalsia, po-vidimomu, s pechatnogo otzyva G[umile]va o *Cor Ardens* na stranitsakh *Apollona*. [. . .] V. Ivanov emu chego-to etoi retsenzii nikogda ne prostil' ('Iz dnevnikovykh zapisei', edited by V. A. Chernykh, *Literaturnoe obozrenie*, no. 5, 1989, p. 11).

31. 'Dar druzhby u nego byl sviazan s despotizmom, s zhazhdoi obladaniia dushami ... No v kontse kontsov liudi ot nego ukhodili.' See Nikolai Berdiaev, *Samopoznanie: Opyt filosofskoi avtobiografii*, 2nd edn, Paris, 1983, p. 178.

32. The diary entry for 17 April 1912 appears in Aleksandr Blok, *Sobranie sochinenii*, edited by V. N. Orlov, 8 vols, 1960–3, Moscow–Leningrad, vol. 7, 1963, p. 140. It was written the day after Blok's letter to Andrei Belyi of 16 April 1912 (printed in vol. 8, pp. 386–8), which criticised the first issue of *Trudy i dni* and attacked Ivanov's despotism and covert polemics with Gumilev. This issue of *Trudy i dni* contained Ivanov's essay, 'Myslio simvolizme', with its celebrated declaration 'ia ne simvolist, esli slova moi ravny sebe, esli oni – ne ekho inykh zvukov' (*Trudy i dni*, no.1, 1912, p. 6).

33. The age-difference was undoubtedly a very important factor in Gumilev's case. One can contrast his response to Ivanov with that of the older Briusov, who, despite an open polemical disagreement with Ivanov over the nature of art, was still able to write two very positive reviews of *Cor Ardens*.

against Viach. Ivanov and even as the desire to break free from his authority and despotism'.[32]

This statement contains the key to the ambiguities and distortions of Gumilev's reviews – born of the conflicting pressures of Ivanov's pervasive and somewhat despotic influence, exerted over a younger poet whose intense desire for independence was not yet matched by a sufficiently strong sense of direction.[33]

By the time Gumilev came to review Ivanov's next collection, he had overcome some of these earlier unresolved conflicts.[34] His short review of *Tender Mystery*, published in *Apollon* in 1913, praises the simplicity and clarity of Ivanov's new collection and describes it as the work of a great poet at the peak of his powers. Although Gumilev concludes his review by reiterating the profound distance between Ivanov's path and Acmeism ('between Viacheslav Ivanov and Acmeism there is an abyss which no talent can fill'), his awareness of this difference no longer prevents him from recognising the older poet's gifts, as it previously had.[35]

Gumilev's reviews of *Cor Ardens* are not only key documents for understanding the gradual stages of the emergence of Acmeism from the symbolist chrysalis; they also reveal the many ways in which a writer's criticism can contribute to his own literary development – as a means of self-definition, as an indirect form of literary manifesto, or as a tool in the polemics of literary succession.[36]

34. In 1913 he published his prose manifesto 'Nasledic simvolizma i akmeizm' (*Apollon*, no. 1, 1913); this was followed later in the same year by the programmatically Acmeist drama 'Akteon' (*Giperborei*, no. 7, 1913), written as a further endeavour to overcome Ivanov and Symbolist attitudes (see the perceptive analysis by Michael Basker, 'Gumilyov's "Akteon": A Forgotten Manifesto of Acmeism', *Slavonic and East European Review*, vol. 63, 1985, pp. 498–517).

35. *Apollon*, 1913, no. 3, pp. 74–5. Gumilev's other review of *Tender Mystery*, published in *Giperborei*, no. 4, 1913, p. 27, was even more positive in its praise and untinged by any form of negative comment.

36. The author would like to thank the British Academy and the Leverhulme Trust, whose generous support of research for a complete annotated bibliography of critical works about Ivanov has facilitated work on this essay.

6

Missing Links: Russian Women Writers as Critics of Women Writers

Catriona Kelly

This essay is not an attempt to set out a general historical survey of Russian women writers as critics; still less is it an annotated bibliography of criticism by women. My concern is more narrowly defined: I intend to examine what criticism can tell us about the history of women's writing in general, and about the links between women writers in particular. In examining these questions, I do not intend to suggest, as some early feminist literary historians have, that 'the women's literary tradition' is separate from the 'men's literary tradition', and subject to entirely idiosyncratic laws of development.[1] On the contrary: one cannot overlook the enormous role which male writers and literary journalists, such as Belinskii, Nekrasov, Pisarev and Chukovskii, played in the denomination of a feminine readership, and of tastes relating to women's writing.[2] But it would also be an over-simplification to see the history of Russian women's writing merely in terms of a conspiracy by men to keep women down. Women writers have historically played an important part in disseminating, diluting and modifying, though rarely in directly challenging, the views expressed in criticism written by men.

The recovery of criticism by women writers is vital, then, in constructing a properly nuanced perspective of 'the women's tradition' as a

1. For a separatist view of the 'women's tradition', see particularly Sarah Gilbert and Sandra Gubar, *The Madwoman in the Attic*, Yale, 1984. Their approach is cogently criticised in Marilyn Butler's new introduction to *Jane Austen and the War of Ideas*, 2nd edn, Oxford, 1987. Elaine Showalter's *Sister's Choice*, Oxford, 1991, represents an interesting recent attempt to theorise the 'women's tradition' where it intersects with, as well as where it departs from, the 'men's tradition'.

2. Two extensive surveys of male critics' role in denominating feminine authorship and the reading public are Barbara Heldt, *Terrible Perfection*, Bloomington, 1987, and Arja Rosenholm, 'Auf den Spuren des Vergessens: zur Rezeptionsgeschichte der russischen Schriftstellerin N. D. Chvoščinskaja', *Studia Slavica Finlandensia*, vol. 6, 1989, pp. 63–92.

dialectic of separatism and assimilation. It is also of crucial importance in establishing an adequate narrative of articulations within this tradition. And here I would emphasise that we need not necessarily be evolutionists in the vulgar Darwinian sense, chroniclers of constant progress towards higher entities, to wish to search for missing critical links. Far from establishing a naïvely progressivist causality, the analysis of criticism by Russian women helps to illuminate what one recent feminist commentary has called the 'ruptures' of history, the moments of uncertainty and shifting value when women's social and cultural position has come under interrogation.[3]

The argument that follows is informed by the theoretical position just stated, but its main purpose is to consider two specific issues in the history of criticism. First, I shall show that criticism, as opposed to the composition of literary essays or the evocation of other women through the literary subtext, has been a difficult area for Russian women writers, and shall suggest some of the reasons why that should have been so. Then I shall illustrate the importance which criticism as an analytical practice has nevertheless had in a few scattered, but significant, instances, concentrating especially on its role at one important era of 'rupture', the breakdown of Symbolist ideology.

The initial difficulty experienced by Russian women writers in contemplating women writers has lain in the status of women's writing itself. The institution of writing as a professional activity of national importance, in which writers have been perceived in the public role of *vlastiteli dum*, mental leaders, made entry to letters more difficult for Russian women than it was, say, for English women in their cosier, more empirical and more domestic tradition. Large numbers of Russian women writers practising as critics have, accordingly (like Russian women critics in general), turned their eyes to texts written by men rather than women. Amongst such instances are Zinaida Gippius and Liubov´ Gurevich.[4] In cases where Russian women writers in fact have written on other women writers, they have often conformed to the pattern described by Cora Kaplan in her essay, 'Pandora's Box': 'if texts by women reveal a "hidden" sympathy between women, as radical feminist

3. Cécile Dauphin *et al.*, 'Women's Culture and Women's Power: Issues in French Women's History', in Karen Offen, Jane Roach Pierson and Jane Rendall (eds), *Writing Women's History: International Perspectives*, London, 1991, pp. 107–34. See also Catriona Kelly, 'History and Post-Modernism: II', *Past and Present*, vol. 133, November 1991, pp. 209–13. A more extensive analysis of shifting values in Russian literary culture, and their effects on the position of women's writing, will be found in Kelly, *A History of Russian Women's Writing*, 1920–1992, Oxford, 1994.

4. Zinaida Gippius, *Literaturnyi dnevnik 1899–1907*, St Petersburg, 1908; on Gippius's criticism see also Temira Pachmuss, *Zinaida Gippius; an Intellectual Profile*, Carbondale, 1971, Chapter 5; Liubov´ Gurevich, *Literatura i estetika*, Moscow, 1912.

critics often assert, they equally express positive femininity through hostile and denigrating representations of women'.[5] An outstanding early example of such 'hostile and denigrating representations' is the realist writer Mariia Tsebrikova's article on English women novelists, written in 1871.[6] Tsebrikova sees the entire history of English women's writing as simply an expression of English women's social subordination in reality, which is most particularly expressed in the dreary didacticism of Jane Austen, the 'vicarage morality' of Charlotte Brontë and Mrs Gaskell, and the half-baked philosophical formulations and vacillating heroines of George Eliot. To this Tsebrikova opposes a contrasting, emancipatory tradition of 'outstanding women heroines', which will always be beyond the reach of English women writers.

Tsebrikova's arguments are supported by long, boring and disturbingly pedestrian readings of individual texts. And it is notable that where she comes across English writers such as Mary Wollstonecraft, whose attitudes prefigure her own, she mentions their names, but passes their work over in silence. The primary material of other women writers is useful only as a point from which to argue for the ineffable superiority of her own aesthetic views.

Another, and complementary, manner of using women's writing was demonstrated by Tsebrikova, again, in an article on George Sand which appeared six years later.[7] Here Sand's work, rather than being employed to demonstrate what women should not do, is pressed into service in order to demonstrate what they should do. Sand's long and varied *œuvre* is reduced to a straightforward manifesto for women's emancipation within marriage in accordance with the terms of the 'woman question' as then debated in Russia.

Where Russian women writers have written on other Russian women writers, disincentive evocations have been more prevalent than incentive evocations. In the 1840s and 1850s, the two leading women poets of the day, Evdokiia Rostopchina and Karolina Pavlova, titillated metropolitan literary circles with a poetic exchange of insults which reads like a bizarre adumbration of the spiteful verbal fisticuffs in which Dostoevskii's women characters were later to indulge.[8] Neither of these poets practised as critics, but some of their successors who did proved equally capable of rival-hating outbursts in prose. Marina Tsetaeva's

5. Cora Kaplan, *Sea Changes: Culture and Feminism*, 2nd edn, London, 1990, p. 168.
6. Mariia Tsebrikova, 'Anglichanki-romanistki', *Otechestvennye zapiski*, no. 8, 1871, pp. 403–60; no. 9, pp. 121–72; no. 11, pp. 175–205.
7. Mariia Tsebrikova, 'Zhorzh Zand', *Otechestvennye zapiski*, no. 6, 1877, pp. 439–72; no. 7, pp. 255–92.
8. Evdokiia Rostopchina, 'Pis´mo po povodu perepiski ...', *Stikhotvoreniia, proza, pis´ma*, Moscow, 1986, p. 372; Karolina Pavlova, 'Kak serdtsu vashemu' and 'My sovremennitsy, grafinia', ibid., p. 396, p. 397.

essay 'The Poetess's Evening', a section of her memoir of Briusov, 'The Hero of Labour', is one well-known instance; a lesser-known one is an essay by Nadezhda L´vova, also a poet, 'The Cold of Morning', which is critical of the 'derivative' verse written by Akhmatova, Tsvetaeva and Kuz´mina-Karavaeva, and awards the highest laurels to the poetess 'Nelli' – who was in fact no 'poetess' at all, but Briusov writing under a pseudonym.[9] In 1913, the poet Sofiia Parnok, writing as Andrei Polianin, was to attack what she saw as the inflated reputation of Anna Akhmatova:

> The verses of Anna Akhmatova are typical both of contemporary poetry and of women's writing in general. This poetess's field of vision is not so much restricted as miniature in the most genuine sense of the word. Anna Akhmatova has divided herself off a small corner of the world which is so egotistically isolated, so stuffed with all kinds of bibelots and assorted bric à brac, that a visitor feels stifled, claustrophobic, uncomfortable, or sometimes simply bored, just as a guest might on stumbling into someone else's all-too-intimate bedroom. In this close world, in the prison of this diminutive private life, 'rings the wavering voice', the morbidly weak voice of a woman who, according to her own confession has 'become a toy', lives like 'a cuckoo in a clock', who 'cuckoos when they wind me up' ... A week in the time of this world is equivalent to a year in ours: so in the phrase 'many weeks of peace' ... but those for whom a week is simply a unit of time equivalent to seven days will not find that Anna Akhmatova's poetry is likely to detain them for 'many weeks'.[10]

Parnok's attack on Akhmatova formed only part of a review article in which she lamented the current condition of Russian poetry, and took to task the work of two other contemporary poets, Kliuev and Severianin. There was, however, no reference to gender in her scrutiny of these two male poets. Her objections were on aesthetic grounds: Kliuev's style was pretentious, and Severianin's vulgar.

Russian women writers have often compensated for the predominance of disincentive models of femininity in their contemplations of Russian literature by looking for incentive models from outside Russian literature. Part of the massive popularity of Mariia Bashkirtseva's memoirs, published in 1893, derived from their congruence with the rise of interest in the 'decadent', narcissistic, feminine personality. But no less important was Bashkirtseva's exotic, Franco-Russian, background: her memoirs had been composed in French, and she had herself lived much

9. Nadezhda L´vova, 'Kholod utra: nekotorye mysli o zhenskom tvorchestve', *Zhatva*, no. 5, 1914, pp. 250–6; Marina Tsvetaeva, 'Vecher poetess' (Section III of 'Geroi truda'), *Izbrannaia proza v dvukh tomakh*, New York, 1979, vol. 1, pp. 197–210.

10. A. Polianin, [Sofiia Parnok], 'Otmechennye imena', *Severnye zapiski*, no. 4, 1913, p. 114.

of her life in France. In the same way, Russian Symbolist and post-Symbolist women writers, notably Adelaida Gertsyk and Marina Tsvetaeva, developed a positive cult of the German Romantic writer Bettina Brentano.[11]

Tsvetaeva is a notable illustration of the search for incentive models outside Russian literary tradition. Her enthusiasms for Russian women writers were almost all sanctioned by male authority. Adelaida Gertsyk and Cherubina de Gabriack were protégées of Maksimilian Voloshin, as Tsvetaeva recounts in 'A Living Word About a Living Thing'; her enthusiasm for Karolina Pavlova followed on the rediscovery of this important poet by men in the Symbolist movement, notably Valerii Briusov, editor of the first, 1915, critical edition of Pavlova's work.[12] In later life, Tsvetaeva was to devote critical attention to male writers, rather than female. The encounter with a living woman writer which perhaps affected her most in the sense of conscious self-fashioning was her exchange of ideas in Paris with the French-American Natalie Barney.[13]

If the praise of non-Russian women writers manifested one line of compensation, a second was illustrated in Tsvetaeva's moving tribute to another sort of 'women's creativity', the painting of Natal´ia Goncharova. Though Goncharova is descended from 'the male line', not from Pushkin's wife, her namesake, she has inherited the latter's 'wordlessness', and hence is able to be 'feminine' in a positive sense inaccessible to the artist working with words.[14] By implication, Tsvetaeva holds a position akin to that held by Zinaida Gippius, who had baldly declared in her review of Ekaterina Bakunina's novel *Love for Six People*, 'The feminine remains "the feminine" only so long as it is silent. When it begins to speak about itself, it becomes the prattle of a strumpet.'[15]

Views that the 'feminine' was incompatible with appropriate language had direct effects on how criticism was practised, as well as on the nature of its objects. Adelaida Gertsyk, in her 1915 article on the Italian woman poet Annie Vivanti, describes Vivanti as having 'shown me the mysteries of feminine charm and the mysteries of her mother-

11. Bashkirtseva and Brentano are the only two positive models of women writers whom Tsvetaeva acknowledges in 'Vecher poetess' (see note 9 above); Brentano is celebrated also in Adelaida Gertsyk, 'Istoriia odnoi druzhby', *Severnye zapiski*, no. 2, 1915, pp. 110–28.

12. Marina Tsvetaeva, 'Zhivoe o zhivom', *Izbrannaia proza*, vol. 2, p. 9; the Karolina Pavlova edition is *Sobranie sochinenii*, ed. V. Ia. Briusov, 2 vols, Moscow, 1915.

13. Marina Zwétaieva [Tsvetaeva], *Mon frère féminin* (1939), Paris, 1979.

14. Tsvetaeva, 'Natal´ia Goncharova', *Izbrannaia Proza*, vol. 1, pp. 283–340.

15. Gippius, 'E. Bakunina. *Liubov´ k shesterym. Roman*', *Sovremennye zapiski*, vol. 58, 1935, pp. 478–9.

tongue', equating 'charm' and exoticism of language. She also makes an illuminating distinction between 'criticism' and 'enthusiasm': 'as I began to understand the poetry with greater ease, my love for Annie grew, and I now made no attempt to criticise her, but followed the caprices of her feeling with delight'.[16] Criticism is understood by Gertsyk as scrutiny without feeling, enthusiasm as empathy by means of the suspension of critical judgement. This polarisation of analysis and sensibility maps on to the division between 'mind' and 'heart' current in Russia since the eighteenth century, in which women are regularly identified with 'heart' and men with 'mind'.[17] Women writers have been wary of criticism because, as a mental activity, it is incompatible with 'femininity'. The identification of analysis and masculinity was to lead some Russian women writers to publish criticism under a male pseudonym (Zinaida Gippius employed several, including 'Anton Krainyi'; as mentioned earlier, Sofiia Parnok wrote as 'Andrei Polianin').

Of course, one cannot hang too much upon such strategies: the real names behind 'Anton Krainyi' and 'Andrei Polianin' were so well-known that, like those formulae of recent days, 'helping the police with their enquiries' and 'the alleged criminal', the pseudonyms may, paradoxically, have stressed the critic's identity, rather than masking it. Still, in historical terms the division between 'criticism' and 'femininity' has had important effects. One of these is simply practical. The gender-marked connotations of 'analysis' have meant that there has been an upsurge in the number of women writers producing statements on literature in eras when detached and quasi-academic analysis has been replaced by other, more synthetic and subjective forms of writing. The overwhelming majority of the most important essays on literature by Russian women writers appeared in the Symbolist and post-Symbolist journals before 1917, and in the journals of the Russian emigration between 1917 and 1939.

Another result has been of an intellectual or conceptual kind. There are far fewer really important statements about the process and mechanics of writing by Russian women writers than by men. Even Russian women writers whose work does not, in objective terms, conform to a nineteenth-century realist direction have often baldly asserted their tasks in terms that recall Russian realism's naïve assumptions about the transparency of language and its subordination to reality. Marina Tsvetaeva,

16. Gertsyk, 'Moi romany II: Anni Vivanti', *Severnye zapiski*, 1913, no. 2, p. 84.
17. On the distinction between heart and mind, see for example Viazemskii's tribute to Madame de Stael in 'Biblioteka' ('Po serdtsu zhenshchina i po dushe muzhchina'), *Stikhotvoreniia*, Leningrad, 1986, p. 188; and the Princess's impassioned protest in Pavlova's 'Za chainym stolom' ('Razve oni vse ne uvereny, chto gde um, tam net serdtsa?'), *Russkii vestnik*, no. 12, section 2, 1859, p. 823.

for example, asserted that formal innovation had been no part of her task in writing *The Swain;* she had simply been intrigued by the original narrative material:

> Often, when I read some review about me and hear that 'the formal tasks have been superbly executed', I pause for thought: did I set myself any such formal task? Madame Tsvetaeva wanted to write a folk tale and employ this and this element, etcetera, etcetera.
>
> Was that what I (stress on the I) wanted? No. Was *that* what I wanted? No, no and no. I'd read Afanas´ev's tale 'The Vampire' and it had got me wondering why Marusia, who was terrified of the vampire, should have so stubbornly refused to tell what it was that she had seen, though she knew that to name it was to be saved. ... That was *my* task when I began work on *The Swain*. To uncover the essence of the tale from its bare bones.[18]

It is as though Russian women writers have felt that thematics is far too important to be unsettled by trivial formal or stylistic considerations. To give another example: Liubov´ Gurevich, in her essay 'From "Everyday Life" to "Style"' assaulted Russian realism precisely on the grounds that it was solely concerned, both theoretically and practically, with literature as the representation of 'interesting events from life' in stylistically simplistic terms. However, she then went on to set up an image of the act of writing which allowed no more sophisticated analysis of form: in literature, she stated, the author expressed transcendence of real circumstance in his [sic] own particular handwriting.[19]

I am eager that the argument which I have just stated should not be interpreted too proscriptively. Cora Kaplan's veiled attack on the 'sentimental sisterhood' school carries weight: we should not assume that women writers must look to each other for support in cultural circumstances which make it sensible that they should not. But this is only one of the reasons why one should perhaps not over-emphasise how prevailing conceptions of criticism have hindered Russian women. If Russian women writers could not perform as 'women critics' (whatever such a concept signifies), or as critics, they could certainly write on literature. And when they did, their aspirations to both intellectual and anti-intellectual roles, and uncertainty about their own subject position, could give their work a fluidity which made it exciting. In the best essays of Marina Tsvetaeva, for example, autobiography, literary memoir and abstraction are combined in a bold manner which make these documents

18. Tsvetaeva, 'Poet o kritike', *Izbrannaia proza*, vol. 1, pp. 221–41 (p. 240). Emphasis Tsvetaeva's.

19. Gurevich, 'Ot byta k stiliu', *Literatura i estetika: etiudy*, Moscow, 1912, pp. 248–75.

transcend the serviceable genre of criticism. In an absolute sense, these are amongst the most interesting texts produced by the Russian modernist movement.

I think the reason for arguing as I have done above is concerned less with my views of Russian writers as critics in an absolute sense than with a hypothesis about the possible secondary function of criticism, its role as an articulation of poetics. That is, I am preoccupied with the question of what happens to Russian writer-critics when they write work other than criticism. Here matters become more tricky. The dislike of Russian women writers for analysis is fair enough when one is dealing with a writer who, like Marina Tsvetaeva, was a *Naturgenie*, that is, a writer who works instinctively rather than according to established aesthetic principles. In Tsvetaeva's case such 'instinctive' or 'irrational' gifts included a prodigious verbal memory and capacity for rhythmic innovation; it is not clear how 'critical analysis' in the ordinary sense would have benefited her. For her, in any case, criticism was an activity secondary to poetry: her articles about poetry were, like her memoirs, written when her career as a poet was nearly over.

However, for writers without such 'irrational' gifts, fear of analysis has, I would argue, often been a direct cause of thematic and especially linguistic banality. Conversely, criticism in the sense of informed, but not necessarily approbatory analysis of other women's work, and consequently of the possibilities of women's writing in general, has been of great benefit to those few women writers who have practised it. Parnok's hostility to the decorative love poetry which she associated with Akhmatova's early work was more productive than the sickly reverence with which many other Russian women poets have treated this work, which has directed them towards a woefully second-rate imitativeness.

Analysis is an essential part of women poets 'with a history', because it can convey an appreciation of what a literary tradition means for a woman writer. Despite Russian women writers' perennial protests (in the twentieth century at least) that they do not want to be classified by gender, classified by gender is what they have been. Attempts to avoid such generalisations have on the whole been fruitless; by contrast, criticism can be an important part of the process of distancing or even transforming them.

Parnok's deliberate separation of her own path from Akhmatova's had considerable resonance for her own self-fashioning as a poet, both directly and indirectly. The iconoclasm with which she slams this 'noted name' heralded a determination to make independent aesthetic judgements which was to be re-iterated in a poem written the following year, 'Ia ne liubliu tserkvei':

Я не люблю церквей, где зодчий
Слышнее Бога говорит,
где гений в споре с волей Отчей
в ней не затерян, с ней не слит,

где человеческий дух тщеславный
как бы возносится над ней –
мне византийский купол плавный
колючей готики родней.[20]

The substance of Parnok's criticisms is also important, since it points towards her intention, realised in the poems from 1915 onwards, to adopt a persona of explicitly feminine gender to which 'femininity' in the conventional sense would be alien. The sexual disgust with which Parnok speaks of Akhmatova's 'intimacy' is also indicative, for here was a lesbian poet profoundly dissatisfied with the expression of female desire which was permissible in the contemporary heterosexual love lyric, and determined not to transfer the patterns elaborated in this lyric to her own work.

If analysis was in some sense a starting-point for Parnok, it might be described, on the other hand, as a turning-point in the case of a second poet of the Silver Age, Anna Akhmatova herself. In 1914, Akhmatova published a review of a collection brought out by the young poet Nadezhda L´vova shortly before her death. The review is significant not only as a rare piece of published criticism by Akhmatova, but also as a statement which has something of a programmatic character, and which, further, dates from a year which Akhmatova herself was later to assert had been crucial to her biography.

Akhmatova's review, whilst tactfully avoiding the impropriety of an overt attack on L´vova, given that the latter was then scarcely in her grave, also avoids the converse danger of sentimental overstatement. More importantly, though, she also makes some illuminating statements about love poetry, the central genre for L´vova, as for so many other women poets:

Her poems are so unskilled and touching, they do not reach a level of enlightened clarity sufficient to engage everyone in intimacy, but one simply trusts them, as one would a person in tears. The main and almost the only theme of *An Old Tale* is love. And here we observe something odd. In real life, women are so strong, so acutely aware of all love's capacity for disappointment; yet

20. Parnok, *Sobranie stikhotvorenii*, Ann Arbor, Michigan, 1979, p. 112.

Catriona Kelly

no sooner do they begin to write than they seem to know only one kind of love: tormented, morbidly sensitive and hopeless. ... Submission almost to the point of entire surrender of will is the most typical state conveyed in N. L´vova's work. Her suffering seeks an outlet in dreams. These are not dreams of the Romantic kind, capable of conquering the world by force of will; no, they are intensely lyrical dreams, and they transform every moment of life for her ... I think that N. L´vova did violence to her delicate gifts by making herself write rondos, gazuls and sonnets. Of course the high mastery of form is within the grasp of women too, Karolina Pavlova is an example of that; not there, though, does their strength lie, but rather in the capacity to express the most intimate and miraculously simple aspects of themselves and the surrounding world.[21]

Akhmatova's polarisation of 'women in life' and 'women's writing' may not be particularly wide-ranging or subtle, but it does suggest a self-conscious and determined anti-biographical stance, prefiguring developments in her poetry. Of course, even her earliest collections, *Evening* and *The Rosary*, could only be perceived as a 'lyrical diary' by a naïve reader insensitive to the lack of a unified persona across the lyrics, and to the literary resonance of the various personae (plural) which Akhmatova employs. Sometimes she speaks as the 'Stranger' of Blok's poems (in 'Vecherom', for example); sometimes she puts words into the mouths of other fictional heroines from male texts. In 'Chitaia Gamleta' she first adopts the voice of Ophelia, addressing Hamlet directly, rather than simply responding, as Shakespeare's heroine does. Then, in the second part, 'I kak budto po oshibke/ Ia skazala "Ty"', she rephrases Pushkin's 'Ty i vy' from the point of view of his addressee. In other poems, she follows traditions established in the work of Symbolist poems, adopting, for example, the mysterious 'sister' figures of Adelaida Gertsyk (in 'Ia prishla tebia smenit´, sestra').[22] But most frequently of all Akhmatova speaks in the guise of a 'novelistic heroine', combining an emphasis on failed love relationships with a set of traditional loci and a studiedly 'prosaic' choice of lexicon and metre. (So, for example, in 'On liubil tri veshchi na svete'.)[23] Often erroneously held to be Akhmatova's own invention, this 'novelistic heroine' persona is in fact widely developed in the work of such nineteenth-century woman poets as Iuliia Zhadovskaia and Evdokiia Rostopchina, the latter of whom also shares Akhmatova's fascination with dressing-up. However, Akhmatova has a sense of background as disharmonious and bizarre in itself, rather than as simply out of harmony with the lyric heroine's feelings, which is novel.

21. Anna Akhmatova, 'O stikhakh N. L´vovoi', *Russkaia mysl'*, no. 1, 1914, pp. 27–8.
22. Anna Akhmatova, *Stikhotvoreniia i poemy*, Leningrad, 1976, p. 77.
23. Akhmatova, 'Vecherom', ibid., p. 56; 'Chitaia "Gamleta"', ibid., p. 52; 'Ia prishla tebia smenit´', ibid., p. 76.

For all the diversity of her early lyric, though, in the poems which
Akhmatova wrote after 1914 she both developed and deepened the
interplay of different masks and subtexts. She began to emphasise the
fictionality of a statement within a given poem, rather than letting such
fictionality be construed from the contradictions across a cycle or a collection. In important poems composed over 1914 and 1915, she evolved
a personal mythology of the 'muse-double' (as in 'U samogo moria' and
'Uedinenie').[24] At the same time, in poems such as 'Net, tsarevich, ia ne
ta', she questioned the assignation of pre-scripted subject positions.
Most significantly of all, she initiated a process of referring to her own
early work, most particularly her own versions of the love lyric, in a
new, ironic, context:

> Нет царевич, я не та
> Кем ты меня видеть хочешь,
> И давно мои уста
> Не целуют, а пророчат.
>
> Не подумай, что в бреду
> И замучена тоскою
> Громко кличу я беду:
> Ремесло мое такое.[25]

Here Akhmatova's earlier self-identification as the heroine of a folk tale
is rejected in favour of a new role as 'prophetess'. But unlike the
Symbolist women poets, she sees her prophecy as self-conferred, rather
than the gift of an external agency: it is her *métier* or trade.

Further development of this device, contrasting different levels of
awareness in a different context occurs in some poems written by
Akhmatova in 1917, in which identity is portrayed as divided across
time and space: 'Ne znali my, chto skoro/ V toske predel´noi pogliadim
nazad'.[26] Or sometimes a subtext, or imagined subtext, may be used in
much the same way, to jolt a reader expecting the former manner:
'Sochinil zhe kakoi-to bezdel´nik/ Chto byvaet liubov´ na zemle'.[27]

In the case of Akhmatova versus L´vova, as well as in the case of
Parnok versus Akhmatova, I would argue that the confrontation with a
distinguished woman contemporary was of fundamental and central
importance to the poetic career of each poet-critic: examination of 'the

---

24. 'U samogo moria', ibid., p. 339; 'Uedinenie', ibid., p. 85.
25. 'Net, tsarevich, ia ne ta', ibid., p. 120.
26. 'Tot golos, s tishinoi', ibid., p. 107.
27. 'Dvadtsat´ pervoe. Noch´', ibid., p. 122.

other' was at the same time the examination of self. A larger historical process is also evident, in my view. The enormous interest amongst male Symbolists, especially Ivanov, Voloshin and Briusov, in 'feminine creativity' had been very helpful to young women poets after 1905. But the views of these male poets had been coercive as well as incentive, dictating a particular form which was to be adopted by 'feminine creativity'. Besides, the Symbolist enthusiasm for 'feminine creativity' had been succeeded by a reversal of fashion, which was reflected, amongst other things, in the misogynistic and masculinist tenor of the Acmeist and Cubo-Futurist manifestos.

In Parnok and Akhmatova's reviews, published during the years 1913 to 1914, we see, I think, two particular women writers getting to grips with the problems of how to find an appropriate poetic persona, and with the implications of using a gendered voice in poetry, which had been raised by this conflict of values. And in Nadezhda L´vova's review article of 1913, 'Cold of Morning', we see one woman poet home in on the nub of the question, the issue of how that contingent 'femininity' (a word she herself floats with quotation marks) should be represented:

> In general, as we have seen, the collections of all these women poets [Kuz´mina-Karavaeva, Akhmatova, Tsvetaeva and 'Nelli'] are typically feminine in terms of their 'contents'. The 'masculine' in poetry exists alongside the 'feminine' in the sense which we give it. It is interesting that the verses of certain male poets also have a feminine flavour. The most significant example is the work of Igor´ Severianin, who has purely feminine feelings and perceptions.
> But for these, *their own*, 'feminine' experiences women have not yet managed to find '*their own*' and adequate language, have not managed to clothe these experiences in *their own* forms.[28]

And it was precisely the question of finding '*their own* language' (the emphasis is L´vova's) which was to be more effectively explored by woman poets after 1913 than it had been before. The years between 1913 and 1935 were not only to see a rise in authority amongst many poets (Tsvetaeva, Akhmatova) who had published work before 1913, but also the emergence of several new poets (Parnok, Vera Merkur´eva, and later Anna Prismanova) whose work matched that of the most talented women Symbolists, Gippius and Gertsyk in linguistic originality, whilst considerably surpassing that of the best-known post-Symbolist woman poet, the pseudonymous 'Cherubina de Gabriack'.

Some recent feminist or proto-feminist work on Russian women writers has stressed the ironic deployment of stereotypes as a radical

---

28. L´vova, 'Kholod utra', p. 256. Emphasis L´vova's.

gesture in women's writing.[29] Whilst it is fair enough to suggest that some Russian women's writing does work like this, it is not the only possible strategy, nor even necessarily the most sophisticated strategy for women writers. A feeling of alienation from all possible 'feminine identities' is another, and perhaps more stimulating, possibility. It was precisely this feeling which separated the post-Symbolists, some of whom one might label 'modernists' in a full sense, from their predecessors the Symbolists. The cases of Akhmatova and Parnok indicate how important a role criticism might play in the new shift of consciousness and in the emergence of a modernist sensibility.

What I have attempted to do in this essay is to set down some of the difficulties and constraints which women writers faced if they attempted the practice of criticism. I have then shown that criticism has nevertheless had valuable functions in the development of women's writing, both in an individual and in a collective sense. I have argued that it was one historical factor which made the years around 1913 an important era of 'rupture' in the culture of women, as in Russian culture in general. Finally, I should just like to comment on the importance to our own critical practice, as observers, of recognising that women writers could and did practise as critics. A great deal of criticism, Russian and Western, still tends to see women's writing as the unmediated product of biography. Criticism is important evidence that a mediation process does, on the contrary, take place. Perhaps the most important point is that women's writing is not just an 'organic' activity, to be found and catalogued. It is the result of analysis, of imagining the self and imagining others. The study of criticism can play a vital part in recognising this point, since it is immediately evident that Russian women writers as critics are peculiar, unnatural beasts. They are not so much found as they are invented, or as they have to invent themselves. Improbable, fantastical creatures that yet fill an important logical and historical role – that is the final sense, perhaps, in which we can describe women writer-critics as 'missing links'.

---

29. See for example Helena Goscilo, 'Tat´iana Tolstaia's "Dome of Many-Coloured Glass": The World Refracted through Multiple Perspectives', *Slavic Review*, vol. 42, no. 2, 1988, pp. 280–90.

7

Marina Tsvetaeva as Literary Critic and Critic of Literary Critics

Sibelan Forrester

Marina Tsvetaeva's literary criticism has long been overshadowed by her poetry and, more recently, her autobiographical prose.[1] Like most of her readers, I know her best as a poet, and this identity both authorises and complicates her critical position and authorial voice. Her critical texts tend to be used to illumine her work in genres that reveal and create an individual speaking self, although they also call attention to the 'critical' content of her poetry. Tsvetaeva's criticism offers much more, however: while accepting most of the Russian poetic canon of her age, it conveys ambiguous messages both about the critic's authority and project and about her relationship to her predecessors. The critical articles merge in many ways with her other prose (memoirs, autobiography, and especially literary theory);[2] the difficulty of drawing genre boundaries in Tsvetaeva's prose reflects her intentional genre-mixing, as well as her challenge to the literary hierarchies that contribute to genre definitions. Her urge to claim authority, expressed through her use of accepted critical tone and terminology in parts of her texts, alternates with subversion of authority to provide a flexible critical position. The critic still holds a kind of status, but this status turns out to be due to the critic's primary identity as a poet. Tsvetaeva's critical prose reveals the interplay of gender, genre and authority and the tremendous political stakes in establish-

1. This situation may change now that several of Tsvetaeva's critical and theoretical articles are available in a very readable English translation, *Art in the Light of Conscience. Eight Essays on Poetry,* trans., introd. and notes by Angela Livingstone, Cambridge, Mass., 1992. This volume includes the essays 'Downpour of Light' and 'The Poet on the Critic'. I have not used Livingstone's translations in this article because her English versions do not always preserve the elements I examine.

2. Whether one calls it 'literary theory' or invents terms such as 'essays on poetry', articles such as 'Poets with History and Poets without History' and 'Art in the Light of Conscience', while containing many elements of literary criticism, are clearly also concerned with broader, theoretical issues of art.

ing the criteria by which literature must be judged, especially for someone as invested in her art as she is.

In this study I shall concentrate on three of Tsvetaeva's early critical articles, 'Downpour of Light' (1922), an idiosyncratic review of Boris Pasternak's book *My Sister Life*, 'Hero of Labour' (1925), a critical memoir of Valerii Briusov and his work and 'A Poet about Criticism/the Critic' (1926), an attack on *émigré* criticism and critics.[3] These three pieces are used to structure references to a wider range of other works and to demonstrate the place of the physical body in her criticism, the nature and effects of the style of her criticism, her maintenance of ambiguity, and the implications of her criticism of critics.

Tsvetaeva writes criticism almost exclusively about her own specialty, poetry and poets.[4] Her literary criticism offers interpretation of work, criticism proper (judgement of the work), her own readings and reactions to the work, and guidance to her reader on what to read and how to read it. She is only one of the many Russian poets who have written literary criticism; like Pushkin and his circle, or the Symbolists, she attempts to form a reading public capable of fully appreciating the writing she values, especially her own. It is already a cliché that Russian literature often sublimates political concerns because of the historical succession of oppressive climates which allowed no better forum for public discussion. Though Tsvetaeva and many others reject the mandatory connection of literature with politics, the pressure exerted by this tradition of political concern and content makes even that rejection a political position. Thus, it is no surprise that literary politics informs Tsvetaeva's criticism of critics.

On the whole, the values Tsvetaeva assigns to works and poets may seem far from controversial to today's reader. Even her vision of the poet and the poetic process is clearly derived from nineteenth-century poetics, and her own experience, located at the centre of her descriptions

---

3. 'Svetovoi liven″' is Tsvetaeva's first published piece of literary criticism, and 'Geroi truda' is the first of her literary memoirs, while 'Poet o kritike' is her first substantial critical article and, according to Simon Karlinsky, her 'single most successful and valuable piece' of prose written in the 1920s (S. Karlinsky, *Marina Cvetaeva. Her Life and Art*, Berkeley, 1966, p. 274). My choice of two works of critcism proper and one work of metacriticism also duplicates the relationship of Tsvetaeva's criticism to the writing that it criticises.

All three pieces will be cited from the edition: M. Tsvetaeva, *Izbrannaia proza v dvukh tomakh*, New York, 1979, vol. 1; all translations are my own.

4. It is interesting and indicative that Tsvetaeva's concentration on poetry (Russian as well as German and occasionally French) effectively prevents her from devoting critical attention to the prose works written by women (for example, Sigrid Undset, Selma Lagerlöf, Pearl Buck) which she was reading in the 1930s. Her comments on these works appear only in her letters to other women (Vera Muromtseva Bunina and especially Anna Tesková), perhaps reflecting Tsvetaeva's sense that her female correspondents would be more interested than the general reading public in 'women's writing'.

of poetry, is strongly mediated by the theories and practice of her many favourite nineteenth-century authors. Almost all the poets she recurrently mentions are now generally recognised as great (Goethe and other German Romantics, Pushkin, and among her contemporaries Blok, Rilke, Maiakovskii, Pasternak, Akhmatova, Mandel´shtam),[5] or are considered secondary but still significant in the context of the Russian Silver Age (Briusov, Bal´mont, Voloshin, Esenin, etc.). The poets she cites whose status was or is not so high (Karolina Pavlova, T. Churilin, Adelaida Gertsyk) rarely appear in her criticism, and then are often associated with a higher-status poet (as Gertsyk and de Gabriack illumine Voloshin).[6] Indeed, Tsvetaeva would seem interested only in writing about winners,[7] and not at all attracted by the daily journalistic grind of book reviews.

Given that her assignment of poetic value can rarely be faulted, one might ask why Tsvetaeva's criticism has not been read and cited with the sort of reverence that is often paid to the criticism of such poet-critics as Gumilev or Mandel´shtam. One obvious possible reason is that Tsvetaeva was never part of a literary group, unlike her contemporaries Gumilev, Mandel´shtam, Maiakovskii, Briusov, Blok and others.[8] Her criticism shuns even the political polarisation of Russian literature into Soviet and *émigré* camps. All the same, Khodasevich was not a member of any literary grouping but still wrote much-quoted criticism, and D. S. Mirsky remains a critical classic in spite of (or perhaps precisely because of) his refusal to limit his judgements of literature to one or another political system. A second obvious distinction is Tsvetaeva's gender; among women of her era who published literary criticism, many chose to sign their work with masculine pseudonyms (for example, Zinaida Hippius as 'Anton Krainii', Sof´ia Parnok as 'A. Polianin').[9]

5. It might be useful to recall that in *émigré* Paris in the 1920s Pasternak and Maiakovskii were hardly fixtures of any generally accepted literary canon.

6. See 'Zhivoe o zhivom,' in *Izbrannaia proza*, vol. 2, pp. 36–40; 45–6.

7. Even the biting depiction of the hopeless would-be poet Mariia Papper in 'Zhivoe o zhivom' (ibid., pp. 68–9) illustrates Voloshin and Khodasevich more than it describes Papper's own work from any angle.

8. This rejection of poetic groupings was the result of a principled position: 'Poeticheskie shkoly (znak veka!) – vul´garizatsiia poezii...' ('Poet o kritike', ibid., p. 239). Tsvetaeva's critical projects differ considerably from those of poet-critics who wish either to attack competing groups or to establish parameters for their own groups. As Barbara Heldt points out, women poets were much less likely than men to belong to the literary groupings of the Silver Age and early post-Revolutionary period (Barbara Heldt, *Terrible Perfection. Women in Russian Literature*, Bloomington, Indiana, 1987, p. 98).

9. Though it is probable that knowledgeable readers were well aware of the identities that these pseudonyms concealed, Tsvetaeva still emphasises the importance of the author's true name as a guarantee of quality: 'Firma, v dannom sluchae, imia avtora' ('Poet o kritike', *Izbrannaia proza*, vol. 1, p. 225), complaining that a critic who does not cite from a poet under review gives no guarantee of trustworthiness other than 'Imia v kontse stolbtsa' (ibid., p. 236).

Though Tsvetaeva signs her criticism with her own name and writes with explicitly female language (use of verb forms, etc.), at least one later article suggests that the signature was an issue for her as well.[10]

Finally, and perhaps most significantly, Tsvetaeva's criticism struck many readers as idiosyncratic and even 'hysterical' in its style and reasoning. It was difficult to read according to the standards for criticism of her time, not fulfilling the critical ideal of 'a tone of detachment and objectivity'.[11] Her very idiosyncrasy and refusal to duplicate the canonical style of literary criticism makes every word detract from her critical authority; the impression of 'hysteria' produced by her writing on some readers ties her style back to her gender and to the presence of a female body (in this case a womb, Greek *hystera*) lurking behind a text written by a woman who uses woman's language. Her stylistic innovations might still have attracted approval and attention if they had served some overt critical purpose, like the Futurists' flashy and quotable rejections of the recognised canon;[12] unlike the Futurists, however, Tsvetaeva accepts the better part of the Russian poetic canon of her age in order to perform a radical re-reading of its texts and authorial personalities. This ambiguous relationship to the Russian poetic tradition makes the explicit content of her critical prose appear more conservative and less interesting than that of many other poet-critics. The relative lack of study of Tsvetaeva's critical works suggests that the full significance of these texts can only be found by examining them as works of literature, reading below their surfaces.

10. In 'Zhivoe o zhivom' Tsvetaeva recalls how she was tempted by Voloshin's suggestion that she begin writing poetry under a variety of pseudonyms. She refused, but, 'A khoroshii byl by Petukhov poet! A tekh poeticheskikh bliznetsov po sei den´ oplakivaiu' (Tsvetaeva, *Izbrannaia proza*, vol. 2, p. 41).

11. René Wellek, *A History of Modern Criticism 1750–1950*, 8 vols, New Haven, 1955–93, Vol. 7, German, Russian, and Eastern European Criticism, 1900–1950, 1991, p. 280. Interestingly, this formulation occurs in a part of the text where Wellek is evaluating the criticism of Viacheslav Ivanov, a Symbolist poet whose writing and theories Tsvetaeva admired very much.

Mandel´shtam is generally taken seriously as a critic despite the syntactic and logical games he plays in some of his critical works. See, for example, Svetlana Boym's respectful use of evaluations of Tsvetaeva and Maiakovskii from his essay 'Literary Moscow,' in *Death in Quotation Marks*, Cambridge, Mass., 1991, pp. 192–6. Perhaps a certain stylistic freedom is acceptable as long as one is calling for 'manliness' in poetry, as Mandel´shtam does in this piece.

12. One obvious example here is the much-quoted injunction that the classics of Russian literature should be thrown from the steamship of modernity, and the entire 1910 manifesto 'Slap in the Face of Public Taste'.

Tsvetaeva's Critical Body

Tsvetaeva's criticism treats poetry as an organism, whether the unit under discussion is one poem, one cycle, one book, or one poet's opus. Her review of Pasternak's *My Sister Life* describes the book as if it were a tree, complete with chirping birds.[13] By contrast, Briusov's poetry and career are a granite embankment or marble sculpture, monuments to labour rather than offspring of a poetic gift.[14] Tsvetaeva's comprehension of poetry as a physical organism leads her to speak of poetry as a living, human body, as in this description of the relationship of form and content from 'A Poet about Criticism/the Critic':

> It isn't a plaster cast! No I am seduced by the essence. afterwards I'll embody [it]. *That* is a poet. And I will embody [it] (here already the question of form) as essentially as possible. The essence is the form – a child cannot be born different from itself! Gradual revelation of features – that is the growth of a person and the growth of a work of art.[15]

Repetition of the verb 'voploshchu' ('embody'), formed from the root 'plot´' ('flesh'), could make the poet analogous to God, the great incarnator; but the assertion that the child cannot be born differently equates the poet and poem more to parent and child. Tsvetaeva mentions the well-known comparison of poetic incubation to pregnancy and childbirth but considers it too obvious and widely-known an analogy to need either elaboration or justification: 'everybody knows about this – and it is universally known'.[16] The 'femininity' of the poet's activity is also expressed by descriptions of the possibilities contained like babies within the poet: 'It's not Pasternak who is a newborn..., it's the world that is newborn in him.'[17] Thus Tsvetaeva feminises the 'organic' metaphor of male Romantic poets, applying the analogy of pregnancy to Pasternak as well as to herself. Her concern for the presence of the body in the writer's voice is surely one factor underlining Hélène Cixous's analysis of Tsvetaeva's prose as *écriture féminine*.[18]

If the poet's writing is somehow identical to a human body, it is not surprising that Tsvetaeva interprets not only poetry but also parts of

13. Pasternak, *My Sister Life*, p. 136.
14. Ibid., p. 177.
15. Tsvetaeva, *Izbrannaia proza*, vol. 1, p. 240.
16. Tsvetaeva, 'Iskusstvo pri svete sovesti', ibid., p. 381. This idea is also a significant element in Tsvetaeva's poetry; see for example 'Kazhdyi stikh – ditia liubvi' (1918), in *Stikhotvoreniia i poemy v piati tomakh, New York,* 1983, vol. 2, p. 14.
17. Ibid., p. 137.
18. See Hélène Cixous, 'Difficult Joys', in *The Body and the Text. Hélène Cixous, Reading and Teaching*, ed. Helen Wilcox *et al.*, New York and London, 1990, pp. 16–17.

poets' biographies and even poets' bodies. One example is her description in 'Downpour of Light' of Pasternak's appearance as having something both of an Arab and of his horse, 'both of the Arab and his horse: wariness, listening closely, – and just about to ...'.[19] This both reacts plausibly to Pasternak's face, which early photographs show as somewhat exotic for a Russian, and suggests a thoroughbred quality, a perfect unity between rider (intention?) and steed (execution?), even an archaic, less-civilised quality which would fit Tsvetaeva's other descriptions of Pasternak's verse as somehow closer to (non-Western) nature than to (Western) culture. Similar examples include Briusov's wolfish look and 'shod face' and Maiakovskii's gladiator features.[20] The changing nature of Tsvetaeva's own poetry evokes the ageing of her face,[21] phrased in a manner that suggests an acceptance of women's objectification in art and social standards of beauty.[22] Physical traits and biographical details, like elements of a poem, are interpreted as literary elements full of significance, and clues to the poet's work.[23]

This attitude can also apply to the physical look of a book itself, as even that factor, something that influences the book's reader, is introduced into Tsvetaeva's criticism. The first two sentences of 'Downpour of Light' describe the gloomy appearance of the newly published Soviet edition of Pasternak's *My Sister Life*, which to her suggests death more than the life its title promises: 'In a khaki dust-cover, ... a bit crude, uncomforting, all covered in some sort of funereal bruises, – not quite a catalogue of mortuary wares, not quite the last gamble on life of some expiring publisher.'[24] The 'funereal' bruises, 'mortuary' accessories and 'expiring' publisher emerge from the book's physical appearance and belie the life force that Tsvetaeva goes on to find on every page. Starting her reader off with these gloomy expectations allows her to surprise her reader with the book's actual liveliness, as if to claim that it will retrieve readers from death (or, perhaps, Russian literature from its bruising in the Revolution).

However, the book as a physical object is not important only for the way its cover can mislead; Tsvetaeva goes on to describe herself waking

19. Tsvetaeva, *Izbrannaia proza*, vol. 1, p. 136.
20. Ibid., p. 198, while the reference to Maiakovskii is in 'Epos i lirika sovremennoi Rossii', ibid., vol. 2, p. 21.
21. Ibid., vol. 1, p. 223.
22. In the 1916 poem 'Nastanet den' – pechal'nyi, govoriat!', the fourth poem of the cycle 'Stikhi o Moskve', Tsvetaeva explores the links between stillness, decorum, and death. The sixth line, 'Skvoz´ legkoe litso prostupit lik', could also be applied to a reader's image of a poet's work once that poet has died and ceased to evolve (*Stikhotvoreniia i poemy*, vol. 1, p. 216).
23. One may note a corresponding presence of poets' looks and bodies in Tsvetaeva's poems to other poets, Mandel´shtam, Blok and Akhmatova.
24. Tsvetaeva, *Izbrannaia proza*, vol. 1, p. 135.

in the morning with the book open on her breast.[25] Lower on the same page, she describes the book's content: '[Pasternak] intentionally let everyone say – everything, in order at the last second, with a perplexed gesture – [to pull] a notebook out of his breast pocket: "And I ...".' The book that now lies on her breast is transformed into the notebook that Pasternak pulls from his breast pocket, closest to the heart and its rhythmic beat, and this common touch of book to breast gives the poet and his reader heart-to-heart contact via the poems. What is more, the 'wide-opened' book on the critic's breast exactly parallels the later description of Pasternak's wide-openness: 'Pasternak – that is an utter wide-open[ness]: eyes, nostrils, ears, lips, arms.'[26] Through the openness shared by Pasternak's poetic image and the book as his incarnation, in effect, she wakes in the morning with the poet himself spread out on her breast. A secret erotic contact of poet and reader is encoded in Tsvetaeva's admiring review of Pasternak's poetry; this contact in turn underlines the inspiring weight of the book, which leads to the conception of this essay.

If we recall the original associations with death and gravestones, however, it is also somewhat threatening that the narrator awakes with this dual burden of death and life on her breast. As Tsvetaeva points out later in the piece, her pleasure in discovering Pasternak's poetry has been mediated by a threat to her ability to breathe properly and to her own poetic 'voice,' since Pasternak is the first contemporary 'for whom I don't have enough of a ribcage [grudnoi kletki]'.[27]

The sense of not having enough ribcage or breath to encompass Pasternak's work is only one example of how Tsvetaeva's criticism traces the effect of poetry on the reader's body: her readings are often performed as a meeting of two bodies. Another wonderful example, also from 'Downpour of Light', stresses what the poetry in the book does to her body: 'My first action, having endured the whole of it: from the first blow to the last – arms wide: this way, so that all [my] joints cracked. I wound up under it, as if under a downpour.'[28] The gender of the speaker is clear in the feminine verb form *popala* ('wound up'), while the 'unfeminine' detail of cracking joints underlines the common human effort that reading this poetry demands. Once again, the body of our critic contacts the body of Pasternak himself, here in repetition of the word *nastezh´* ('wide open'), used to describe the movement of her arms and the state of his entire body, as mentioned above. Pasternak's wide-open arms make her open her own arms wide, so that the two can now embrace.

25. Ibid., p. 135.
26. Ibid., p. 138
27. Ibid., p. 147.
28. Ibid., p. 136.

Other examples of physical reactions convey the critic's impossible desire to rewrite the whole book with her own hands: 'my hands are burning to cite it here entirely', 'I gnaw my hands [in frustration]', 'my hands really will be gnawed to shreds', and a phrase which describes both the result of the critic's erotic contact with Pasternak's poetry and the threat of being possessed by his work and talent: 'let us make way for the one bursting out of me even more: P. himself'.[29] The process of reading has introduced the poet into the critic's body, and now he (as words, the body comprised by his poetry) rushes from her body in birth-like violence. Evidently the organic paradigm can fit the practice of critical citation as well as the poetic process. Tsvetaeva as critic must let Pasternak out in order to avoid being smothered or choked by his power, so that his rebirth in her review serves her as a kind of exorcism.

Although the distinctive role of the body in her criticism provides Tsvetaeva a way to convey her experience of inspiration as a reader and writer, it would be unfair to imply, as does Réné Wellek,[30] that inspiration was her central explanatory conceit. Her references to craft in the poetic process and rejection of the idea that a 'divine spark' in the poet's soul compensates for lack of talent and skill reflect a concern with conscious processes in literary production not unlike that of the Formalists, though use of the term 'craft' is more often associated with the Acmeists.[31] In her theoretical articles Tsvetaeva rejects the idea that poets are elevated beings bringing moral lessons to the rest of the world, and she posits an 'in-between' world where art takes place that partakes of both the 'heaven' of inspiration and the 'earth' of poetic technique. Along with her attention to craft, Tsvetaeva's understanding of the poem as a body nonetheless leads her to reject Formalist emphasis on scholarly dissection of poetic processes; craft and inspiration can be invoked to correct one another, and Tsvetaeva allows neither to assume greater importance or stability than the other.[32]

29. Ibid., pp. 140, 144, 141.
30. Wellek, who devotes several pages to the criticism of Blok, Ivanov, and other Silver Age poets in the seventh volume of his monumental *History of Modern Criticism*, dismisses Tsvetaeva with one phrase: 'The Symbolists and Acmeists believed in inspiration (and so did, e.g., Marina Tsvetaeva)' (p. 251). I would suspect that this oversimplification is not unrelated to Tsvetaeva's equally summary description in 'Poet o kritike', '("formal´nyi metod", to est´ vidoizmenennaia bazarovshchina)' (*Izbrannaia proza*, vol. 1, p. 224). Even sixty-five years after its first publication, 'Poet o kritike' has the power to alienate and incense certain readers.
31. Ibid., *Izbrannaia proza*, vol. 1, p. 224. Note that Tsvetaeva's use of the term *remeslo* ('craft'), as the title of one book of poetry and as a term in criticism comes not from the Acmeists and their 'Tsekh poetov' but rather from a poem by another outstanding poetic craftswoman, Karolina Pavlova's 'Ty, utselevshii v serdtse nishchem' (1854).
32. Indeed, Tsvetaeva's critical theories, like her poetic use of gender, reject dualism in favour of more flexible dichotomy, as described by Anya Kroth in 'Androgyny as an Exemplary Feature of Marina Tsvetaeva's Dichotomous Poetic Vision', *Slavic Review* vol. 38, 1979, pp. 563–82.

As the first-person feminine past-tense verb *popala* cited in the previous paragraph indicates, Tsvetaeva often emphasises her own gender and authorial voice in her critical prose. However, at times she moves away from concentration on the person and reactions of this self through two strategies common in more traditionally structured literary criticism: first, occasionally hiding her gender behind pseudonymous terms such as *pishushchii*, which allow the use of masculine word forms,[33] and second, drawing her readers into a sort of critical community through use of the first-person plural, *my*. This position is implied in a number of statements concerning the overall effects of poetry on reader's bodies: '...this is a book – for everyone. And it's necessary for everyone to know it. This book is for souls what Maiakovskii is for bodies: a discharge into action. Not only healing – like those sleepy herbs of his – [but] miracle-working.'[34] Readers, as common possessors of both souls and bodies, are invited to join the critic in healing both by reading Pasternak's poetry. At other times, readers are drawn into a critical 'we' that is less conventional, since it implies not a commonality of literary and cultural values so much as a joint process of critical activity: 'But enough choking. Let us try sanely and soberly.'[35] Here the first-person plural verb form, 'let us try' ('popytaemsia'), draws the reader into the critic's overwhelmed choking ('zakhlebyvaniia') in reaction to Pasternak's poetry, and so into the movement of the whole text.

The reader's involvement through various linguistic devices brings us to the larger question of Tsvetaeva's critical style, and indeed of the style of all her prose works. What readers such as Simon Karlinsky[36] and Barbara Heldt have noted in describing Tsvetaeva's prose in general is particularly true of her critical essays. Heldt writes:

> By choosing a style of highly-mannered subjectivism when not talking ostensibly about herself, Tsvetaeva is declaring her freedom from conventions of objective narrative while still retaining the right to historicity ... and to critical judgment of her fellow poets. She establishes her own identity through her evaluations of other poets, as well as through her juxtaposition of self with family. She is alternatively [*sic*] epigrammatic – as in her judgment of two Symbolist poets: 'All that is not Bal´mont is Briusov, and all that is not Briusov is Bal´mont' – and digressive. Simulating anti-logic, she makes judgments whose logic then becomes inescapable.[37]

33. In 'Epos i lirika sovremennoi Rossii', *Izbrannaia proza*, vol. 2, p. 9.
34. Tsvetaeva, *Izbrannaia proza*, vol. 1, p. 148.
35. Ibid., p. 138.
36. Karlinsky, *Marina Cvetaeva*, p. 272.
37. Heldt, *Terrible Perfection*, p. 98.

The Soviet critic Aleksei Pavlovskii makes the valuable point that Tsvetaeva's works are often constructed according to principles more common to music: 'Tsvetaeva frequently builds her works and conducts motifs not so much by logical paths as by musical ones.'[38] Tsvetaeva does not adopt an academic tone 'of detachment and objectivity', as Wellek would have it, but rather transforms the genre of criticism with ellipses, sound allusions and morphological associations like those found in her poetry. Towards the end of 'Downpour of Light', for example, the critic stresses the power of Pasternak's book by abdicating her own responsibility: 'I am stopping. In despair. I've said nothing. Nothing – about nothing – for it is Life before me, and I don't know any words of that kind' ('Konchaiu. V otchaianii. Nichego ne skazala. Nichego – ni o chem – ibo peredo mnoi Zhizn´, i ia takikh slov ne znaiu').[39] The assonance of the elliptic 'Konchaiu. V otchaianii' links the necessity of ending her piece with ending's 'rhyme', despair, and this rhyme negatively expresses the critic's desire to continue writing until she has recopied all the poems in Pasternak's book, echoing her earlier positive statements of the same desire.[40] Like the rest of her prose, Tsvetaeva's critical articles call attention to and create meaning through their own aesthetic structures, and they are not only expressions of opinion and judgement, but also works of art.

Tsvetaeva began writing and publishing criticism as a mature and confident poet, sure that her status as an artist conveyed the right to make pronouncements on literature in general,[41] and this may well have eased her refusal of the 'smooth' prose more usually found in works of criticism. Rather than hiding her voice and person behind a standardised tone of authority, Tsvetaeva writes in an individual and even an eccentric voice. She is aware of her departures from the critical tradition, as she adds at the end of 'Downpour of Light': 'One doesn't [literally, "they don't"] write this way about contemporaries. I repent.'[42] Here the community of 'we' composed of writer and readers is opposed to and grammatically excluded from the alienating 'they' who do not write this way. The repentance the critic displays may be due to what Svetlana Boym calls the 'tastelessness' of this kind of text, its passionate self-exposure, which includes display of the writer's marked, feminine gender.[43]

---

38. A. Pavlovskii, *Kust riabiny. O poezii Mariny Tsvetaevoi*, Leningrad, 1989, p. 259.
39. Tsvetaeva, *Izbrannaia proza*, vol. 1, p. 147.
40. Ibid., p. 140.
41. Since Tsvetaeva's critical authority depends on her primary stressed identity as a poet, any 'nodes' of uncertainty and anxiety in her self-confidence as an artist have more to do with being a poet than with being a critic *per se*.
42. Tsvetaeva, *Izbrannaia proza*, p. 147.
43. See Boym's *Death in Quotation Marks*, pp. 194–9, for a discussion of 'obscenity' and lack of taste in women's writing.

Nonetheless, the eccentric and self-revelatory function of the prose can be balanced by the more 'classical'[44] objections attributed to her readers. At times her readers' comments are set apart by the quotation marks she otherwise uses for titles of poems: '"A set of words, all for the sake of the repeating "ch""'.[45] To these imagined objections she responds: 'Yes, gentlemen', 'But, gentlemen', 'Gentlemen, you now know' and, humorously, 'after all I'm not pulling [you] by the ears'.[46] Of course this device allows her the last word; but her need to draw her readers into her argument as interlocutors reflects the same ambiguity present in her attitude toward authority in general. It may be that Tsvetaeva the critic, as a woman, is forced by the language and traditions of Russian literature to formulate a 'voice' whose claim to authority must constantly be defended from the imagined or remembered voices that challenge it.

Tsvetaeva's critical texts may strike some readers as 'hysterical' because they frequently give the impression of improvisation (only the impression, since her critical prose, like her poetry, resulted from long and painstaking work over drafts); this element undercuts the whole notion of the critical text as a finished, perfected piece of judgement and of the critic as a monumental authority. She corrects statements made earlier, including examples of her own poetry, makes self-deprecatory comments about her own writing, and creates texts which, like her scrupulously finished but apparently spontaneous poetry, preserve traces of their own history of composition. Thus she adds a footnote to 'Downpour of Light'[47] which corrects her statement on the first page that *My Sister Life* is Pasternak's first book but also suggests that she intuitively used the expression *poverkh bar´erov* ('over the barriers') in her text before learning that this was in fact the title of another of his books. Her comments on specimens of her own writing include 'Not a brilliant line' and 'from my helpless splashes';[48] in a footnote to 'Hero of labour' she comments that *ne povtoriu* ('I won't repeat') would be a better line than *ne utaiu* ('I won't conceal') in her early poem 'Vospominan´e slishkom davit plechi'.[49] After 'rationally' picking apart Georgii Adamovich's criticism of her poetic voice as 'impertinently-breaking' ('derzko-sryvaiushchimsia'),[50] she offers a Cyrano-like list of

---

44. I say 'classical' here because of this technique's echo of Dostoevsky's Underground Man, with his obsession for anticipating and responding to his opponents' objections. Compare Livingstone, in her introduction to *Art in the Light of Conscience*, p. 10.

45. Tsvetaeva, *Izbrannaia proza,*, vol. 1, p. 139.

46. Ibid., pp. 135, 140, 146, 141.

47. Ibid., p. 138.

48. Ibid., p. 137

49. Ibid., p. 191.

50. Ibid., p. 223.

adverbs which she considers more suitable for use in this case, outdoing Adamovich's criticism with apparent criticism of herself: 'Wrathfully-breaking, yes. Manifestly-breaking, yes. Wrathfully, manifestly, languidly, noticeably, maliciously, nervously, pathetically, amusingly ...'. After the first few words, however, the repetitive rhythm and lack of grammatical anchor make the words seem to apply to the entirety of Adamovich's critical practice, especially since the words she suggests grow increasingly pejorative. After stating that Briusov went against the current of his own ungiftedness, she redefines the latter as something that cannot have a current, since it does not flow: 'I leave the mistake, as a useful one for those who read and those who write.'[51] Leaving her own 'mistake' in the text as useful to readers and writers sets up a kind of textual instability, where the author comments on her own writing and her own place in the process of criticism and literature, lowering her own position to that of a fallible authority. This also gives her room to deviate and assert her own claim to authority through the 'mistake'. All these digressions from standard critical posture underline Tsvetaeva's own claim that she is a poet, not a 'specialist' in poetry: 'That's the business of specialists in poetry. My specialty is – Life.'[52] Her critical article is constructed not as a monument to the critic's taste, but rather as part of a mutual activity of reading and writing.

Finally, Tsvetaeva's demanding prose style, commentary on writing, and sense that the reader participates in the process of writing, interpreting and making meaning, underlie her explicit insistence on reading as co-creation: as she says in 'A Poet about Criticism/the Critic', 'Tired of [reading] my piece – that means you read well and – you read something good. The reader's weariness is not a devastating weariness, but a creative one. Co-creative. It does honour both to the reader and to me.'[53] In writing criticism she aims to stretch and even to strain her reader. The greatest effect of the author's primary and even stressed identity as a poet is apparent in the making of her prose itself: the reader is educated and transformed not through lecture, but rather as an active participant in the demanding co-creation of a text. Like her inclusion of physical reactions to a poem, this increases the reader's involvement in the text and that text's conclusions, emphasising the process of reading through a text rather than presenting a fixed and final set of judgements.

51. Ibid., p. 213.
52. Ibid., p. 136.
53. Ibid., p. 238.

Tsvetaeva the Meta-Critic or Poet on Top

The title of 'A Poet about Criticism/the Critic' allows its author the sat-
isfaction of making the poet the grammatical subject of her verbless
phrase, while the critic (and/or criticism) is distanced from reader and
writer by its oblique case. Tsvetaeva both emphasises that she is a poet
who will write as such and immediately upsets the traditional hierarchy
in which the critic creates a higher work of art by writing about the poet
and poetry – a hierarchy which she herself goes on to invoke, as we shall
see below. The title, as mentioned earlier, can also be translated ambigu-
ously, as either 'A Poet about the Critic' or 'A Poet about Criticism'.
Russian grammar makes this possible by requiring the same ending in
the prepositional case for both masculine *kritik* and feminine *kritika*, as
if to unite the two platonically in their identical form. This has the effect
of making the critic potentially identical to the critic's writing, implying
that the criticism is the critic's body, just as poetry forms the poet's
body. The writer and the writing are essentially identical, they can be
spoken of at the same time with the same language. The question
remains, however: if Tsvetaeva is a poet, as she keeps insisting, then is
her article criticism, poetry, or something else?

The inversion of the hierarchy of critic and poet implicitly stresses
the issue of power in literary relations. In Tsvetaeva's reading, poets
want power more than anything else.[54] Her juxtapositions of critic and
poet point out the inherent power of the critic's position and so the
importance of protecting the poet from irresponsible criticism. The fact
that this poet writes criticism suggests that she herself must assume the
position of critic if she wishes to have the right of reply when faced with
bad criticism of her own work. It is no surprise that she sets out to correct her critics, since poets complain about critical reviews of their work
all the time, and Tsvetaeva, like many women writers, had more than
adequate grounds for feeling that she had been misunderstood.[55] Her
criticism of critics is no more virulent than that of many other poets, but
it is less usual for a poet to undertake such detailed and substantial
instruction in how to avoid critical errors.

At its appearance, 'A Poet about Criticism/the Critic' caused a scandal and alienated a good part of the *émigré* literary community from

54. Ibid., pp. 183, 232.
55. Compare Dale Spender, *The Writing or the Sex? Or why you don't have to read
women's writing to know it's no good,* New York, 1989, esp. p. 63: 'What can be stated at
the outset is that reviews have always been taken seriously by writing women. The literary
history of women is so replete with protests about unjust reviews that the topic stands at
the centre of women's literary traditions and suggests how different literary history and literary criticism could be if women's version of experience had been equally represented.'

Tsvetaeva.[56] Though she may have been naïve in assuming that an attack phrased in such personal terms would not be taken personally, the epigraph from Montaigne,[57] insisting that one can work for a very small audience or for none at all, suggests that she was quite conscious of the possible results of what she did. Her article sets out to defend both poet and reader[58] from the flawed criticism of bad critics. She supports her attack with numerous examples of inconsistent criticism in the appended 'Flower-bed', a series of quotations from articles by Georgii Adamovich interspersed with Tsvetaeva's own humorous and devastating comments. Although there are examples of Adamovich's comments about her own work, she includes many more statements about other poets, living and dead, which she considers just as bad. The element of self-defence expands to include the entire class of poets (so long as they are not playing critic). Despite the biting humour throughout the article, Tsvetaeva is deadly earnest in her typical defence of the underdog, in this case, of the poet. Her defence is to place herself above the critic, turning that customary hierarchy on its head. One might argue, after all, that a hierarchy of commentary and judgement that is continually reversed eventually assumes the form of a dialogue.

Tsvetaeva's demands on the critic reflect the dual nature of the critic's activity as both reader and writer, or as she puts it, 'an absolute reader who has taken up the pen'.[59] As an absolute reader, the critic must know the poet's entire opus in order to judge it competently and chronologically, must not expect to be amused and entertained by a difficult work, and preferably should have the vision to sense immediately what other readers will grasp only after ten or a hundred years. Bad readers, who either read with ill will or do not actually read at all, are damned.[60] Tsvetaeva compares the critic's judgement to a cobbler's ability to evaluate the soundness of a pair of boots,[61] which both humorously refers to the utilitarian critics of the 1860s and challenges the idea

56. Karlinsky, *Marina Cvetaeva*, pp. 70–1.

57. "'Souvienne vous de celuy à qui comme on demandoit à quoi faire il se peinoit si fort en un art qui ne pouvoit venir à la cognoissance de guère des gens, –

"J'en ay assez de peu", répondit-il. "J'en ay assez d'un. J'en ay assez de pas un'" ('Poet o kritike', *Izbrannaia proza*, vol. 1, p. 221).

The same quotation is used as the epigraph to the second notebook of Tsvetaeva's last published collection of poetry, *Posle Rossii*, in 1928 (*Stikhotvoreniia i poemy*, vol. 3, p. 77). This repeated use as an epigraph to works of differing genre links Tsvetaeva's critical agenda once again with her poetic experience and production.

58. Karlinsky points out that in 'Poet o kritike', 'Tsvetaeva uses a multiple vantage point, in this case that of an innovating creative artist and that of an intelligent and inquisitive reader' (*Marina Cvetaeva*, p. 274).

59. Tsvetaeva, *Izbrannaia proza*, vol. 1, p. 227.

60. Ibid., pp. 234–5.

61. Ibid., p. 225.

that there is a hierarchy of values among different arts and even crafts. Her insistence on the poet's need for money also deflates the generally lofty position of the poet in Russian society.[62] In another section of the article a certain hierarchical positioning remains, as the critic observes the poet's work from a higher (if not a superior) level and creates in criticism a new work of art based on creative and co-creative reading: 'The folk, in a fairy tale, interpreted the dream of the elements, the poet, in a poem, interpreted the dream of the folk, the critic (*in a new poem!*) interpreted the dream of the poet.'[63] Hierarchy and non-hierarchy interplay as the poet requires the critic to be more like the poet and yet capable of seeing farther and more clearly.

Tsvetaeva demands that the critic as a writer provide copious citation in reviews[64] and have the taste to refrain from printing her or his own bad poetry. She advances the idea that a good critic must not only love poetry, but 'live in it' and know it well, somewhat self-servingly recalling her own critical qualifications as a poet. She damns the activity of critical dilettantes but also questions the value of the new Soviet Formalists, who merely dissect the living text, thereby killing it: 'A dissection, but a dissection not of a corpse, rather of a living [being]. Murder.'[65] The poem, again, is a living body whose integrity must be respected.

In addition, the article 'A Poet about Criticism/the Critic' unifies the two terms of its title by discussing the criticism of poets. Here, of course, what is at stake is the author's own position and her right to appropriate cultural standards (such as the image and work of Pushkin) in support of her own agenda. Given a poet's obvious natural qualifications as a critic (living in and knowing poetry, presumably loving it, and reading a great deal), at best the criticism of a poet illuminates two bodies of work, the poet's and the poet-critic's. At worst, only the poet-critic is revealed, though if the poet is of sufficient stature the criticism

---

62. Ibid., p. 232.
63. Ibid., p. 240. Emphasis Tsvetaeva's.
64. Tsvetaeva consistently cites at some length in her own reviews. At times, as in 'Svetovoi liven'', she makes her reader's head spin with a succession of brief, unconnected fragments.
65. Ibid., p. 238. If the poet is a being who incarnates, as described above, then the Formalist project appears as a desire to dis-incarnate. Tsvetaeva finally labels the Formalists scholars rather than critics ('Poet o kritike', *Izbrannaia proza*, vol. 1, p. 239); the metaphor of biological dissection, perhaps meant to recall Bazarov with his frogs, makes a humorous contrast to her later comparison of formalist criticism to cookbooks. Here the fact that some would-be poets lack the wherewithal to produce real poetry reminds her of the economic 'zhestokii zakon neravenstva' which deprives the poor of luxurious ingredients in their cooking (ibid., p. 239).

may still be worth reading.[66] A poet's criticism is not dispassionate but rather expresses the passionate relation of two writers, their relatedness and unrelatedness. When this passion predominates, the result is opinion rather than judgement, or what Tsvetaeva calls 'otnoshenie'. It is in essence an entry into dialogue with the other poet rather than a final, monumental judgement.

Tsvetaeva adds that anyone, poet or bootmaker, is entitled to a personal opinion, as long as the words 'I' and 'me' are included. 'I' and 'me' do not bear the responsibility of a statement made without these qualifiers, and she claims that most lyric poets choose to be partisan and thus to abdicate critical objectivity. The lyric genre's traditional association with strong emotion (especially love) and poetic personality implies that a lyric poet's passionate temperament would lead to a 'passionate' tone and style in criticism rather than to 'dispassionate' style or objectivity in judgement. At the same time, the inclusion of 'I' and 'me' mark the author as a historical individual and make that individual more present in the text, especially since in Russian the first person singular is one important site of gender-marking. The demand for personal accountability, a personal voice, and the possibility that a different kind of criticism should be practised are undercut by the later suggestion that an epic poet, unlike the lyric, has not only a more 'objective, detached tone' but also a creative vantage point that can duplicate the position of society at large. 'Society at large', of course, speaks in the voice of the part of society that controls discourse and the formation of literary tradition – perhaps the very 'gospoda' ('gentlemen') whom Tsvetaeva addresses from time to time in her early criticism. In 'A Poet about Criticism/the Critic' her style ranges from the Dostoevskian 'Gentlemen, some fairness, and if not – even some common sense!' to emphasis on her own self and experience, 'To whom I listen' and 'For whom I write', an interplay of styles that positions the speaker variously.[67]

Once more, Tsvetaeva creates a position for herself as critic that intertwines an idiosyncratic, individual voice with existing notions of the poet as a conduit for general poetic truth, the latter being much closer to cultural ideals of the critic as discerner and disseminator of 'truth' in judgements of literary value, the myth of critical objectivity. If we

66. As Tsvetaeva puts it, 'A na Bal´monta gliadet´ i Bal´monta videt´ – stoit' (ibid., p. 227). She distinguishes between poetic and academic criticism, mentioning Khodasevich as an example of a lyric poet who can produce good academic criticism when he wants to but implying that most poets do not want to (ibid., p. 228). The question of where she falls in this split is not addressed; for the purposes of this article she clearly sides with the poetic critic, but her later articles 'Pushkin i Pugachev' and 'Dva lesnykh tsaria' certainly pretend to (and, many would argue, achieve) the status of academic criticism.

67. Tsvetaeva, *Izbrannaia proza*, vol. 1, pp. 225, 227, 231.

recall images of the poet in her poetry, such as a voice crying in the wilderness or an oracular voice of the gods, it appears that here too Tsvetaeva relies on a mystical subtext of the poet's value and vocation. It is no accident that the epigraph to the subsection of the article entitled 'To whom I listen' is taken from the story of Joan of Arc.[68] Tsvetaeva herself invokes the critic's interpretative function, as if to pay lip-service to critical authority, in the statement we have already seen: 'The folk, in a fairy tale, interpreted the dream of the elements, the poet, in a poem, interpreted the dream of the folk, the critic (*in a new poem*!) interpreted the dream of the poet.'[69] The critic, a higher instance of the poet, makes meaning of material which, like a dream, is raw and unprocessed. This time, however, I would like to point out that if the critic's work is indeed a 'new poem', then the critic has been transmogrified, with truly Tsvetaevan solipsism, into the poet, recalling Joseph Brodsky's point that her prose is just a continuation of her poetry 'by different means'.[70]

The ending of 'A Poet about Criticism/the Critic' goes even further in describing the critic's powers of interpretation, as the ideal critic becomes 'The Sibyl above the cradle'.[71] As a Sibyl leaning over a cradle, the critic is no longer a rational, masculine interpreter, but a prophet who is female, inspired by the god of poetry, Apollo, and (perhaps most strikingly) known for speaking in riddles which must then be deciphered. Like her image of the Poet Himself, Tsvetaeva's more conventional theories reveal the power of tradition in genre and text but may be undercut by her practice in critical writing, even containing their own subversion, as in this case. One might argue that an attempt to destabilise a system is furthered by incorporating what one opposes into one's objections, as no statically extreme position can be defended: extreme positions evoke and provoke their own opposites, while ambiguity allows freedom of movement. Ambiguity, too, is surely part of the heritage of a woman who refuses to keep silent. Her 'hysteria' as a woman writer is both concealed and confirmed by the discovery of a Sibylline womb in her ideal critic.

Clearly, Tsvetaeva's literary criticism and critique of critics lead beyond the stylistic traits common to all her prose work, to issues of the writer's authority in any genre. While her critical prose conveys her passionate belief in the importance of writing and poetry and the special issues that concern all major poets, the very form of the writing seems to modify, if not to undercut, the kinds of authority invoked in her content. Her individual identity as a writer, anchored by the invariable signature,

68. Ibid., p. 230.
69. Ibid., p. 240.
70. Iosif Brodskii, 'Predislovie. Poet i proza', in *Izbrannaia proza*, vol. 1, p. 8.
71. Ibid., p. 241.

is performed with great mobility for the reader. Her critical agenda is defined by her own experience, experience that is in turn clearly mediated by tradition. The main critical project of educating her reader in her own manner of thinking through apparent contradictions draws the reader into a co-creation of the text that must finally have consequences for the reader's own self-creation. As the penultimate part of 'A Poet about Criticism/the Critic' states, the reader, not the critic, is the final instance of interpretation and judgement in literature for Tsvetaeva.[72]

72. Ibid., p. 240.

–8–

Air. Suffocation. Muteness: Akhmatova, Mandel´shtam, Pasternak and Tsvetaeva

Anatoly Naiman

'Our four have made it at full tilt', Akhmatova was fond of saying in the sixties with reference to Mandel´shtam, Pasternak, Tsvetaeva and herself at a time when they had received complete and total recognition. The phrase sounded intentionally vulgar and unexpectedly solemn. Pasternak, in Tsvetaeva's words, resembled simultaneously an Arab and his horse and somehow the disrespectful metaphor suited him, as the others harnessed with him in a team might well have snorted. The solemnity stemmed from the image of the triumphal quadriga, like one of those adorning the pediments of magnificent buildings – such as on the arch of the Staff Headquarters on Palace Square in St Petersburg.

Decades of degradation and pain have coloured the inner drama of each of the four with tragic shades. Over four recent years, from 1989 to 1992, their poetry and fate have passed before us one after the other, inspired by the common denominator of their centenaries. That epoch: those directly responsible for creating it, as well as those who meekly obeyed orders, has now collapsed beneath the accusations both of people who had the right to accuse and of others who have conferred upon themselves that right without prior tribulations. From that bloodstained era we request an explanation of everything: the executions, the camps, persecution, of the suicides, human weakness and baseness. And even as to why for so many years the poet kept silent.

'Things are somewhat more complicated,' wrote Akhmatova in 1960. 'Apart from all the difficulties and disasters on the official side [two resolutions by the Central Committee],[1] artistically I always had serious difficulties with my work on the creative side; it may even be

---

1. Publication of Akhmatova's work was banned by a Resolution of the Central Committee of 14 August 1946. In 1925 a similar ban was placed on publication of her work. Akhmatova was of the opinion that the same body was responsible then, but I have no documentary confirmation of this. In any case, the ban was effective.

that official difficulties partly obscured the real problem.' Artistic censure of a poet might intensify or relax according to the political situation, but to view him or her as a product of the regime's pressure is not valid because it is too simplistic. The poet's inclination to write particular poems or not to write at all come as a consequence of a number of impulses, which are not always subject to analysis or even observation. The so-called 'present moment' is simply the most noticeable of these impulses, the most accessible to external view.

The traditional merits of Russian criticism and the literature it has nurtured, reacting to what is going on – on occasion almost like a newspaper – have been held up regularly during the last two centuries as deficiencies, flaws that have ruined art. If the poet speaks of his 'homeland' this means first and foremost Poetry, the space in which he or she was born not as Ania and Osia but as Akhmatova and Mandel´shtam. Their birthplace where they are known by the short version of their first names serves only to lend concrete authenticity and warmth to this space.

In the same way when they say 'air', this signifies not only the human world but also the resonant air of their habitat, a substance which is necessary not only for the physical act of breathing but also for poetic inhalation/inspiration, that sole medium in which their poetry can ring out and without which it falls silent.

I

In the sixties Akhmatova recorded in her diary: 'Marina [Tsvetaeva] has retreated into trans-rational language ['zaum´']. Look at her *Poema vozdukha* ('Poem of Air'). She became restricted in the confines of Poetry. She is "dolphin-like" as Shakespeare's Cleopatra remarks about Antony. One element was not enough for her so she withdrew into another or into others.' Subsequently, Akhmatova was to repeat more than once, both in conversations and in the written notes acompanying these conversations, that there was no internal connection between *Poema bez geroia* ('Poem without a Hero') and Tsvetaeva's poems. Let us not forget, however, that in the night between their two meetings in 1941, Tsvetaeva wrote out *Poem of Air* for Akhmatova. At this time *Poem without a Hero* already existed in rough outline and was being worked on, and it was the beginning of the first chapter that was, as it happens, written in Tashkent in 1942.

Poem of Air was written, as its author emphasises, 'in the Lindberg days', that is the days of the first solo flight across the Atlantic. It is viewed by critics, not without reason, as a continuation of her poem 'Novogodnee' (1927), addressed to Rilke who had recently died. The conflict described in 'Novogodnee' is the same as in *Poem without a Hero*:

Я зажгла заветные свечи,
И вдвоем с ко мне не пришедшим
Сорок первый встречаю год , -

The one whom the poet addresses, with whom she sees in the New Year,
is not able to appear. Tsvetaeva's phrase from the poem 'S nastu-
paiushchim!' relates equally to New Year's Eve and to Rilke's birthday:
'(Rozhdalsia zavtra!)' – 'V Al'kazare budete? – Ne budu', refers to a
Parisian restaurant where a noisy New Year's party is to take place. It
may be noted here that this verbal exchange can be found reflected,
should one so wish, in a fragment from *Poem without a Hero*:

«Мы отсюда еше в «Собакуя»...»
«Вы отсюда куда?» -
«Бог весть!»

The posthumous journey of the hero's soul, perhaps corresponding to
the Orthodox formula of 'aerial peregrinations',[2] is described concretely
by Tsvetaeva in the poem as a flight through the air: 'Dukh zakhvatyva-
lo? ... Kak gliadel ... So svoei stol'ko-to (skol'ko?) mil'noi/
Beskonechnoi ibo beznachal'noi/ Vysoty nad urovnem khrustal'nym/
Sredizemnogo i prochikh bliudets'.

There are clear parallels between the beginning of *Poem without a
Hero* and *Poem of Air*:

'Ia sama kak ten' na poroge,/ Steregu poslednii uiut./ I ia slyshu zvonok
protiazhnyi ...' (Akhmatova)
　'Dver' iavno zatikhla,/ kak dver', za kotoroi gost'.' (Tsvetaeva)
　'I kak budto pripomniv chto-to,/ Povernuvshis' vpoloborota ...'
(Akhmatova)
　'Kak gost, za kotorym zov/ Khoziaina, bden'e/ Khoziaiskoe .../ Kak
gost', za kotorym znak/ Khoziaiki – vsei t'my znak!' (Tsvetaeva)
　'Kto stuchitsia? Ved' vsekh vpustili.' (Akhmatova)
　'No kto zhe bez stuka – zhdet?' (Tsvetaeva)
　'Ledeneiu, stynu, goriu ... ' (Akhmatova)
　'Ta sladkaia (igry v strakh!)/ Osobogo roda/ Ottiazhka – s kliuchom
v rukakh.' (Tsvetaeva)

---

2. According to Orthodox teaching, the soul after death journeys to the Other World.
En route it must undergo aerial trials involving encounters with demons who exact dues
for what has been done by the soul during its earthly life. If payment is not made, the soul
is dragged off to hell.

It would, however, be both groundless and erroneous to consider the question of the dependence of the beginning of *Poem without a Hero* on *Poem of Air* solely on the basis of like concurrences and echoes. Let us risk a cautious formulation: it is possible that the opening stanzas of the first part of *Poem without a hero* reflect an awareness of Tsvetaeva's poem – especially as Tsvetaeva was the special object of Akhmatova's attention in the years 1940–2.

In 1940 Akhmatova wrote a poem addressed to Tsvetaeva, 'Nevidimka, dvoinik, peresmeshnik', which maintains the tonality of *Requiem,* which was in the process of composition both before and during this period. As she read *Poem of Air*, she probably observed the similarity between the lines: 'Grunt, kak budto grud´/ Zhenshchiny pod stoptannym Voe-sapogom' and her own 'I bezvinnaia korchilas´ Rus´/ Pod krovavymi sapogami' from the introductory poem to *Requiem* and 'Slovno grubo navznich´ oprokinut' from the dedication; similarly the connection between Tsvetaeva's lines: 'V pesne, v bol´sherotoi/ Pamiati narodnoi' and her own from the second epilogue: 'I esli zazhmut moi izmuchennyi rot/ Kotorym krichit stomil´onnyi narod'.

Akhmatova continues her remark about Tsvetaeva's escape into trans-rational language by comparing her creative path to Pasternak's and Mandel´shtam's: 'Pasternak did things the other way round: (in the Peredelkino cycle of 1941) he returned from his Pasternakian version of *zaum´* into the bounds of ordinary (if poetry can be ordinary) Poetry. Mandel´shtam's path was more complex and mysterious.' If Akhmatova expressed herself quite definitely about Tsvetaeva and Pasternak, she said in effect nothing about Mandel´shtam. One can only surmise that underlying the 'complexity and mystery' she had in mind the fusion of what might be called *zaum´* with the 'unheard-of simplicity' of his later poetry. In any case, Akhmatova's verbal pronouncements on this theme led to a similar conclusion, even though they do not spell it out. Attempts to establish internal links between Tsvetaeva and Akhmatova by an intermediate means, but one equally important to both – the text – appear relatively fruitful.

Akhmatova called Mandel´shtam's *Verses on the Unknown Soldier* the pinnacle of world poetry in the twentieth century. In the early sixties she kept a copy in her desk. She overtly cited Mandel´shtam's line 'Araviiskoe mesivo, kroshevo' in 'Rodnaia zemlia', one of the final poems of her later years: 'I my melem, i mesim i kroshim'. By the time she read *Poem of Air* she was familiar with the *Verses* and she could not have overlooked the persistent, albeit unintentional, response of two poets greeting each other:

Compare 'Rastsediv sechatkoiu/ Mir na sei i tvoi,/ Bol´she ne zapachkaiu/ Oka – krasotoi' (Tsvetaeva) with 'I svoimi kosymi podosh-vami/ Svet stoit na sechatke moei.' (Mandel´shtam).

Or 'Slava tebe, dopustivshemu breshi... ' (Tsvetaeva) and
'I vozdushnaia iama vlechet... Vperedi ne proval, a promer ... '
(Mandel´shtam);

'Otstradano. V gazovom meshke/ Vozdukha. Bez kompasa – Vvys´!' (Tsvetaeva) and 'Kak mne s etoi vozdushnoi mogiloi/ Bez rulia i kryla sovladat´ .../ Milliony ubitykh zadeshevo/ Protoptali tropu v pustote ...,' (Mandel´stam);

'V polnoe vladychestvo/ Lba. Predel? – Osil´ ...' (Tsvetaeva) and 'Dlia togo l´ dolzhen cherep razvit´sia/ Vo ves´ lob – ot viska do viska,' (Mandel´shtam);

'V chas, kogda goticheskii/ Khram nagonit shpil´/ Sobstvennyi – i vychisliv/ Vse, – kogorty chisl!' (Tsvetaeva) and '– Skvoz´ efir desi-atichnooznachennyi/ Svet razmolotykh v luch skorostei/ Nachinaet chis-lo, oprozrachnennyi/ Svetloi bol´iu i mol´iu nulei' (Mandel´shtam).

In 1942 Akhmatova wrote a poem 'Kakaia est´. Zhelaiu vam druguiu ...'. She finished it by comparing her own fate with the fate of Marina Tsvetaeva who had hanged herself, and in turn linked both to the fate of Marina Mniszech[3], who was incarcerated in a tower of the Kremlin in Kolomna. She awaits death, which appears in the guise of a Catholic priest coming to hear her last confession:

> И ты придешь под черной епанчою,
> С зеленоватой страшной свечою,
> И не откроешь предо мной лица ...
> Но мне не долго мучиться загадкой:
> Чья там рука под белой перчаткой
> И кто прислал ночного пришлеца?

In this tragic merging of three fates the most significant point is where Akhmatova sees the similarity between her path to death and Tsvetaeva's:

> Но близится конец моей гордыне,
> Как той, другой, - страдалице Марине, -
> Придется мне напиться пустотой.

3. Marina Mniszech, daughter of a Polish aristocrat, married the False Dmitrii in 1606. After his death she married another impostor, the Second False Dmitrii, and bore him a son. She died in prison in 1614.

'Emptiness' is the key word. It is also the pivotal epithet for air in the *Poem of Air*: 'Tretii vozdukh – pust'. Tsvetaeva is here anticipating by several years and almost verbatim one of Kliuev's lines, in the form that Akhmatova had remembered it and used it as an epigraph to the second part of *Poem without a Hero*: 'Akhmatova – zhasminnyi kust,/ Gde Dante shel i vozdukh pust'. Kliuev's poem of the early thirties, 'Ia gnevaius´ na vas, i gorestno braniu', reads somewhat differently:

> Ахматова - жасминный куст,
> Обложенный асфальтом серым,
> Тропу утратила ль к пещерам,
> Где Данте шел и воздух густ …

(Tsvetaeva's line, written earlier in 1927, reads: 'Pervyi vozdukh gust'.)

The contiguity of empty air and Dantesque space is significant in Akhmatova's work. In 'Novogodnee' Tsvetaeva's topography of the other world is also Dantesque:

> Не один ведь рай, над ним другой ведь
> Рай? Террасами? Сужу по Татрам -
> Рай не может не амфитеатром
> Быть.

When talking about Tsvetaeva, Akhmatova used the expression 'Marina suffocated' particularly when referring to the trans-rational language of *Poem of Air*. Further developing and emphasising her remark cited earlier regarding the difference between the creative paths of the four poets, she said: '*Pro domo sua* I say that I *never* flew from nor crept away from Poetry, although more than once as my numbed hands clinging to the side of the boat were battered by powerful blows from the oar, I was invited to descend to the bottom. I admit that now and again the air around me lost its moisture and resonance, the bucket was lowered into the well and instead of a comforting splash it produced a dry blow against the stone. Generally *suffocation* then set in and lasted for years.'[4] Notable here is the enumeration of the three elements one can inhabit 'outside of Poetry': air (never flew away), earth (did not creep away) and water (descend to the bottom). It illustrates how the different elements can be inhabited simultaneously by the same Shakespearian 'dolphin-like' hero.

---

4. Emphasis Akhmatova's.

Poetic suffocation, however, does not take root (according to Akhmatova) because the poet consciously or unconsciously rejects one element in favour of another, but because of the destruction of the elements' natural interplay: 'the air ... lost its moisture', and consequently its 'resonance'. Resonance disappears and 'the interchange of voices' becomes impossible 'on aerial ways', which Akhmatova once again remembered in connection with Tsvetaeva, Pasternak and Mandel´shtam in the poem 'Nas chetvero' (1961). In other words the remarks 'Marina escaped into "zaum""' and 'She became too restricted in the confines of Poetry', signify that the air surrounding the poet became empty, air 'of the Other World' and that 'Marina suffocated' firstly as a poet, her physical death coming as a natural conclusion to poetic 'suffocation'. 'Marina suffocated' like a sea creature ('creatura marina') on the shore, cast out of her native element.

The combination of words, 'to drink in the emptiness' ('napit´sia pustotoi'), conveys the very process of such suffocation. It is not a momentary gulp but an incessant, non-stop imbibing of the air of poetry, an imbibing which is more important than breathing. The poet, seized with a devilish black thirst ('besovskoiu chernoi zhazhdoi') drinks it in every drop ('ee v kaple kazhdoi') and as he drinks the air he drains the air, defined by Tsvetaeva as 'gúdok', until the moment when: 'Konchen vozdukh. Tverd´'. As Akhmatova said in 'Prolog' (1946), the poet finds himself in one of Dante's circles and he anticipates the approach to it partly by the alteration to conventional scales and measures: 'I iarkie do uzhasa tiul´pany/ Kovrom zatkali mnogo soten mil´'. 'Mile' ('milia') in this context is a unit of measure belonging to 'another world', neither native Russian nor indigenous Asiatic, but other-worldly. The phrase about cheeks aflame with fire ('shcheki opalennye pozharom') is a direct reference to Dante, whom his close contemporaries already regarded as one who had been There, and whose image – of a person scorched by hell's flames (the fourth element) – became universal tradition in poetry. Alongside this, it is striking that for Akhmatova that world is hell, for Tsvetaeva – paradise.

The line 'Sedoi venets dostalsia mne nedarom' calls to mind first and foremost a verse from Proverbs (16:31): 'The hoary head is a crown of glory, if it be found in the way of righteousness.' This line also interconnects with a reference to grey hair in *Poem of Air*:

Седью, как сквозь невод
Дедов, как сквозь косу
Бабкину ... –

It follows immediately after 'Tretii vozdukh – pust' and anticipates definitions of air such as 'rarefied' ('redok'), 'sharp' ('rezok') and 'sparse' ('tsedok').

I would venture to say that while Akhmatova in all probability rejected the poetic method and manner of *Poem of Air*, it must have given her confidence that Tsvetaeva divined things in the same way as she, Akhmatova, did, yet independently from her. It is difficult to imagine that Akhmatova could have read with indifference Tsvetaeva's lines:

> Так, пространством всосанный,
> Шпиль роняет храм –
> Дням –

when she herself had written a few months before: 'Kto znaet, kak pusto nebo/ Na meste upavshei bashni'. It is not known exactly in what order the new stanzas of *Poem without a Hero* appeared, thus giving the critic less by which to judge the influence of *Poem of Air* on *Poem without a Hero*. We reiterate that it can only be a question of echoes, of precisely which verses in both poems carry on a dialogue. The 1942 version does not yet include the line about the unclean spirit ('nechistyi dukh'), 'Khvost zapriatal pod faldy fraka', nor the line 'V blednykh lokonakh zlye rozhki' about Kozlonogaia,[5] lines echoing Tsvetaeva's poem 'Kak farnovy rozhki/ Vstavali'. The line 'U skatulki zh troinoe dno' has yet to be included but already we have 'Bes poputal v ukladke ryt´sia', both connected in one way or another with Tsvetaeva's 'Raskolotyi iashchik Pandorin, larets zabot' in *Poem of Air*. Finally, the stanzas beginning 'A ved´ son – eto tozhe veshchitsa' which in some form reflect the line, 'Sniu tebia ili snius´ tebe', from *Poem of Air* have yet to be written. The main point is that another existence is physically co-present in earthly here-and-now reality. We have Tsvetaeva's Guest 'alive or a spectre' ('zhivoi ili prizrak'), Akhmatova's Guests – 'a swarm of some kind of spectres' ('kakikh-to prizrakov roi') where she alone is alive ('odna ia iz nikh zhiva'). In 'Novogodnee' Tsvetaeva says:

> Связь кровная у нас с тем светом:
> На Руси бывал – тот свет на – этом
> Зрел, –

---

5. The name given to Akhmatova's old friend Ol'ga Glebova-Sudeikina in 'Poem without a Hero'. She had been a dancer, but the nickname Kozlonogaia means 'goat-foot' and has demonic/satyric cloven-hooved overtones.

And in 'Requiem' Akhmatova echoes this when she writes: ' Po stolitse odichaloi shli,/ Tam vstrechalis´ mertvykh bezdykhannei'. That is why in *Poem of Air* the Guest:

> Стоявший – как хвоя
> У входа, спросите вдов –
> Был полон покоя... –

and in *Poem without a Hero* – '... tol´ko khvoia/ Mogil´naia ...', and the Guest[6] from the other side of the looking-glass has a pale brow and wide-open eyes ('bleden lob i glaza otkryty').

In one of the comments she made in her later years about *Poem without a Hero*, Akhmatova remembered that 'in June 1941 when I read a bit of the poem to M[arina] T[svetaeva], the first draft, she said quite scathingly: 'You need considerable daring to be writing about Harlequins, Colombines and Pierrots in 41', evidently supposing that the poem was a stylisation in 'World of Art' manner after Benois and Somov, the thing which she may have wrestled with during her emigration as outmoded rubbish. Time proved otherwise. Time worked on *Poem without a Hero*. If this remark is accepted as polemical, then it makes no sense at all if we say that time worked on *Poem without a Hero* but not, let us say, on *Poem of Air*. This simply explains what Tsvetaeva may have overlooked that *Poem without a Hero* used time, or speaking in Akhmatovan terms 'the flight of time', as an instrument of creativity. This instrument is located within the poem and by constant work acts as a continually enriching mechanism: the mechanism being the text itself. We get an idea of how she valued Tsvetaeva's creative work in the twenties and thirties, and in particular *Poem of Air*, from a short extract written for an essay about Mandel´shtam but omitted from the main text: '[Mandel´shtam said] "I am an anti-Tsvetaevan". This perhaps because he never got to know Tsvetaeva's work written abroad.'

Beginning from the late fifties, readers, and especially critics and literary scholarship, have tended to contrast Akhmatova and Tsvetaeva or even portray them as antagonists. This approach has been based on oral remarks, as a rule taken out of context and therefore not entirely reliable, as well as on a handful of written comments about each other. Most frequently cited in support is Tsvetaeva's diary entry for 9 October 1940:

6. The guest from beyond the mirror in this instance is not so much a reference to the folk belief that the Devil or a girl's intended can be glimpsed in the mirror at midnight at New Year or to the widespread use of this image in Symbolist writing, but rather to *Alice through the Looking Glass*, which is usually translated into Russian as *Alisa v Zazerkal´e*, and hence to England and Sir Isaiah Berlin.

Yes, yesterday I read and re-read almost the whole of Akhmatova's book and it is old and feeble. Frequently (it's a bad but reliable sign) there are utterly weak endings leading nowhere ... First there was love, then verses ... But now: I am the book. There were some good lines ... An irretrievably blank page ... But what did she do between 1917 and 1940? She was caught up in herself. This book is an irretrievably blank page.

Tsvetaeva's admission, 'At first there was love, then verses' is ignored like other comments from the early years, for example, in the memoir 'An Otherworldly Evening': 'in a certain sense there was competition between Akhmatova and myself, but not "to outdo her", for it is impossible to outdo her, and this impossibility of doing it better – should be laid at her feet'.

Even the poetry fails to confirm the idea of opposition. Surely it is only the poetry, and not the diaries, letters and more significantly private conversations that should be the object of discussion and a basis for conceptual statements. Meanwhile the dialogue between Tsvetaeva and Akhmatova is surprising and particularly meaningful. In it can be discerned a reply, half a century on, to the remarks Tsvetaeva tossed out in the second decade of the century. In 1916 in the cycle *Verses to Akhmatova* she addressed the following lines to Akhmatova:

> Не отстать тебе. Я - осторожник.
> Ты конвойный. Судьба одна.
> И одна в пустоте порожней
> Подорожная нам дана.
> Уж и нрав у меня спокойный!
> Уж и очи мои ясны!
> Отпусти-ка меня, конвойный,
> Прогуляться до той сосны!

The extract from *Poem without a Hero* which Akhmatova addressed to her double is identical to these lines in both subject-matter and rhythm (we may also recall the beginning of the poem dedicated to Tsvetaeva, 'Nevidimka, dvoinik, peresmeshnik'):

> А за проволокой колючей,
> В самой сердце тайги дремучей
> Я не знаю, который год,

Ставший горсткой лагерной пыли,
Ставший сказкой из страшной были,
Мой двойник на допрос идет.
А потом он идет с допроса,
Двух посланцам Девки Безносой
Суждено охранять его.
И я слышу даже отсюда –
Неужели это чудо! –
Звуки голоса своего ...

Another poem, which also comes from Tsvetaeva's *Verses to Akhmatova*, is dedicated to Akhmatova and Gumilev's son. It seems a prediction of his cruel fate:

Рыжий львеныш,
С глазами зелеными,
Страшное наследье тебе нести!
Северный Океан и Южный
И нить жемчужных
Черных четок – в твоей горсти.

Was it not to this prophetic, compassionate premonition that Akhmatova responded in the sixties with a touching quatrain:

Ты любила меня и жалела,
Ты меня как никто поняла.
Так зачем же твой голос и тело
Смерть до срока у нас отняла?

II

Akhmatova's poetry of the last decade of her life includes a particularly large quota of poems, which could be described as a summing-up. Though it is natural for a poet who has reached the edge of life on earth to concentrate on this theme, this should not obscure the what and how of Akhmatova's summing-up; which people, events and subjects became the prime focus of her attention. These poems are essentially different from *Poem without a Hero*, also part of her 'review', begun in 1941 and written continuously over the next twenty-five years. Like the accompanying poems of the forties and fifties, also some in the sixties, for example the cycles *Shipovnik tsvetet* and *Polnochnye stikhi*,[7] *Poem without a Hero* is addressed clearly from the 'past' to the 'future', whereas the poems which sum up (for example, 'Trilistnik moskovskii' (1961–3), 'Primorskii sonet' (1958), 'Tsarskosel´skaia oda' (1961), 'Rodnaia zemlia' (1961), 'Pamiati V. S. Sreznevskoi' (1964), 'Zemlia khotia i ne rodnaia' (1964) and others) are addressed from the posthumous future to the past. 'Komarovskie nabroski' (1961) also belongs to this group.

All these poems are linked directly, albeit not in any straightforward fashion, to the prose of her final years. This includes diary entries, letters to concrete and hypothetical addressees, and lastly the literary sketches *Amedeo Modigliani* and *Pages from a Diary* (with their more or less rounded plots), as well as adjunct essays, reminiscences, and autobiographical notes, that is, everything which is included in the prose section of recently issued collections of Akhmatova's verse.

Let us recall the text of 'Komarovskie nabroski', with its three epigraphs from Mandel´shtam, Pasternak and Tsvetaeva:

Ужели и тиане гибкой
Все муки Данте суждены (О. М.)

Таким я вижу облик Ваш и взгляд. (Б. П.)

О Муза Плача (М. Тс.)

...И отступилась я здесь от всего,
От земного всякого блага.
Духом, хранителем «места сего»
Стала лесная корчяга.

Все мы немного в жизни в гостях,
Жить - это только привычка.
Чудится мне на воздушных путях
Двух голосов перекличка.

Двух? А еще у восточной стены,
В зарослях крепкой малины,
Темная свежая ветвь бузины...
Это письмо от Марины.

19–20 November 1961
Leningrad Harbour, in hospital

---

7. *Shipovnik tsvetet* was written in 1946, 1957, 1963 and 1964, *Polnochnye stikhi* in 1963.

The poem is dated 1961, regardless of the fact that Akhmatova continued to work on it during the following year. Changes affected the title, the sequence and the number of stanzas, and other minor corrections were also incorporated. It would appear that the poet was pursuing a more important aim by dating it specifically 19–20 November, thereby 'tying' the poem to the time of its creation in the Leningrad Harbour hospital. Akhmatova had been taken there with a serious heart attack and for some time hovered between life and death. 'Harbour' (Gavan´) is the key word in the postscript to the poem. Apart from the place of composition it is also suggests port of destination, ('poslednee pristan-ishche') and the 'desired haven' ('zhelannyi pritin') from 'Trilistnik moskovskii'.

The poem, imbued with the foreboding of imminent death, is dedicated to her three contemporaries, who by then had departed this life, and whom in the early sixties readers had begun to group together with Akhmatova in the category of 'great Russian poets of the twentieth century'. Her half-joking story told about a young man, who slipped into the room, 'while I was lying there with drip and oxygen bag', in order to find out who was the best – Mandel´shtam, Pasternak, Tsvetaeva or Akhmatova – relates to the same stay in the Harbour hospital. Approaching death signified not only the death of Akhmatova but of the 'foursome', of whom she was the last survivor. The validity of this is confirmed by the three epigraphs to the poem – which conferred on her the power of attorney three times over to conclude their common case.

The first stanza, that is, first according to its position in the poem but possibly not according to its time of composition, describes the setting for her life on the eve of death; for the last couple of years she had been living in Komarovo in the simple little house allocated to her by the Literary Fund. She had christened it, ironically, her Cabin, just as the twisted tree-root brought from the forest nearby was termed the guardian spirit ('dukh khranitel´') of the dacha. The formula, 'this place', ('mesto sie') brings to mind the curse of Evdokia Lopukhina,[8] forcibly exiled to a convent – 'Byt´ pustu mestu semu' – which is used as an epigraph to the third part of *Poem without a Hero*. The play on the incongruity between the lofty diction and the down-to-earth subject-matter, lowers and, as it were, puts in its place the elevated gravity of the two first lines, which mimic an almost monastic rejection of the world.

The last stanza is entirely devoted to Marina Tsvetaeva. That the line, 'Temnaia svezhaia vetv´ buziny', is written with Tsvetaeva's poem 'Buzina' (1931–5) in mind (and the accompanying poem 'Dom', which

---

8. Evdokia Lopukhina was the first wife of Peter the Great. She was forced to take the tonsure for her support of the Streltsy in their revolt against Peter.

she describes as a daisy and burdock house ('lopushnyi, romashnyi'), is self-evident. A month before 'Komarovskie nabroski' was composed, an official volume of Tsvetaeva's poetry containing both poems had appeared in print.[9] Of no less importance, however, is reference to her prose, in part to the sketch known as *Kirillovnas*. At the end of the fifties and early sixties, typescripts of now well-known essays and articles by Tsvetaeva circulated widely, and were read and discussed by Akhmatova, and *Kirillovnas* came out in the same year (1961) in *Pages from Tarusa*.[10]

In this short piece Tsvetaeva constantly underlines the wildness of the place: 'dampness, and by a forked post, deeply embedded in the earth, as if it had grown up out of it, through the cold, black, noisy and swift stream, behind the first willow fence on the left, invisible behind the willows and elderberry bushes'; 'on the left – burdock, sand'; 'more than anything I loved this second of descent, of entry, of lowering – into the green, cold, darkness of the stream, moments of grey, endless willow-elderberry hedge, behind which ... is for ever summer, all of summer immediately, with everything about it that is beautiful and sweet, where all you have to do is to enter (but we never did go in!), everything is immediately within reach – the strawberries and cherries and currants and especially the elderberries!' This landscape resembles the 'unexpected' ('neozhidannyi') scenery of Tsarskoe Selo in Akhmatova's poem of 1917, 'Pochernel, iskrivilsia brevenchatyi most': 'I stoiat lopukhi v chelovecheskii rost,/ I krapivy dremuchei poiut lesa'; and further on 'cherez reku vplav´' and 'Sladok byl ustam/ Chernyi dushnyi med'. It is also reflected in a much later poem 'Iva' (1941): 'Ia lopukhi liubila i krapivu/ No bol´she vsekh serebrianuiu ivu' as well as in Akhmatova's prose writing on Tsarskoe Selo. In speaking about the place of Tsarskoe Selo in the poetry of Akhmatova, I have already noted that for Akhmatova burdock, nettles, weeds and the like made up the flora of that garden where the poet composes, comparable to the myrtle, laurel and roses of the ancients.[11]

In Akhmatova's later poetry the landscape of Tsarskoe Selo merges with that of Komarovo. It would be tempting to see in the initial two lines of the third stanza of 'Komarovskie nabroski', 'A eshche u vostochnoi steny,/ V zarosliakh krepkoi maliny', a straightforward depic-

9 Marina Tsvetaeva, *Izbrannye proizvedeniia,* ed. Ariadne Efron and Anna Saakiants, Moscow–Leningrad, 1965.
10. *Tarusskie stranitsy,* Kaluga, 1961. An English version, *Pages from Tarusa,* edited by Andrew Field, was published in Boston in 1964.
11. 'Rodnaia i nerodnaia v tvorchestve Akhmatovoi', published in *A Sense of Place. Tsarskoe Selo and Its Poets. Papers from the 1989 Dartmouth Conference Dedicated to the Centennial of Anna Akhmatova,* ed. Lev Loseff and Barry Scherr, Columbus, Ohio, 1993, pp. 113–19.

tion from nature, a Komarovo sketch. It is more likely, however, that it echoes stories about Tsvetaeva's unmarked grave in Elabuga which emanated from people who had been to the graveyard and then were passed on by word of mouth. A comparable description of the locality which mentioned a wall and thickets featured in the stories. Evidently similar stories lay at the basis of Pasternak's stanza in the early edition of his poem 'Pamiati Mariny Tsvetaevoi' (1943): 'Nado zapechatlet´ na medi/ Etu zhizn´, etot put´ proezzhii,/ Etot dozhd´, etot sad vperedi.'

The two concluding lines of the second stanza of 'Komarovskie nabroski', 'Chuditsia mne na vozdushnykh putiakh/ Dvukh golosov pereklichka' allude to Mandel´shtam and Pasternak. Apart from the meaning naturally suggested by 'aerial ways' – the peregrinations of the soul in the air after death – there are several more levels to this image. Pasternak's story *Aerial Ways* forms one of the major thematic knots tying together his novel *Doctor Zhivago*. In 1958 scandal erupted over its publication abroad and the award to Pasternak of the Nobel prize for literature. With his death following within two years this topic retained its crucial significance and was discussed by Akhmatova. Her evaluation of his novel, though on the whole negative, did not detract from a constant and impassioned interest in the man. At that time she was deeply absorbed in reflections about prose; there was her own attempt to measure up, her attempt to fit ('primerka') in her own prose compositions into twentieth-century Russian prose in its late period. The items that came first within her field of vision were Mandel´shtam's *The Egyptian Stamp* and *Noise of Time* and Pasternak's *Safe Conduct*, followed by Tsvetaeva's prose, mentioned already, and, possibly, some of Khodasevich's essays. The allusion to Pasternak's story in 'Komarovskie nabroski', which had originally been entitled 'Nas chetvero', is not, it appears, coincidental, as it also establishes a link with the aphoristic maxim in *Aerial Ways*, a narrative piece published abroad: '*three human figures* glimmered indistinctly on the edge of the field and across from them the vanishing echo of the distant sea eternally thundered and heaved. It bore these four only from the past into the future and never brought them back' [my emphasis – A.N.].

Reference to Pasternak's *Aerial Ways* also introduces a marked political aspect to 'the interchange of two voices' ('dvukh golosov pereklichka'): 'These were the aerial ways, along which the single-track thoughts of Liebknecht, Lenin and a few minds on their wave-length departed daily like trains. These were the ways laid out at a level that permitted them to traverse any border whatever it might be called.' It was along these aerial ways that the well-known telephone conversation between Stalin and Pasternak on the subject of Mandel´shtam travelled; and likewise, after Mandel´shtam's arrest, the efforts made on his behalf, in which Pasternak participated. The interchange of voices was continued even after his death in Akhmatova's *Pages from a Diary* and in Nadezhda Mandel´shtam's memoirs.

It does not appear unfounded to suggest that the ways which facilitated the interchange of two poets' voices are for Mandel´shtam saturated with this 'air', which from the inception of his work and with increasing clarity towards the end, was vital to him for sound, just as for breathing and for poetry, just as for inhalation/inspiration:

> Люблю появление ткани,
> Когда после двух или трех,
> А то четырех задыханий
> Придет выпрямительный вздох.

Or take the end of the poem 'Eta oblast´ v temnovod´e':

> В гуще воздуха степного
> Перекличка поездов
> Да украинская мова
> Их растянутых гудков. -

alongside the opening lines: 'Ia kruzhil v poliakh sovkhoznykh,/ Polon vozdukha byl rot'.

But it is surely *Verses on the Unknown Soldier* that represents the most direct source, the deepest receptacle of Mandel´shtamian air:

> Нам союзно лишь то, что избыточно,
> Впереди - не провал, а промер,
> И бороть ся за воздух прожиточный -
> Это слава другим не в пример.

Akhmatova writes about this 'vital air' ('prozhitochnyi vozdukh') in *Pages from a Diary*: 'It is striking how a sense of breadth and space and deep intakes of breath appeared in Mandel´shtam's Voronezh poetry precisely when he was not free at all: 'I v golose moem posle udush´ia/ Zvuchit zemlia – poslednee oruzh´e' ('Stansy', 1935). Akhmatova chose two of Mandel´shtam's lines which, as it were, contain the scheme for the final two stanzas of 'Komarovskie nabroski' from the voices, which have found the air necessary for sounding forth, to the earth of the grave. And in this instance her remark revolves around yet another point: 'When I was young I loved water and architecture most but now I love *earth* and *music*.'[12] Her entry in *Pages from a Diary*

12. Emphasis Akhmatova's.

about her last meeting with Mandel´shtam: 'Osip was breathing poorly, he caught the air with his lips', may be read not merely as the end of the man but as the end of the poet – his 'aerial grave' ('vozdushnaia mogila'). Thus emerges the theme that can only be touched upon. For the epigraph to 'Komarovskie nabroski' Akhmatova chose Mandel´shtam's lines written in 1915: 'Uzheli i gitane gibkoi/ Vse muki Dante suzhdeny?' Mandel´shtam's 'aerial grave' is the space beyond the grave of *The Divine Comedy*, condensed into a two-part formula, the same 'place of the Dantesque circle' in Akhmatova's later poetry. The real agony of the outcast Dante and the torments of Hell and Purgatory transformed by poetry are in a direct and figurative sense that air which Mandel´stam and Akhmatova breathed from their youth until the last days of their lives. 'He had only just learnt Italian and he was raving about Dante, reciting pages from memory. We started to speak about "Purgatory". I read a bit from the thirtieth canto (the appearance of Beatrice) ... Osip began to cry. I was alarmed – "What's the matter?" – "No, it's nothing, it is only those words and your reading of them."'

In addition, we will mention another, more overt possible reference to Mandel´shtam in the third stanza, which echoes his comment about Akhmatova's poetry in his article *Sturm und Drang*. He wrote: 'In her poetry there is no psychological fragmentation, but a parallelism typical of folk song, with its clear asymmetry of two contiguous theses, following the pattern: "The elderberry is in the kitchen-garden but ('a') my uncle is in Kiev."'[13] Gathering together what Mandel´shtam had said about her for *Pages from a Diary* and recalling the remark cited above, Akhmatova may have responded to it with the device which he had described by means of the conjunction 'a', 'Dvukh? A eshche ...'. In this instance woven into the allusion to Tsvetaeva's elderberry is the echo of a reminiscence recorded in *Pages from a Diary*: 'The last poem that I heard from Osip: 'Kak po ulitsam Kieva-Viia'. In other words if she really had absorbed his remark then the pattern would have been inverted: 'My uncle is in Kiev and the elderberry is in the kitchen-garden.'

Finally, there is yet another kind of 'Aerial ways' present in 'Komarovskie nabroski' as a real-life backgound. Since 1960 an almanac bearing the same title has been published by R. N. Grinberg in New York. Akhmatova collaborated in its publication and after taking all possible precautionary measures, contributed *Poem without a Hero* and other poems and prose. Only two or three close friends knew about this. The first edition of the almanac (1960) was dedicated to the seventieth anniversary of Pasternak. In the second issue (1961) fifty-seven of

13. *Osip Mandel´shtam. Sobranie sochinenii*, 3 vols, Washington, 1967–9, vol. 2, p. 389.

Mandel´shtam's poems were published, together with two articles about him, Lourié's reminiscenses and *Poem without a Hero* (which had also appeared in the first issue). The third issue (1963) included Akhmatova's poem 'Nas chetvero' ('Komarovskie nabroski') and five of Mandel´shtam's poems. The fourth issue (1965) contained Akhmatova's *Pages from a Diary*, *Amedeo Modigliani*, another five poems by Mandel´stam and a portrait of Pasternak. With this the 'aerial ways' began to resonate and the dialogue of the poets became a visible reality for the reader.

Translated by Joy Bache

Joseph Brodsky on Marina Tsvetaeva

Henry Gifford

In April 1926 Boris Pasternak heard from his father the totally unexpected news that Rilke had read some of his poems in Ehrenburg's anthology of 1922, *Portraits of Russian Poets*, and also others in French translation. He was glad to know of the success his former friend's son now enjoyed. This came like a benediction from the skies. Pasternak, always a fervent admirer of Rilke, at once wrote an ecstatic letter to him in which he declared: 'I owe to you the basic traits of my character, the entire mould of my spiritual being.'[1] And in the same letter he begged Rilke to send one of his books, perhaps the *Duineser Elegien*, to Marina Tsvetaeva in France, who shared his veneration for the poet. Pasternak was already engaged in a passionate correspondence with her, and had just been reading her *Poem of the End*. When Rilke in due course dispatched to her the *Elegien* together with the *Sonette an Orpheus*, Tsvetaeva wrote to him, in German like Pasternak and in the same exalted tones: 'You are a phenomenon of nature ... You are the fifth element embodied – poetry itself...'.[2] There followed a three-sided exchange lasting through the summer, in joyful recognition of all these poets had in common. It did not flow evenly: Pasternak 'was pained when Tsvetaeva sought to exclude him from her friendship with Rilke'.[3] And Rilke, though he met her on the same level of emotion in his letters, and even wrote a splendid verse epistle to her in the style of the *Elegien*, eventually drew back in alarm. Pasternak and Tsvetaeva had been intending to visit the Master. But he was already ill with leukaemia, and at the end of December he died in a Swiss sanatorium. Tsvetaeva reported in shock to Pasternak: 'Rainer Maria Rilke is dead.' And the next day: 'Boris, we shall never go to Rilke.'[4]

1. K. M. Azadovskii, E. V. and E. B. Pasternak (eds), 'Iz perepiski Ril´ke, Tsvetaevoi i Pasternaka v 1926 godu', *Voprosy literatury*, 1978, no. 4, p. 238.

2. Ibid., p. 243.

3. Ibid., p. 258. See also p. 270.

4. Marina Tsvetaeva, *Neizdannye pis´ma*, ed. G. and N. Struve, Paris, 1972, pp. 316–17.

Tsvetaeva had been in 1926 at the very height of her powers, and was gaining recognition in the *émigré* circles of Paris as their leading poet. She published during that year a series of major works: *Poem of the Hill* and *Poem of the End*, both lyrical monologues with snatches of intense conversation and inward debate; also the last instalment of *The Ratcatcher*, a dazzling satire on the theme of *The Pied Piper of Hamelin*. Further she wrote at this time *From the Sea*, a sea dream with some topical satire on Soviet censors and party journalists, dedicated to Pasternak; *Essay of a Room*, an account of a meeting in dream, dedicated to both Pasternak and Rilke; and finally *Poem of the Staircase*, exposing the poverty and squalor of Bellevue, a working-class suburb of Paris, where she was now living. This great surge of creativity would be her last in poetry. The death of Rilke coincided with a downturn in her fortunes. But before this phase of inspiration ended, Tsvetaeva had still one important task to perform. She wrote a final letter to Rilke, a New Year's greeting in verse, 'Novogodnee', in the first weeks of 1927. It is an extraordinary poem, and one that only Marina Tsvetaeva could have achieved so triumphantly.

'Novogodnee' was chosen by Joseph Brodsky to be examined 'in lieu of an introduction' ('Vmesto predisloviia') to the Russica edition of her poetical works.[5] The year before he had provided a Foreword, 'The Poet and Prose', to a selection of the prose from the same publishing house.[6] The essays are neatly dovetailed. At the close of 'The Poet and Prose' Brodsky claims that Tsvetaeva, 'the most passionate voice in Russian poetry of the twentieth century', resembles the star 'in a poem by her beloved Rilke, translated by her beloved Pasternak', that shines like the light in the farthest house of a village. Thereby it changes the parishioners' perception of the extent of their parish. This essay, notable in itself, prepares the way for the much ampler introduction to Tsvetaeva's poems. There will be need sometimes to refer back to it. However, the sequel on 'Novogodnee' is so obviously free-standing, a sustained celebration of Tsvetaeva's own *tour de force*, that it fully merits being taken on its own. Simon Karlinsky has praised this Foreword as not only 'a splendid and highly personal line-by-line exegesis', but also 'a prose poem about the nature of Tsvetaeva's art and thought'.[7] Nothing could demonstrate more tellingly the value of a practitioner's response to a poem that he has understood as no ordinary critic can, by identifying with the poet in her creative experience – identifying, that is to say, as the artist does, with whatever he describes, at one remove. His

---

5. *Stikhotvoreniia i poemy v piati tomakh*, New York, 1980, vol. 2, pp. [39]–[80]).
6. *Izbrannaia proza v dvukh tomakh*, New York, 1979, vol. 1, pp. 7–17.
7. Simon Karlinsky, *Marina Cvetaeva: The Woman, her World and her Poetry*, Cambridge, 1985, p. 169.

'enthusiasm and feeling profound or vehement', as Coleridge put it, will always be accompanied by 'judgement ever awake and steady self-possession'.[8]

One other essay by Brodsky, appearing with these two on Tsvetaeva in his selection of critical and autobiographical pieces, *Less Than One*,[9] follows the same pattern as that on 'Novogodnee'. There he carries out a similar exploration in detail of the well-known poem by Auden 'September 1, 1939'.[10] It was originally given as a lecture to a group of American students, for whom much had to be explained. Their generation knew little of the historical background to Auden's poem, or of Auden's own situation, or of the subtle, sometimes deep differences between the English and the American poetic sensibilities. As an exposition of the poem it answers its purpose admirably. The audience would have been able to share Brodsky's sympathetic regard for Auden in this representative poem – representative too of his habitual uneasiness, for subsequently he rejected it on account of one false note that he would not let pass. The exploration of 'Novogodnee' is very different in manner: Brodsky does not need to coax or encourage his audience. ('Well, a little bit of history shouldn't hurt, should it?') He can assume that the reader of the Russian text is no stranger to Tsvetaeva's poetry; but this poetry is so agile and so many-faceted, that we must bend our attention to match his. Tsvetaeva herself sets the level at which he must write. Criticism of this stamp is a kind of athletics, wary and powerfully concentrated.

Tsvetaeva confessed to Rilke, after receiving his elegy: 'Rainer, all my life I have given myself in verse – to everyone... But I always gave too much, I stifled the possible reply, scared it away.'[11] What masks more than anything else her final communication with Rilke in 'Novogodnee' is the exquisite tact. For example, when she sent a book of her own to him, it disquieted her to learn that the Russian had proved too difficult for Rilke. As Brodsky points out, she felt a certain discomfort in not having used for her poem German rather than Russian. All her letters had been in German, as would be the prose draft of one after Rilke's death which she copied out for Pasternak. This was later abandoned, for further development in 'Novogodnee'.[12] Everywhere the poem reveals her anxiety, in so addressing Rilke, not to let herself intrude. The elegiac mode abounds in temptations to do this, and

8. S. T. Coleridge, *Biographia Literaria*, ed. J. Shawcross, 2 vols, Oxford, 1907, vol. 2, p. 12.

9. Joseph Brodsky, *Less Than One: Selected Essays*, New York, Toronto and Harmondsworth, 1986.

10. 'On "September 1, 1939", by W.H. Auden', Brodsky, *Less than One*, pp. 304–56.

11. Azadovskii *et al.*, 'Iz perepiski', p. 272.

12. Tsvetaeva, *Neizdannye pis'ma*, pp. 319–20.

Tsvetaeva especially had always been addicted to passionate mono-
logue, with the extremes of self-delight and self-exposure.

The elegist, Brodsky notes, normally takes the position of a spectator
in the front row of the stalls. But Tsvetaeva felt an imperative need in
this poem to step onto the stage herself, thereby doing what was essential to her purpose: she enlarged the genre. 'Novogodnee' becomes her
confession to another poet: Rilke is her ideal listener, if only because,
unlike the Almighty beyond the horizon of this poem, he possesses the
gift of perfect pitch. Tsvetaeva's confidence as an artist would have fal-
tered without her perception that through the medium of poetry she
could be at ease with Rilke. The opportunity to make her confession to a
supremely responsive poet enhances the sheer linguistic energy of
'Novogodnee'.

Akhmatova used to say that Tsvetaeva always begins on a high C.[13]
The opening line of the poem illustrates her procedure, the ascent still
possible to her and the measure of her control: 'S Novym godom – sve-
tom – kraem – krovom!'[14] Brodsky observes that 'krovom' (literally
roof) 'as it were looks back from the height on itself in "godom"' (which
it has transmuted). Then he shows how Tsvetaeva resumes her argument, or poetic thinking:

Первое письмо тебе на новом
– Недоразумение, что злачном –
(Злачном –жвачном) месте зычном, месте звучном
Как Еолова пустая башня.

Characteristically she turns upon herself. It is not the 'zlachnoe mesto'
of Orthodox liturgical language, because 'zlachnoe' entangles with
'zhvachnoe', and no poet would be content with an after-life of chewing
the cud. Brodsky has already observed that Dante's paradise is much
more interesting than its Christian source, because the poetic mind
abhors the static.[15]

In 'The Poet and Prose' Brodsky claims that 'so far as literature
forms a linguistic equivalent of thinking', Tsvetaeva turns out to be 'the
most interesting thinker of her time'.[16] He would like to have identified
Shestov as a precursor who influenced her, had there been documentary
proof. At least it is known that she met Shestov in Paris, finding in him
'nobility personified', and that *Versty*, the 'Eurasian' journal co-edited
by her husband Sergei Efron, was intended, in Karlinsky's words, as 'a

13. Tsvetaeva, *Izbrannaia proza*, vol. 1, p. 10.
14. *Svet* could be rendered by Henry Vaughan's 'world of light'; *krai* also means territory, and gives a hint of paradise ('rai').
15. Tsvetaeva, *Stikhotvoreniia i poemy*, vol. 1, p. [44].
16. Ibid., vol. 1, p. 13.

showcase for the work of the writers they [the editorial board] considered to be the most important poet, the most important prose writer, and the most important philosopher of the Russian emigration'. These were Tsvetaeva herself, Remizov and Shestov ('a great favourite of Tsvetaeva's, both as a writer and as a person').[17] Brodsky, by the way, defines Shestov as being less a thinker ('myslitel´') than a 'razmyslitel´' or 'ponderer' – an apt term which matches Antonio Machado's for Ortega y Gasset, 'joven meditador'. Tsvetaeva, he concludes, could have followed a similar path to Shestov's as a result of 'the professional relations between a poet and his language', which in the last resort determine everything.

Poetic thinking, always strenuously pursued by Tsvetaeva, is described, or accounted for, in the celebrated lines from her poem of 1923, the first of a cycle of three under the rubric *Poets*. 'Poet – izdaleka zavodit rech´./ Poeta – daleko zavodit rech´.'[18] This statement, quoted by Brodsky, is a prime example of poetic thinking in action. The poet takes his thought from afar; thought takes the poet far. Tsvetaeva has exploited the identity of form in the nominative and accusative cases of *rech´*. The effect is of an interior change, a sudden reversal: within the apparently static a dialectic is concealed. In poetic thinking movement is all. Mandel´shtam stresses this point often in his *Conversation about Dante*. And as Brodsky remarks in his examination of 'Novogodnee', poetic thought, impelled by speech itself, achieves a rapidity of its own. No 'concentration of the psyche' can travel so far or so fast.[19]

In 'Novogodnee' she embarked upon a journey exactly suited to her temperament – an exploration of the unknown, the inconceivable which her reliance on poetic instinct, the 'ear', is able to figure. And the exploration is performed under Rilke's eye, in such a way that she sees herself from his new vantage point. She is constantly aware of what would be Rilke's response. This results in a poem of the highest integrity.

The same instinct led her to the accents of Russian folk poetry, with its preference for trochaic rhythms and dactylic endings to the line, as against the firm reassuring march of three- or four-footed iambics. The folk poetry of Russia inclines to the incantation ('zagovor') and especially to the lament ('prichitanie'). Her affinity with it accounts for 'a certain *a priori* tragic note' in her verse, a concealed sobbing, not to be heard generally in the work of her contemporaries. Brodsky does not attribute this to any tragic experience of her own, rather it was the 'by-product' of working on the language, especially in relation to folk poetry.[20]

17. Karlinsky, *Marina Cvetaeva*, pp. 153, 155.
18. Tsvetaeva, *Stikhotvoreniia i poemy*, vol. 3, p. 67.
19. Ibid., vol. 1, p. [43].
20. Ibid., vol. 1, pp. [47–8].

The act of writing poetry is, of course, a matter in the first place of very attentive listening. This Mandel´shtam already knew at the beginning of his career: 'Slukh chutkii parus napriagaet'.[21] The hearing tautens the sensitive sail that catches the wind, and this veers with the time. Or, to put it differently, every age has its characteristic rhythm, and the true poet will recognise it. Brodsky sees Tsvetaeva's essay of 1932, *The Poet and Time*, as central for an understanding of her poetics.[22] There she considers the paradox of a poet whose orientation, in life and ideas, is towards a past already vanishing, while without her knowledge or her own will the poetry itself takes her into an advanced position. The 'contemporaneity of the poet' is revealed in 'so many heart-beats a second, giving the exact pulsation of the age'.[23] So Brodsky can say of her that it is idle to speak of her 'not accepting the Revolution'. Tsvetaeva achieved something greater than that: 'she understood it. Like an extreme baring – to the bone – of the essence of being.'[24] Her poetic thinking brought her to the point where there sounded in her voice 'something unfamiliar and terrifying to the Russian ear: the unacceptability of the world'.[25]

Unacceptable too was the death of Rilke. But, exactly as the sense of a radical alienation began for her as a literary device and became an instinct, so it serves in this poem as both method and theme.[26] The psychological and linguistic cannot be disentangled. Content and form preeminently in her work grow together. Brodsky says that enjambment is the autograph or fingerprint of Tsvetaeva, illustrating this point from the lines quoted above:

> Первое письмо тебе на новом
> – Недоразумение, что злачном –
> (Злачном –жвачном) месте ...

This shows how the one device introduces another – the parenthesis, which here contains another parenthesis in brackets.[27] And thus she is continually commenting upon herself. Elsewhere Brodsky refers to Tsvetaeva's 'constant insurrections against herself' which are 'so typical of her lyricism'. The discomfort and restlessness that characterise her mind were dictated by a 'striving after the realistic', leading her to shift abruptly from one linguistic plane to another.[28]

21. O. Mandel´shtam, *Stikhotvoreniia*, Leningrad, 1973, p. 63.
22. Tsvetaeva, *Izbrannaia proza*, vol. 1, p. 14.
23. Ibid, vol. 1, p. 374.
24. Tsvetaeva, *Stikhotvoreniia i poemy*, vol. 1, p. [58].
25. Ibid., vol. 1, p. [48].
26. Ibid., vol., pp. [53–4].
27. Ibid., vol. 1, p. [50].
28. Ibid., vol. 1, p. [56].

Before investigating the strategy of 'Novogodnee' – strategy in the sense of diplomacy, judging the right move in a newly developing relationship with Rilke – it seems best to consider a little further the singularity of Marina Tsvetaeva. Brodsky in both his essays finds her dedication to absolute truth akin to Calvinism. That is how he describes in 'The Poet and Prose' Tsvetaeva's 'ruthlessness towards herself'.[29] In the account of 'Novogodnee', with regard to her 'psychological realism', he ventures one possible definition of her art in two variants: 'the Russian dependent clause put at the service of Calvinism', or 'Calvinism in the embrace of this dependent clause'.[30] As we have seen above, in discussion of kindred thinkers – Shestov was the one quoted there – who might have influenced her, the emphasis falls on language itself as the determinant. Tsvetaeva's rigour of thought was facilitated by the structure of Russian syntax. As Brodsky explains in 'Catastrophes in the Air', an essay mainly concerned with Andrei Platonov, Dostoevskii in many ways 'was our first writer to trust the intuition of language more than his own ... A born metaphysician, he instinctively realized that for probing infinity ... there was no tool more far-reaching than his highly inflected mother tongue, with its convoluted syntax.'[31] And Tsvetaeva is in Dostoevskii's manner a born metaphysician, as 'Novogodnee' demonstrates.

Her art, for all its extravagance – the exalted pitch, the headlong movement from one surmise to the next – remains under the rule of conscience. A language that excels, as Russian does, in qualification and 'many-planed thinking and the endeavour to take everything into account'[32] might have been designed for her purposes. Tsvetaeva's life and her writing are indivisible. That is also true of D. H. Lawrence in her generation. But although at his best Lawrence can write with marvellous exactitude, even in his poems there can be lacking the sense of measure that, surprising as it may seem, distinguishes Tsvetaeva. The lyrical impulse was supreme in both; so too was the feeling of isolation which accompanied it. Lawrence's intuitions, however, while exploiting the language often to superb effect, cannot be said to derive, or take their direction, from it. The complexity that Russian allows is unsurpassable for self-analysis.

Poets writing in English whom Brodsky admires – Donne for instance or Robert Frost – are also expert in self-analysis. Frost's 'West-

---

29. Tsvetaeva, *Izbrannaia proza*, vol. 1, p.14.

30. Tsvetaeva, *Stikhotvoreniia i poemy*, vol. 1, p. [60]. It is erroneous, though not material to Brodsky's argument, to state that German is the native language of Calvinism. Calvin wrote the *Institutes* in Latin, and subsequently translated them into French. The extreme clarity and relentless logic of his mind are surely French attributes.

31. Brodsky, *Less than One*, p. 278.

32. Tsvetaeva, *Stikhotvoreniia i poemy*, vol. 1, p. [49].

Running Brook' moves with an agility not unlike Tsvetaeva's (or Brodsky's own):

> It seriously, sadly, runs away
> To fill the abyss' void with emptiness.
> It flows beside us in this water brook,
> But it flows over us. It flows between us
> To separate us for a panic moment.
> It flows between us, over us, and *with* us.
> And it is time, strength, tone, light, life, and love –
> And even substance lapsing unsubstantial;
> The universal cataract of death
> That spends to nothingness ...

Impressive as this is, the graces of English syntax here depend upon a music of repetition: 'it flows ... it flows ... it flows' and on a legerdemain with the prepositions: 'between us, over us and *with* us ...'. But Tsvetaeva's statements build up through their own momentum, a perpetual metamorphosis of word and thought. Only in one line does Frost verge upon Tsvetaeva's method: 'And it is time, strength, tone, light, life and love'. But the words glide into one another: there is not the challenge, the dialectic, of Tsvetaeva's simplest utterance.

Brodsky's investigation of 'Novogodnee' combines minute verbal analysis with a remarkable hold on the circumstances of the poet, and all the difficulties of her relationship with Rilke. It might be objected in some quarters that such criticism is painfully old-fashioned, giving undue weight to the poet's intention and actually imposing a single definitive meaning on the poem. (Surely Brodsky's acute ear should have picked up the sounds of the deconstructionists lugging their machinery up the road?) But a poet's criticism assumes for a start that the experience of a poem can only be understood through re-enactment. As Keats has said, 'We read fine things but never feel them to the full until we have gone the same steps as the Author.'[33] Note the capital letter. The legitimate pride of a poet is tempered by modesty. Keats was writing about the greatest English poet of his day, Wordsworth. When one poet discourses at length about another, as Brodsky does on Tsvetaeva, this is an act of homage – not only to an individual, but to the poetic activity itself in which he too participates.

We may expect a fellow practitioner to show extreme sensitivity to changes of key. The general tone of 'Novogodnee' is a rising tone; but if you start on a high C you might be supposed to have kicked away the ladder for further ascent. Brodsky stresses the anxiety of Tsvetaeva to

---

33. M. B. Forman (ed.), *The Letters of John Keats*, Oxford, 1942, p. 142. (Letter to J. H. Reynolds, 3rd May 1818.)

'save her utterance from the poetical *a priori*'.[34] Until his death she, Pasternak and Rilke had communicated, to quote Karlinsky, 'in a world of spiritual essences, not of gross realities'.[35] Rilke had vanished into the empyrean. A poet less sober than Tsvetaeva (as she shows herself to be in 'Novogodnee') would have been tempted to meet Rilke in 'the intense inane'. But she is continually on her guard against 'the poetical *a priori*'. Her mistrust is shared by Brodsky. Here and there she will allow herself a moment of 'pure poetry'. We are referred to ll. 42–7:

> Жизнь и смерть произношу с усмешкой
> Скрытою — своей ее коснешься!
> Жизнь и смерть произношу со сноской,
> Звездочкою (ночь, которой чаю:
> Вместо мозгового полушарья –
> Звездное!

Tsvetaeva has been objecting to these abstract terms 'life' and 'death' – indeed she accuses herself of 'tripping up ('ogovorilas´') as I always do'. Never once, Brodsky points out, does she refer to 'your death' in this poem addressed to Rilke, who is for her still alive. Such a mistake would be the first step 'to a domestication ('k odomashnivaniiu') – that is to a misunderstanding – of the catastrophe'.[36] She prefers to put the words 'life' and 'death' in brackets (l. 28) or to pronounce them here with a hidden smile, to match Rilke's own. These mutual smiles Brodsky sees as an 'existential kiss', to be heard in the whisper-like 'kosnesh´sia'.[37] Then she pronounces them with 'a footnote,/ An asterisk'. Rilke himself has become a star, or is among the stars, and this permits her to indulge in 'two and a half lines of pure poetry', firmly contained within brackets (ll. 45–7). The entire universe is made into a page of asterisks (stars) referring to Rilke. However, she has sensed the danger of such 'exclusively poetical achievements', and it is safer to seal them off. Otherwise there is the risk that she will be distracted by her own virtuosity and thus separated from Rilke.[38] And the one thing she must do in this poem is to keep reality always in view.

Brodsky's suspicion of pure poetry is more characteristic of his time than hers. There have been countless catastrophes since Tsvetaeva wrote her poem sixty-five years ago, and poetry by and large has shied away from them (the Holocaust) or 'domesticated' some of the less monstrous

34. Tsvetaeva, *Stikhotvoreniia i poemy*, vol. 1, p. [56].
35. Karlinsky, *Marina Cvetaeva*, p. 163.
36. Tsvetaeva, *Stikhotvoreniia i poemy*, vol. 1, p. [55].
37. Ibid., vol. 1, p. [58].
38. Ibid., vol. 1, p. [59].

by self-admiring language. A classic case of reaction against this abuse of poetry is the work of Tadeusz Różewicz. As Czeslaw Milosz explains, 'Since he hated art as an offence to human suffering, he invented his own type of anti-poem ... limited to the simplest words.'[39] Tsvetaeva's position is very different. Hers is not the age of Samuel Beckett, even though her existential despair may have been equal to his. She was all too conscious by 1934 of her own 'edinolichie chuvstv', feelings that resisted 'collectivisation', and protested:

Не обольщусь и языком
Родным, его призывом млечным.
Мне безразлично – на каком
Непонимаемой быть встречным![40]

To return to 'Novogodnee'. At this point Tsvetaeva abruptly changes tone. She apologises to Rilke for writing to him not in German but in Russian characters, and with a deliberate coarseness explains that this was not negligence:

То не потому, что нынче, дескать,
Все сойдет, что мертвый (нищий) все съест –

Brodsky sees this descent in language as a kind of self-flagellation, the measure of her abasement before Rilke. And then she proceeds to defend herself by claiming that as a child of thirteen at Novodevichii she had understood the next world to be 'not tongueless but all tongues' ('ne bez- a vse-iazychen').[41] She is constrained by a number of things: embarrassment at her own survival when Rilke no longer is here, the recognition that inevitably the dead man will be forgotten, and a fear that her verses will pave the way to oblivion. Here the strategy, Brodsky insists, is not poetical, rather it is determined by 'the logic of conscience (more accurately, conscientiousness)'. And he considers the true strength of Tsvetaeva to lie in her psychological realism. The voice of conscience is never appeased: it can be heard 'in her verse either as a theme – or (at the least) in the character of a postscript'.[42]

There follows one of the most remarkable feats of the poem, when she finds her way to the transcendental. Recalling how Rilke had asked her in a letter what was the Russian word for the German 'Nest', she

39. *Polish Post-War Poetry*, selected and translated by Czeslaw Milosz, Harmondsworth, 1970, p. 69.
40. Tsvetaeva, *Stikhotvoreniia i poemy*, vol. 3, p. 175.
41. Ibid,, vol. 1, p. [59].
42. Ibid., vol. 1, p. [60].

tells him that the rhyme 'covering all nests' ('gnezda') is stars ('zvezdy'). Thus she looks back to her moment of pure poetry just before. Now, worried that the thought might take her away from Rilke, she reassures him and herself:

Каждый помысел, любой, Du Lieber,
Слог в тебе ведет - о чем бы не был
Толк (пусть русского родней немецкий
Мне, всех ангельский родней!)

Once before in the poem (l. 14) she has played on *liuboi* and *liubimyi*, words cognate but today opposite in meaning. Tsvetaeva is seeking at this point a word of real tenderness for Rilke. As she explains, astonishingly for a poet so much indebted to the Russian language, German is more native ('rodnei') to her than Russian, and one reason for the switch could be that *Du Lieber* makes for a closer intimacy with Rilke. But 'Novogodnee' is not a macaronic work, and a poet of Tsvetaeva's virtuosity certainly had the means to achieve this effect in her own language. It is true that she has just mentioned her childhood, which could bring back memories of those 'German roots, ... "O Tannenbaum, O Tannenbaum" – and all that grew out of them', shared by her with Pasternak.[43] However, the paramount reason for the switch to German was that *Du Lieber* saves her from repeating the collocation of *liuboi* and *liubimyi*.[44] Here then is a striking instance of the ear dictating the right move – that led not only to the avowal of German as the language of her heart, but to another one she may not have foreseen: dearest of all was the speech of angels. Incidentally, for Rilke, who had been much preoccupied with angels, the language was very appropriate.

Brodsky suggests *Du Lieber* is 'a blessed meaningless word' ('blazhennoe, bessmyslennoe slovo') of the kind important to Mandel´shtam.[45] In the context of this poem it becomes 'primarily a sound', neither Russian nor even German – it is used by Tsvetaeva in a 'supra-linguistic sense'. And the reason why she must achieve this 'angelic' effect is that it accords so well with her own genius, always in pursuit of a spiritual quality attained by going beyond the normal reach of words. 'Poetry itself is a kind of *other* language', Brodsky affirms, 'or a translation from it.'[46] We know that poetic speech is endowed for him with the power to outface all the terrors of existence; God may be inconceivable, but the Word remains.

43. Tsvetaeva, *Neizdannye pis´ma*, p. 256.
44. Tsvetaeva, *Stikhotvoreniia i poemy*, vol. 1, p. [61].
45. Mandel´shtam, *Stikhotvoreniia*, p. 117.
46. Tsvetaeva, *Stikhotvoreniia i poemy*, vol. 1, p. [62].

From this angelic height Tsvetaeva now descends abruptly to the 'real' – her own situation in sordid Bellevue. This she would later make almost overwhelming to the senses in *Poem of the Staircase*. Here Tsvetaeva's plight is seen both with Rilke's eyes from on high, and with her own keen perceptions. 'Reality' is always for her the start of an imaginative flight that springs away from it in revulsion. Brodsky calls Tsvetaeva a classical Utopist – 'the more intolerable is actuality, the more aggressive her imagination'.[47] Russian scholars have long insisted on Thomas More's preoccupation with social evils in England when projecting his Utopia.[48] To describe Tsvetaeva as a classical Utopist is once again to emphasise her sense of actualities, her responsibility to brute fact. Henceforward in the poem she will be free to unfold her profoundest theme, the love she feels for Rilke. And since here poetry is at work creating a reality of its own, 'no less significant than the given reality of space and time', the text has to be viewed on the psychological plane it proposes.[49]

At two points in particular Brodsky is able to probe the very recesses of her mind, where she is a poetic intelligence talking to another, Rilke, in appropriate terms. In the first instance Tsvetaeva asks what she must do with the words announcing Rilke's death: 'S etoi vnutrenneiu rifmoi: Rainer – umer' (l. 110) – in Brodsky's own translation: 'With this inner rhyme of Rainer's dying'. The marvel is in the word that precedes the assonance of 'Rainer – umer'. Brodsky senses in each distinct syllable of *vnutrenneiu* the inexorability of what is being said, and a certain physiological inwardness in the word itself. It is a matter of internal realisation, in which phonetics says the whole truth without or above conscious intention. And he notes that the five r's in the Russian line seem to have been prompted by the first and last letters of the name Rainer. There is, he adds, for a poet like Tsvetaeva significance in the fact that the full name, Rainer Maria Rilke, sounds to a Russian ear as having a masculine, a feminine, and finally a neuter component. A 'definite metaphysical element' is thereby indicated.[50]

In the second instance the psychological explanation is again to the fore. Tsvetaeva now has to face the pain of yielding up Rilke to time, and time is the essence of all tragedy. Brodsky quotes a letter she wrote to Pasternak about Rilke's aloofness from all human ties, something ultimately true of herself.[51] For a moment in the poem she imagines all

47. Ibid., vol. 1, p. [65].
48. M. P. Alekseev, *Angliiskaia literatura: Ocherki i issledovaniia*, ed. N. Ia. D´iakonova and Iu. D. Levin, Leningrad, 1991, p. 7.
49. Tsvetaeva, *Stikhotvoreniia i poemy*, vol. 1, p. [65].
50. Ibid., vol. 1, pp. [67–8].
51. Azadovskii *et al.*, 'Iz perepiski', p. 257.

the meetings she might have had with Rilke, and finally breaks out with the cry: 'Nichego u nas s toboi ne vyshlo', (l. 136). 'Nothing came out right for us two.' This is no affirmation made, as often in poetry, under the guise of a negative. Now she has to accept that nothing came out right in their relationship. But the reader may guess that what she most needed, in the moment itself of renunciation, was to use the words 'for us two'.[52] Brodsky is always sensitive to the concealed – here one might almost say surreptitious – intimacies of 'Novogodnee'.

He sees the remainder of the poem as a postscript to Tsvetaeva's rueful admission: 'Nothing came out right for us two.' She makes two attempts at a finale (more than once Brodsky has resorted to musical analogies). The tone changes to one of pure lyricism, as Tsvetaeva speculates about the topography of the next world, with memories of lessons in the schoolroom, and ideas about God that are unashamedly heterodox. Is He 'a growing *baobab* tree?' (her emphasis). Is there another God above God? These are the puzzled questions of a child. But one of her questions could be given a sensible answer: how in Rilke's 'new place' is writing done, with no table on which to lean his elbow, no forehead for the palm of his hand to support? She has already told him, as she did in her first letter, that he is poetry itself. Now 'writing becomes a euphemism for existence in general', and poetry comes to her rescue. It describes what is now absent from the scene, with 'a negative tangibility' which poetry can always bestow. And since she is thinking about a poet, 'the linguistic reality' of the other world 'materialises as a part of speech, as grammatical time'.[53]

Now this, as Brodsky concedes, is 'the scholasticism of grief'. Tsvetaeva's fearless logic could offer little comfort on its own: rather it made her 'a poet without compromise and in the highest degree uncomfortable'. The 'destructive rationalism' of 'Novogodnee' is at odds with the traditional attitude of Russian poetry, always in Brodsky's view seeking to end positively or at least on a consolatory note. Tsvetaeva is fiercely rational not in 'Novogodnee' alone, but many other poems. She may well be unique among the poets of her time and their precursors, yet it is they who are out of step with the Russian consciousness, determined as it is by the syntax of the language. Brodsky attributes this longing for spiritual comfort to the Orthodox version of Christianity. Tsvetaeva is prepared for the worst, and Brodsky respects her judgement. After all, he maintains, poetry is much older than any particular faith, and more universal. It may espouse a faith, and breed children, but it does not die with that faith.[54]

52. Tsvetaeva, *Stikhotvoreniia i poemy*, vol. 1, p. [73].
53. Ibid., vol. 1, pp. [76–7].
54. Ibid, vol. 1, p. [78].

Issues of huge importance are raised here, at a time when in the Western world, if nowhere else, religious faith has little hold on the majority of the people. It is therefore the more necessary for a poet to proclaim his certitudes. For him, every word is not a conclusion, but the beginning of a new thought: it cries out for a rhyme. Tsvetaeva's whole effort in this poem has been to hold back Rilke from oblivion. In the very last lines she gives his new address, and while having to acknowledge their 'manifest and utter separation', asks for the letter to be given into the hands of Rainer Maria Rilke. Thus he stands at the conclusion of the poem, even though her voice breaks with the onset of tears. Tsvetaeva has gone to the farthest bounds of the imagination. And she has given Rilke a magnificent poem.

–10–

Nabokov and Dostoevskii: Aesthetic Demystification

Nora Buhks

Nabokov's characterisation of Dostoevskii was both harsh and eccentric. With unwavering insistence throughout his whole life – in correspondence, conversation, interviews, lectures and in his own novels (*Despair, The Gift* and *Look at the Harlequins!*) – Nabokov called Dostoevskii 'a mediocre writer of mystery stories'.[1] The shockingness of this judgement has often drawn sharp reactions,[2] been taken as an aesthetic provocation, and, in the context of Nabokov's literary behaviour as a whole, been deemed more of an artistic pose than an artistic position.[3]

Nabokov did not write much about Dostoevskii. We know two early verses, a lecture in Russian entitled 'Dostoevskii without *dostoevshchina*' given at an evening of the Union of Russian Writers in Berlin on 20 March 1931, and the *Lectures on Russian Literature* comprising six essays on six writers, including one on Dostoevskii. These lectures, prepared posthumously from manuscript notes for university courses, cannot be considered as complete literary entities (with the exception of the essay on Gogol´ which was published in 1944). This fact, however, has preserved in the texts the impression of the living spoken word, and

1. V. Nabokov, *Lectures on Russian Literature*, London, 1983, p. 98. Quotations from this edition will hereafter be noted by page numbers in the text.
2. Nabokov's embittered attacks on Dostoevskii provoked irritation in *émigré*, and later, American literary circles. They led to complications in his relations with the students at Cornell, which nearly got Nabokov into trouble. See B. Boyd, *Vladimir Nabokov. The American Years*, Princeton, 1991, pp. 181, 308. Boyd considers that Nabokov's criticism of Dostoevskii was the reason for Roman Jakobson's refusal to invite him to Harvard: ibid., p. 303. Thus his attitude to Dostoevskii may be seen to have played a fateful role in Nabokov's life.
3. A. Dolinin, 'Tsvetnaia spiral´ Nabokova', in V. Nabokov, *Rasskazy. Priglashenie na kazn´. Esse. Interv´iu. Retsenzii*, Moscow, 1989, pp. 440-1. Dolinin's article comprises a rich compilation of various assessments of Nabokov's works.

reveals the devices of Nabokov's teaching methods, with the inevitable repetition of basic principles and the developed argumentation of critical observations. In accordance with the law of parody, so beloved of Nabokov, the main features with which he reproached Dostoevskii – domination of ideas over style, philosophising and moralising – were demonstrated by Nabokov himself in the utilitarian and didactic form manner typical of lectures.

Nabokov's attitude to Dostoevskii, despite its obvious consistency, was formed and realised over a period of years. Andrew Field and Brian Boyd quote in English translation a poem about Dostoevskii by Nabokov dating from 1919: 'Listening to his nightly howl/ God wondered: can it really be/ that everything I gave/ was so frightful and complicated?'[4] This was the first aesthetic protest by the young poet against a view and presentation of the world which he found repulsive and outrageous. The semantic emphasis of the verse is shifted from the subject to the action. The inability of an artist to see beauty is understood as lack of creative vision. A year later Nabokov embodies this theme in a separate poem:

> Мой друг, я искренне жалею
> того, кто в тайной слепоте,
> пройдя, всю длинную аллею,
> не мог приметить на листе
> сеть изумительную жилок,
> и точки желтых бугорков,
> и след зазубренный от пилок
> голуборогих червяков.
>
> (1920)[5]

In 1921 Nabokov wrote a poem on the fortieth anniversary of Dostoevskii's death. Entitled 'Skazanie', it was printed in *Rul´* on 11 November 1921 with the subtitle 'Iz Apokrifa'. It tells how Christ and his disciples were walking through a garden and saw 'on the sunlit sand ... the corpse of a dog'. The apostles and Christ interpret the scene differently, and the difference reveals the true Creator:

---

4. Boyd, *Vladimir Nabokov. The Russian Years*, London, 1990, p. 7. A. Field, *Vladimir Nabokov: His Life in Art*, London, 1967, p. 71. The poem was published in the collection *Gornii put´*, Berlin, 1923.

5. The poem was published in *Gornii put´* and reprinted in V. Nabokov, *Krug*, Leningrad, 1990, pp. 38–9.

Говорил апостолу апостол:
'Злой был пес и смерть его нага,
мерзостна...'

Христос же молвил просто:
'Зубы у него как жемчуга...'

In this poem Nabokov enters into open dispute with Dostoevskii and his famous philosophical assertion that 'beauty will save the world'. According to Nabokov, the creative strength of art, the strength that creates beauty, consists in the ability to see the world in its unexpected brightness, in the freshness of new perception. The concept of beauty in such an interpretation is displaced from the natural realm of spirituality to the creative realm, perceived and produced in verbal form by the skill of the writer. The chosen form of the poem, a parable, lends Nabokov's ideas a religious and moral nuance analogous to the sense of Dostoevskii's idea.[7]

In his biography of Nabokov, Brian Boyd mentions a lecture on Dostoevskii given by Nabokov ten years after the above verse was written.[8] This was an unusual kind of turning over of ideas, in preparation for a new novel – *Despair*.

In Nabokov's lectures all his earlier remarks and thoughts about Dostoevskii are brought together in a coherent text of investigative analysis. The author's dual viewpoint – as writer and as teacher – is realised by the following method: Nabokov reconstructs Dostoevskii's poetic world, exposes the devices of his poetics of expressiveness, and reveals the influences, but does it within the bounds of literary text analysis and terminology. His position as a writer lends striking individuality to Nabokov's exposition, and the tactics of literary scholarship allow him to carry out his express task: 'to debunk Dostoevski' (p. 98).

Dostoevskii's fiction had, in Nabokov's view, undergone the strong influence of European sentimental and Gothic novels: 'The sentimental influence implied that kind of conflict he [Dostoevskii – N.B.] liked, placing virtuous people in pathetic situations and then extracting from these situations the last ounce of pathos' (p. 10). Richardson, Radcliffe, Dickens, Rousseau, Sue – such were the immediate literary 'ancestors'

6. The poem was published in *Gornii put'* and reprinted in Nabokov, *Krug*, pp. 24–5.

7. Nabokov in his essay 'Good Readers and Good Writers' wrote: 'The art of writing is a very futile business if it does not imply first of all the art of seeing the world as the potentiality of fiction. The material of this world may be real enough ... but does not exist at all as an accepted entirety: it is chaos ... The writer is the first man to map it and to name the natural objects it contains.' See V. Nabokov, *Lectures on Literature*, New York and London, 1982, p. 7.

8. Boyd, Nabokov. *The Russian Years*, p. 363.

of Dostoevskii. It was their influence that determined the domination of sentimental melodrama in his prose. As for Dostoevskii's basic philosophical formula 'egoism – Antichrist – Europe' and its opposite 'brotherhood – Christ – Russia' (p. 103), it was formed, in Nabokov's opinion, as a result of borrowing ideas from the West. This brings Nabokov to an unexpected and striking conclusion: 'Dostoevski, who so hated the West, was the most European of Russian writers' (p. 103). It may be supposed that this playful conclusion was a reply to the numerous *émigré* critics who had criticised Nabokov himself for the 'unrussianness' of his novels.[9]

This disputing of Dostoevskii's literary authority is conducted by Nabokov from the point of view of artistic mastery. His starting-point is the definition of literary art in Nabokov's own understanding. He writes:

> art is a divine game ... It is divine because this is the element in which man comes nearest to God through becoming a true creator in his own right. And it is a game, because it remains art only as long as we are allowed to remember that, after all, it is all make-believe, that the people on the stage ... are not actually murdered, in other words, only as long as our feelings of horror or disgust do not obscure our realisations that we are as readers or as spectators, participating in an elaborate and enchanting game: the moment this balance is upset we get on the stage ridiculous melodrama ... (p. 106).

In the balance between 'le vrai' and 'le vraisemblable' Nabokov sees the main condition for art. The concept of the real and the true in art is understood by him not in the accuracy of imitation of life but in the strength of creative expressiveness. For this reason Dostoevskii's works, marked by artistic carelessness, stylistic inexpressiveness, imprecision of details and definitions, is assessed by Nabokov as mediocre and unreal literature.

The landscape of Dostoevskii's novels, as Nabokov observes, 'is a landscape of ideas, a moral landscape' (p. 104), his characters, bearers of the author's ideas, 'are merely puppets' (p. 129); only the plot is lively, as in detective stories.

Nabokov bitterly criticised Dostoevskii's approach to literature as a means of seeking the truth, mocked the writer's predilection for using the extreme conditions of psychopathology and criminal plots for the

9. The *émigré* critics reproached Sirin for breaking with the humanitarian traditions of Russian literature and emphasised his 'unrussianness'. For instance, G. Ivanov, in a review of the novel *King, Queen, Knave*, wrote that it had been made 'according to the latest model of the "most advanced Germans"', and that '*The Defence* had been copied from a mediocre French model'. See *Chisla*, no. 1, 1930, p. 234. In the same issue of *Chisla* G. Adamovich published a review of *The Defence* in which he asserted that 'the novel could appear in *Nouvelle Revue Française* and pass there unnoticed amongst the host of middling works of current French belletristics'. Zinaida Shakhovskaia also writes about Nabokov's 'unrussianness' in her book *V poiskakh Nabokova*, Paris, 1979.

demonstration and affirmation of his religious and moral ideas. In *The Gift* this criticism is expressed in a witty form: Dostoevskii's works are called a 'reverse transformation from Bedlam to Bethlehem'.[10]

For Nabokov, who saw in art not a moral but an aesthetic meaning, the works of Dostoevskii, the moraliser and philosopher, were without artistic value. He expounded this position in his lectures, and this is, as it were, the declarative, external layer of Nabokov's attitude to Dostoevskii. There is, however, another layer, deeper and more hidden, reflected in literary allusions, in parodic references, in the intertextual links between Nabokov's works and Dostoevskii's novels.

The object of reflection in Nabokov's works is culture, i.e. a world which has already once been reconstituted by art, and this explains the extensive presence of other texts in Nabokov's novels. But what is surprising is that on equal terms with authors whom Nabokov respected and loved we find Dostoevskii, a writer who was, in Nabokov's opinion, 'mediocre' and aesthetically inimical to him.

Some critics have written of the direct influence of Dostoevskii on Nabokov, thus of course arousing the latter's wrath. In one interview Nabokov declared unequivocally that Dostoevskii had no influence at all on Russian literature.[11] It would seem that in Nabokov's novels the 'traces' of Dostoevskii's texts can be regarded as examples of parody, but realised on various poetic levels. They are both extensive and varied. Here are some of them.

Commentators have more than once pointed out the link between *The Eye* and *The Double*.[12] Nabokov's novel *Despair* is an open parody of Dostoevskii's *Crime and Punishment* and *The Double*. The addressee is named directly in the text through the device of misquotation: '"Mist, vapour ... in the mist a chord that quivers." No, that's not verse, that's from old Dusty's great book, *Crime and Slime*. Sorry: *Schuld und Sühne* (German edition).'[13] Raskol´nikov's idea about the permissibility of crime for 'people possessing the gift and talent'[14] is given literal incarnation by Nabokov. Crime is accomplished as a work of art, and the murderer sees himself as an artist. The banality of the plan reveals lack of talent, and the novel repeats Nabokov's judgement that crime is always untalented and mediocre.[15] The profit motives behind the mur-

---

10. V. Nabokov, *The Gift*, Ann Arbor, 1975, p. 83.

11. Brian Boyd quotes this story in his *Nabokov. The American Years*, p. 308.

12. One of the first to notice this was Andrew Field in his *Vladimir Nabokov: His Life in Art*, p. 168.

13. V. Nabokov, *Despair*, London, 1969, p. 172.

14. F. M. Dostoevskii, *Polnoe sobranie sochinenii v 30-i tomakh*, 1972–86, Leningrad, vol. 6, 1973, p. 200.

15. V. Nabokov, 'The Art of Literature and Commonsense', in *Lectures on Literature*, p. 376.

der, although they are disguised by the work's ideology, cast the shadow of hypertrophied ambitions on Dostoevskii himself.

In *Invitation to a Beheading* the parodic coding of the image of Rodion Romanovich Raskol´nikov, the criminal, in the names of the personnel at the fortress, Rodion, Roman, Rodrigo, has been noted.[16] This does not exhaust all the parodic allusions. There are, for example, Cincinnatus and M. Pierre, who repeat the pairing of Raskol´nikov and Porfirii. Attention is drawn not only by the similarity of appearances (M. Pierre is literally copied from Porfirii) or the similarities in behaviour (compare the fainting fits of Cincinnatus and Raskol´nikov), but, most important, the similarity of the situations in which both pairs of characters find themselves. This last factor reveals the strained, hidden moral struggle upon which, according to Dostoevskii's design, his characters are entering. Their parodic incarnation, as Cincinnatus and M. Pierre, placed in the fortress, destroys the unpredictability of the result of the ideological encounter. The conversations between Porfirii and Raskol´nikov with their intellectual struggle are turned by Nabokov into the farcical conversations of M. Pierre with Cincinnatus.

In his own works Nabokov realised artistically what he had constantly reproached Dostoevskii for, namely using the criminal plot and narrative technique of the police novel. The criminal theme and the clichéd, melodramatic plot are used by him especially frequently in his Russian novels. But Nabokov's demonstrative use of the clichéd theme reflects, as a contrast, the high artistic quality of his particular use of it. In this Nabokov realised one variant of Flaubert's dream of the ideal novel, the narration of which would be supported not by the plot but by style. Nabokov's solution was an exciting story-line which, on account of the rich imagery and the expressiveness of language, becomes of secondary importance in the novel.

In Nabokov's relations with Dostoevskii this is a regular argument, namely that even in the most banal material the artist sees and reconstitutes the unique beauty of life.

Another example of intertextuality may perhaps be seen on the thematic level, in two novels about a gambler: *The Defence* is a parodic response to Dostoevskii's *The Gambler*.

When *Lolita* appeared, critics pointed out the similarity of Nabokov's work to Dostoevskii's novels, having in mind the presence of psychopathological deviations. But the link between them would seem to be of a somewhat different nature. One possible reading of *Lolita* is as a parodied transformation of the famous chapter from

---

16. G. Shapiro, 'Russkie literaturnye alliuzii v romane Nabokova *Priglashenie na kazn´*', *Russian Literature*, vol. 9, 1981, p. 373.

Dostoevskii's *The Possessed*, 'At Tikhon's'. The parodic interrelations of the two texts are reflected not only in the semantic overthrowing of the moralising theme – the corruption of a minor in which the victim turns out to be more corrupt than the criminal (the roles change) – but in the demonstrative parallelism of form and characters: 'Lolita, the Confession of a Blonde Widower' and 'Stavrogin's Confession', both intended for publication, fall respectively into the hands of Dr John Ray and his parodic double Archpriest Tikhon, philosopher, psychologist and expert in human souls.[17]

This theme of a terrible sin, the corruption of an innocent child's soul, runs through very many of Dostoevskii's works. One example is Svidrigailov's secret crime in *Crime and Punishment*. Nabokov's story *The Enchanter* is a parodic attempt at this theme. 'Svidrigailov, the embodiment of evil', wrote Nabokov, 'is purely romantic invention' (p. 115). The romantic nature of the image is transformed by Nabokov into the degraded romanticisation of a committed crime.

Thus even a swift enumeration of the intertextual links between Nabokov's novels and Dostoevskii's works shows that Nabokov's attitude to the classic whom he criticised so cruelly was far from unequivocal. Our suspicions are also aroused by a fact from his biography: in 1950 Nabokov agreed to translate *The Brothers Karamazov* for Pascal Covici of Viking Press, but was subsequently obliged by illness to withdraw from the project.[18]

Nabokov in his lectures, which were designed, as he himself acknowledged, for an audience which was ill-informed about art (p. 98), as a teacher strove for the literary demystification of Dostoevskii. In his own novels, on the other hand, Nabokov the writer demonstrated a more complex artistic response to him. It was embodied in numerous literary echoes, in an acute need to engage in a literary polemic, and simply in the constant feeling of Dostoevskii's presence as an artistic opponent. And this attitude of Nabokov the writer lends ambivalence to the demystification of Dostoevskii by Nabokov the teacher.

Translated by Arnold McMillin

17. In Russian there is clear assonance between Ray's surname and Tikhon's title: arkhie*rei*.

18. Boyd, *Nabokov. The American Years*, pp. 146–7.

The Myth of the Poet and the Poet of the Myth: Russian Poets on Brodsky

Valentina Polukhina

> Geniuses arrive like storms – frighten people,
> cleanse the air, go against the flow.
>
> Søren Kierkegaard

> The knowledge a poet's contemporaries have
> about him can never be exhaustive.
>
> Lev Loseff

The myth of the ideal poet is extremely tenacious, and it is poets themselves, it would appear, who create this myth. Brodsky, who inherited the title of First Poet from Akhmatova, lives this myth, having come as close as is possible to it. 'Great poets, like great trees, attract lightning', remarked Kushner in 1987,[1] and it is above all poets themselves who cast the thunder and lightning: for thirty years they have been dedicating poems to Brodsky, writing forewords to his collections of poetry, monographs, academic articles, essays, giving interviews about him, composing parodies and epigrams on him. From the very beginning Brodsky has been surrounded by a crowd of poets and admirers. His poetry 'in *samizdat* won the hearts and minds of the Russian intelligentsia in the mid-1960s. Set to music, 'Piligrimmy' was known by heart from Tallinn to Vladivostok. His behaviour (swimming in icy water in the Crimea in winter), his character (abrupt, uncompromising, spontaneously generating superb epigrams), his external appearance (thin, freckled, red-haired) have become legendary.'[2] Today Brodsky is the only Russian poet termed a genius by many of his fellow-writers, whether sincerely or through clenched teeth.[3] Comparisons not only with Mandel´shtam, Tsvetaeva and Akhmatova, but even with Pushkin, have become con-

---

1. Kushner, *Apollon v snegu*, p. 393. Short references only are given here in the notes. Full references may be found in the bibliography to this chapter.
2. Savitskii, 'Un parasite chez les Nobel', p. 38.
3. Kuz´minskii, *Blue Lagoon*, vol. 3B, p. 754.

ventional.[4] If Krivulin called him with a degree of sarcasm 'the last poet',[5] then Naiman can write in all seriousness: 'He completes the history of Russian poetry in the shape which it has up to the present moment. He does this as if he is its last poet and posterity had to judge Russian poetry as a whole from his poems.'[6] Lev Ozerov conveys the same idea in his epigram: 'And he has spoken for all poets once and for all.'[7]

It is not without interest to trace how the myth of Brodsky arose and what sustained this myth.[8] It is significant that although the great poet Akhmatova clearly favoured Brodsky from their very first meeting on 7 August 1961, calling him 'a grandiose poet',[9] and his poems 'magical',[10] it was not she who laid the foundation stone for the Brodsky legend, but rather his contemporaries. In the opinion of Viktor Kulle, Brodsky 'embodied the figure of the ideal poet ... long before he corresponded to it'.[11] We find corroboration of this in the articles, memoirs and passing comments scattered throughout the ten volumes of *The Blue Lagoon Anthology of Modern Russian Poetry*, compiled by Kuz´minskii and Kovalev. In 1962 these two collected everything written up to that point by the 22-year-old Brodsky, and managed to transport it to the USA, where the poet's first collection of poems, *Stikhotvoreniia i poemy*, appeared in 1965. Kuz´minskii admits that at that time he was 'infatuated' with Brodsky.[12] Viktor Krivulin, describing the first public performance by the young Brodsky in March 1959 at the so-called 'tournament of poets' at the Gor´kii Palace of Culture,[13] calls him 'a living classic': 'The thing that struck me most when I heard Brodsky for

4. Naiman, 'Zametki dlia pamiati', p. 13, *Iosif Brodskii razmerom podlinnika*, p. 147; A. Loseff, 'Iosif Brodskii. Predislovie', p. 23; L. Loseff, Prazdnik spravedlivosti', p. 9, *Brodsky through the Eyes*, pp. 131–2; Gordin, ibid., pp. 42, 46–8; Meilakh, ibid., p. 165; Sedakova, ibid., p. 252; Krivulin, 'Slovo o nobeliate', pp. ii–iii.

5. Krivulin, *Poetika Brodskogo*, p. 222.

6. Naiman, 'Velichie poeticheskogo zamysla', p. iii.

7. 'Nu, kak tam Flavii', p. 16.

8. The scale of this essay does not permit attention to all the poets who have written about Brodsky. I have tried to use not only the most important material, but also that which is inaccessible to most Western readers. The appended bibliography covers not only those included in the essay, but also offers an idea of those who, perforce, were outside its scope. It does not pretend to total comprehensiveness. I cannot here touch on the opinions and evaluations of Brodsky expressed by Western poets, which form part of a separate study.

9. Gordin, 'Delo Brodskogo', p. 149.

10. E. Etkind, *Protsess Iosifa Brodskogo*, London, 1988, p. 36.

11. Kulle, 'The Linguistic Reality', p. 81.

12. Kuz´minskii, *Blue Lagoon*, vol. 1, p. 24.

13. Iakov Gordin, who took part in this 'tournament', dates it 1960. See 'Delo Brodskogo', *Neva*, no. 2, 1989, p. 136; see also K. Kuz´minskii, *The Blue Lagoon*, vol. 2B, p. 177: '... LITO "Narvskaia Zastava", where the much-discussed "Tournament of poets" took place on the fourteenth of February 1960. Kushner, Sosnora and Gorbovskii gave readings while Brodsky produced a poem about a Jewish cemetery.'

the first time (and it hit not only me but many of my friends of that period), was the genuine feeling that beside me, beside us there existed a LIVING CLASSIC ... We – the young men standing alongside ... – were simply stunned by the sensation of something new, an unheard-of music; that element captured us and carried us away.'[14] Krivulin's testimony is to be trusted, given that he has subsequently put a considerable amount of effort into debunking the Brodsky myth. In another article he accuses Brodsky of not being equal to the main aspect of the myth that had become established, remarking that 'he was not a prophet, because at the beginning of the 1960s the existential pathos of his poetry could only have turned into the genuinely prophetic if it had broken into the religious, if the position of the poet had lost its hysterical, desperate assertion of its own rights to existence, individualism, and if his speech had become supra-individual, that is, the speech of one who speaks not *for himself*, but who can say with conviction: "Thus speaks God ...".'[15] So high, evidently, is the price demanded of the poet for what is expected of him.

In his short essay 'From the Poet to the Myth', Vladimir Ufliand wittily ridicules the origin of the Brodsky myth, particularly the fact that Brodsky himself more than once named Ufliand as his teacher.[16] The second of Brodsky's 'teachers', Evgenii Rein, who for a while did in fact act as Brodsky's poetic mentor and who introduced him to Akhmatova in 1961, treats 'Brodsky's passion for creating teachers for himself'[17] more sceptically.[18] Even Mikhail Kreps, author of the first monograph on Brodsky's poetic art, has made a contribution to the legend of the poet in his own way, by rivalling Brodsky in wit and paradox. Lev Loseff is apparently the only poet who has for several years, and with varying degrees of success, been trying to turn us 'from the myth to the poet'.[19]

To be a poetic legend in Russia it is not enough to be young and charming, to have talent and a striking personality, although these qualities are also indispensable for the making of a legend. In Russia myths are richly mingled with blood: it is also necessary to be killed (Pushkin, Lermontov, Gumilev), commit suicide (Esenin, Maiakovskii, Tsvetaeva), fall victim to the system (Mandel´shtam), find oneself the focus of its prolonged and indefatigable attention (Pasternak, Akhmatova), or, at the very least, try one of the dishes on the govern-

14. Krivulin, 'Slovo o nobeliate', p. ii.
15. Krivulin, 'Iosif Brodskii (mesto)', p. 221.
16. Ufliand, 'Belyi peterburgskii vecher', pp. 163–4.
17. Gorbanevskaia, 'Neskol´ko strannoi', p. 9.
18. Rein, *Brodsky through the Eyes*, pp. 58–9.
19. Loseff, 'Brodskii: ot mifa k poetu', pp. 7–15.

ment's menu: arrest, prison, psychiatric hospital, exile and deportation. The number of literary figures who have supped in this canteen makes up a long list; but in the post-Stalin period the list of poets who have been drawn into unequal single combat with the State is headed by the name of Brodsky. This direct contact with history at such a young age perhaps spurs Brodsky to be first everywhere and in all respects. He was the first to graft English onto Russian poetry, the first to publish his books in the West, the first among the young literary figures to receive the Nobel prize, to become the first Russian poet laureate of a foreign state.

'The paradoxes in the reception' of Brodsky[20] are created by several factors. Here we will limit ourselves to discussing only three that have promoted the inception and growth of the myth: the personality of the poet, the originality of which cannot fail to be felt in his poems; his tragic fate, which is an important component of the 'biographical legend' (Brodsky 'took as a pattern the tragic model of life');[21] the nature of Brodsky's talent and, in particular, of his aesthetics and poetics, which are alien to the Russian poetic tradition. To comment on Brodsky's personality in any detail is for the present unethical: the poet is alive and writing. It is, however, essential to speak about one most important facet of his character, since it is precisely this, in a direct or deeply hidden form, which lies at the root of the many diametrically opposed evaluations of the poet. Close acquaintances of Brodsky maintain that right from a very early age he was 'the most free of people' even compared with those who were far from servile psychologically.[22] Brodsky radiated freedom, attracting many people to him: 'Be independent. Independence is the greatest quality, the best word in every language', he wrote to Gordin from exile.[23] But such rare independence was taken as an act of provocation or rebelliousness by many people. In Gordin's opinion, it was precisely Brodsky's free style of behaviour in life and in art which in the 1960s provoked the implacable hostility of the authorities in Leningrad towards him. It is difficult to agree with Kushner, who maintains that 'from the very beginning Brodsky entered into direct conflict with the demands of the state. Such was the romantic model of a poet's behaviour in the world';[24] the authorities' persecution of the poet was, above all, the persecution of his personality and not his poetry, which they did not know.

Ol'ga Sedakova speaks about the striking personality of Brodsky

20. Kulle, 'Paradoksy vospriiatiia'.
21. A. Loseff, 'Niotkuda s liubov'iu', p. 326.
22. Ufliand, *Brodsky through the Eyes*, p. 148; Gordin, 'Delo Brodskogo', p. 135.
23. Ibid., p. 138.
24. Kushner, *Apollon v snegu*, pp. 500–1.

which shows through his poetry. For her, Brodsky's independence has nothing contentious about it; it is completely calm and unconstrained. The basic liberating element in Brodsky, Sedakova claims, is his consciousness of death:

> There was some sort of early and extremely powerful intimacy with death, mortality, temporality. It is the key motif in many of his poems. The fact that a man does not close his eyes to his own mortality liberates him from a host of things; it frees him from petty demands, insults and ties. It is also a liberation from the self (Brodsky's belittling portraits of himself in his poetry also seem like views 'from the moon'). This is what connects Brodsky with the poetry of the Middle Ages and the Baroque, but above all else, with the poet of Ecclesiastes.[25]

Witty and lively according to Gordin, sarcastic and affectionate according to Savitskii,[26] Brodsky provokes irritation in some people on account of his ability to keep any interlocutor at a certain distance: 'one always feels that no matter what he is doing, in any situation he is above personal attitudes, that in any, even the most intimate situations, he acts as a Poet, and that all his actions are facts of his biography'.[27] This arrogant aesthete and highly sensitive person, generous friend and dangerous enemy, who is, invariably, in all things a discontented misanthropist, is a very charming man when he wants to be. Few can resist his arrogant charm. Describing the appearance of the young Brodsky (distinctly reddish complexion and slightly gingery hair) and his manner of reading poetry ('Reading out his poetry his delivery would reach such resounding levels, that sometimes the words and lines were drowned out'), Naiman remarks: 'It was not they [the poems, V. P.] but the person reading them out who produced such an impression of talent.'[28] Similarly Krivulin emphasises the unusual nature of Brodsky's personality. Comparing him with Pushkin, he points out the 'most radical' similarity: 'The fact is that both Brodsky and Pushkin, recognising themselves to be unique personalities, were aware of the necessity of somehow hiding that uniqueness, of wearing a mask.'[29]

Brodsky's fate has ben written about even more than his poetry, but not, as a rule, by poets.[30] Arrests and interrogations following one after

25. Sedakova, *Brodsky through the Eyes*, p. 245.
26. Gordin, 'Poet tragicheskii', p. 7; Savitskii, 'Un parasite', p. 38.
27. Krivulin, 'Slovo o nobeliate', p. iii.
28. Naiman, 'Bukvy, prostupaiushchie na tsene', p. 6.
29. Krivulin, 'Slovo o nobeliate', p. iii.
30. See the bibliographies in Valentina Polukhina, *Joseph Brodsky: A Poet for our Time*, Cambridge, 1989 and *Brodsky Through the Eyes of his Contemporaries*, Basingstoke/New York, 1992. The following should also be noted: N. Iakimchuk, *Kak sudili poeta (delo Brodskogo)*, Leningrad, 1990, and Ia. Gordin, 'Delo Brodskogo'.

another (1959, 1961, 1962, 1964), the fabrication of a 'court case' (1963–4), confinement to a psychiatric hospital (1964), trial and exile (1964–5); all, undoubtedly, added a new dimension to the myth: even in the second half of the twentieth century, poets in Russia are still martyrs. Akhmatova wittily remarked: 'What a biography they are making for our redhead! It is as if he had deliberately hired someone.'[31] Poets, writing about Brodsky from a non-literary position and not knowing him well, are convinced that he is completely indebted to the 'stupid Leningrad authorities of the 1960s' for his fame.[32] The confluence of personality and fate is a process they have overlooked; it is hard for them to accept that in the case of Brodsky the identity of the man and the poet is as justified as in the case of Tsvetaeva. A maximalist of Tsvetaevan proportions, Brodsky gives considerable grounds for regarding him from no less extreme a position. His declarations of the type that in our time, 'Christ is not enough, Freud is not enough, Marx is not enough, nor is existentialism or Buddha' shocked many people.[33] The pronouncement draws attention to one of his most important ideas: no single creed, no single great idea can aspire to comprehensiveness on the metaphysical level. He mentioned this in an interview with David Bethea: 'I always believed, and I still do, that a man, a human being should define oneself in the first place not in terms of ethnicity, race, religion, philosophical convictions, the citizenship or geographic, whatever it is, situation. But first of all one should ask oneself: "Am I a coward? Am I a generous man? Or am I a liar."'[34]

It is necessary to mention another important factor in the biographical legend of Brodsky. Brodsky's poetry, to use Pushkin's words, 'did not appear in print' in the former Soviet Union. By 1987 he had published only four of his poems in Russian journals. The surprising thing is not that Brodsky never became a Soviet poet (despite starting to write poetry in the fortieth year of the Soviet state), but that by virtue of his personality he was incapable of becoming one. 'How does one survive such a thing?' asks Gorbanevskaia, referring to those Soviet poets who did get their work printed. 'It is impossible to survive that – the only interpretation has to be a negative one.'[35] The fact that in the 1960s and 1970s other uncompromising poets were not published also contributes to the myth.

31. Naiman, *Rasskazy*, p. 10.
32. Limonov, 'Limonov o Brodskom', p. 6.
33. Joseph Brodsky, 'Beyond Consolation', *The New York Review of Books*, 7 Feb. 1974, p. 14.
34. Joseph Brodsky, interviewed by David Bethea, 28–29 March 1991, unpublished. Parts of this interview are included in Bethea's forthcoming book, *Joseph Brodsky and the Creation of Exile*.
35. Gorbanevskaia, 'Neskol´ko strannoi', p. 9.

As if in revenge for Brodsky's lifelong avoidance of melodrama, melodrama pursued him. 'Melodrama was courting me with the tenacity of Romeo', Brodsky admitted in a conversation with Bethea in 1991. The dignified behaviour of the poet in court was termed heroic by the world's press. His answer to the judge's question 'Who placed you in the ranks of the poets?' – 'Such things come, I think, from God', has been cited more often than any of his numerous aphorisms. As Naiman testifies, in court Brodsky 'bore himself exactly as if at a poetry reading, and repeated exactly what was in his poems'.[36] Brodsky endured exile equally steadfastly. Rein is convinced that it was in that Northern village to which he was totally unfairly and barbarically driven, that he found in himself the spiritual and artistic strength to come out onto an even higher plane of his poetry.[37] That, however, was merely the first wave of his fame.

'The evolving plot of the myth' of Brodsky received further development after he crossed the frontier of the 'dark closed expanse'[38] of the Soviet Union on 4 June 1972 and his adaptation to the 'foreign' world of the West. The meeting with W. H. Auden (6 June 1972) and the latter's subsequent patronage assisted Brodsky's success in the West to a considerable degree.[39] For people who suffer from the 'disaster that is average taste' (Pasternak) the myth of Brodsky is clear-cut to the point of sketchiness: treated with affection by Akhmatova, arrested, imprisoned, freed through the timely efforts of Shostakovich, Akhmatova and Sartre, he emigrated into the embrace of Auden. Brodsky came on to the American cultural scene without the slightest effort, and settled into it 'as in a second home',[40] receiving recognition and the highest awards. The impression is that Brodsky's fate has never been beyond his control. A Jew to the Russians, a Russian to the Americans and an *émigré* to the rest of the world, Brodsky lives in America just as unpretentiously and independently as he lived in unfree Russia: the door of his basement flat is open to all, and the telephone rings so often one would think it had just been invented. Finding himself outside his own culture, Brodsky continues to serve it by introducing to Russian culture an entirely different sensibility. In trying to rid it of its sentimentalism and provincialism, however, Brodsky has encountered all manner of criticism and fierce resistance.

36. Naiman, 'Prostranstvo Uranii', p. 194.
37. Rein, *Brodsky through the Eyes*, p. 60–1.
38. Iu. M. Lotman, *Izbrannye stat'i*, Tallinn, 1992, p. 64.
39. Brodsky discusses the role of Auden in his poetic fate in two essays: see *Less Than One*, Penguin, 1986, pp. 304–83, and in his poems 'The tree is dark ...', in *W. H. Auden: A Tribute*, ed. S. Spender, New York, 1975, p. 243, and 'York: In Memoriam W. H. Auden', *Part of Speech*, Oxford, 1980, pp. 126–7.
40. Savitskii, 'Brodski, c'est Byzance', p. ix.

Declared a genius by Akhmatova (after she had read 'Bol´shaia elegiia Dzhonnu Donnu' in 1963), Brodsky seemed to have justified this title when in 1987 he became the youngest Nobel Prize-winner for literature. However, this high award has been viewed in a variety of ways, Lev Loseff calling this event 'a meeting of genius and justice'.[41] The envious Limonov was still convinced in 1984 that 'with the help of the Jewish intellectual elite in New-York, I. A. Brodsky will receive the prize named after the inventor of dynamite'.[42] Efim Bershin is similarly inclined to think that Brodsky received the Nobel Prize 'as a consequence of his biography'.[43] The poets in Brodsky's close circle saw the prize as an award to a whole generation (Rein, Ufliand, Kushner). Brodsky himself supported this opinion, naming them in every conversation with journalists. Bella Akhmadulina, taking the news as a personal triumph, was genuinely delighted,[44] and the majority of other Russian poets recognised that Brodsky's success was both natural and deserved. The Nobel Prize is not Brodsky's only prestigious award: as early as 1981 he was one of the first recipients of the MacArthur Foundation's new 'genius' fellowships; in 1986 his book of essays *Less Than One* was awarded the National Book Critics' Circle prize in the USA.

But even Brodsky's second wave of fame was not to be the last. In May 1991, when he took up the post of Poet Laureate of the USA, Brodsky consolidated his exceptional status and justified the nickname given him by Nadezhda Mandel´shtam, who, in a conversation with Kublanovskii, had called him 'the Yankee of Russian poetry'.[45] Not many months after becoming the First Poet of another state, he received from the hands of the French General Consul the Order of the Legion of Honour, and, finally, in June of the same year he received an honorary degree from Oxford University (making him the second Russian poet after Akhmatova on whom this honour was conferred). Bearing in mind that far from all of Brodsky's awards are listed here (he has honorary doctorates from several American and European universities), one does not have to look far for reasons for envy, insults and reproaches. 'One might reproach Brodsky for accepting the title of First Poet as his due (and not even making the best use of it).'[46] On the other hand there are poets, who acknowledge that, 'when he found himself in exile Brodsky's personality became so much stronger, and such an inter-penetration of Russian-speaking and English-speaking cultures took place,

41. L. Loseff, 'Prazdnik spravedlivosti', p. 9.
42. Limonov, 'Poet-bukhgalter', p. 135
43. Bershin, 'Prorok. Eretik. Dezertir', p. 3.
44. In *Brodsky's Poetics and Aesthetics*, p. 197.
45. Kublanovskii in *Brodsky through the Eyes*, p. 205.
46. Aizenberg, 'Nekotorye drugie ...', p. 109.

that since then he has had a thousand times more influence on our poetic youth than "patriots" such as Kuniaev'.[47]

On the poetic and aesthetic level the situation is even more complex. For his poetic achievement and his metaphysical horizons Brodsky's apologists set him beside Mandel´shtam, Akhmatova and Tsvetaeva and compare him to Pushkin. His aesthetic adversaries accuse him of the deadliest of crimes against literature in his treatment of the Russian language. According to Roman Gul´, 'Brodsky has a shallow attitude to the Russian language and to compare him with the Russian Classics is risible'.[48] 'Intellectual sloth', 'lack of verbal power', 'mechanical and strained'; these and other stylistic lapses are detailed by Iurii Kolker in a sixty-page article.[49] His poetry is dry and uninvolved, 'with two exceptions, lacking in charm', and of no use to anyone, declares Igor´ Chinnov in *Ogonek*, agreeing with Naum Korzhavin that the verse is 'spiritually anodyne'.[50] Others acknowledge Brodsky's technical virtuosity but do not grasp his philosophical and moral position. Coldness, bookishness, aestheticism, rationalism and bad taste – this is a far from complete catalogue of the accusations levelled at Brodsky the poet. 'Aren't they a remarkable collection of accusations, especially when you consider how those same faults have contributed to the making of such a fine poet! Any one of them would have been the ruination of another poet', notes Kushner ironically.[51] A third group pretends that Brodsky does not exist at all (Evtushenko, Voznesenskii, Prigov, to name but a few), perhaps because it is not easy to live and work in his shadow. For many his stature occludes the horizon, provoking hostility and aggression. At times we learn more from their statements about these other poets than about Brodsky.

In his own generation and in the younger generation Brodsky stands alone. Indeed, if he can be compared to Tsvetaeva for intellect[52] and technical virtuosity, to Akhmatova for emotional restraint, to Mandel´shtam for richness of cultural references, and to Pushkin for universality, then for the degree of estrangement from himself and from the subject of description, he has no equal in Russian poetry. Several poets have spoken about this: 'I think that not one of us who is writing poetry has mastered those lessons of freedom and courage that Joseph

47. Bek, interviewed in *Literaturnaia gazeta*, p. 3.

48. Gul´, 'O neprilichiiakh', p. 285.

49. Kolker, 'Neskol´ko nabliudenii', pp. 93–152.

50. Chinnov, interviewed in *Ogonek*, p. 14.

51. Kushner, *Brodsky through the Eyes*, p. 110.

52. 'Brodsky has a remarkable mind', said the academic, V. V. Ivanov in an interview with M. Lemkhin in *Russkaia mysl´*, 25 May 1990, p. xi. Gennadii Aigi also considers Brodsky to be 'one of the most intelligent people he has ever had the opportunity to meet' (*Brodsky through the Eyes*, p. 184).

Valentina Polukhina

Brodsky offers Russian poets.'[53] The young poet Mikhail Barash considers that Brodsky 'has to follow a thought through to the end with
peculiar persistence, because no one around him has the desire to spend
time on it'.[54] In Gorbanevskaia's opinion there is no contemporary to set
beside Brodsky either for poetic talent or for degree of artistic personality.[55] Brodsky protests against the Russian tradition of naming a particular poet as the most important at a given time ('naznachat´ glavnym'),
but as long as this situation obtains, the source which feeds the myth of
Brodsky as the ideal poet will not run dry.

In transferring the subject of the Brodsky myth onto the level of poetic reality, discussion of his bilingualism and biculturalism becomes
obligatory. Once again this situation is unique in Russian poetry.
Brodsky has allowed so much of the 'foreigner' into his art, that for
many Russian 'patriots' he has lost his 'Russian soul', or even simply
his Russianness long ago. Brodsky brings to Russian poetry something
uncharacteristic which many find hard to accept. Kublanovskii
reproaches him for the absence of warmth: 'his lyrical hero is lacking in
that spiritual warmth which is the glory of our poetry. Stage by stage,
Brodsky is making his poetry more and more detached from the world –
consciously he makes it colder. His poetry is moulded into a kind of
absolute image, an absolute solitude, an absolute imperfection. It is an
inanimate world, a still-life.'[56] Rein is prepared to look further than
Kublanovskii; in his view Brodsky has rejected the use of what has been
the most characteristic feature of Russian lyric poetry – an excitable,
hot-blooded, hysterical note. In his cycle *A Part of Speech*, the heat has
been lowered and the melody, too, has been tempered, flattened down.
Rein remarks that, 'there is something in those poems that reminds me
of the way time flows past and away from you; and time knows neither
heat nor cold'.[57] Soprovskii rejects 'the all-pervading intonation of
irony' in Brodsky's poems, while Elena Shvarts sees in him a sceptic
and rationalist.[58]

There is in these evaluations a peculiar internal conflict. Brodsky is
indeed relentlessly sober and he cultivates this sobriety in himself. This
manifests itself in the fact that the stylistic vector of Brodsky's poetry is
resolutely directed towards abstraction of emotion and anonymity of
discourse. Bearing in mind that these are very much new qualities for

53. L. Loseff, 'Poka narod zhiv', p. 9.
54. Barash, 'Mramor rechi', unpublished.
55. Gorbanevskaia, *Brodsky through the Eyes*, p. 81.
56. Kublanovskii, *Brodsky through the Eyes*, p. 208, and 'On postoianno vedet', p. 6.
57. Rein, *Brodsky through the Eyes*, pp. 62–3.
58. Soprovskii, 'Konets prekrasnoi epokhi', p. 337; Shvarts, *Brodsky through the Eyes*, p. 220.

Russian poetry, it is not surprising that Russian readers, including some poets, see Brodsky's position of neutral observer as coldness, his use of estrangement as contempt towards people, his lack of discrimination in vocabulary as bad taste, and the many references to world culture as bookishness. Before Brodsky, the typically Russian disease, which Mandel´shtam called 'nostalgia for a world culture', and which hides, as Brodsky himself recognises, an inferiority complex about the West, was considered a noble disease. Brodsky was the first, after Nabokov, to succeed in completely curing himself of this Russian illness. 'The uniqueness of his experience', according to Kulle, 'is above all in something which is rather unusual for our culture, that is an openness to the whole experience of world poetry, conceived as a unified, living organism.'[59] He crosses out many of the stereotypes which are deeply entrenched in both Russian and world culture. This audacity has proved not to be to the taste of a large number of people.

One of the paradoxes in the reception of Brodsky's poems consists in the fact that it is not uncommon for their artistic originality and the relentlessly grand scale of his thinking to form a barrier to the understanding of their true meaning. Loseff remarks that Brodsky's 'poetics remain far above the heads of some readers'.[60] Many critics have disregarded the most important element in Brodsky: his concern 'for the metaphysical potential of the human being', his striving towards 'far greater perspective', his 'quest for self-betterment'.[61] When it comes to evaluating his poetics, nearly all the poets thoroughly familiar with his work agree that, despite all the changes Brodsky has undergone, his is an unusually solid poetic personality. Almost everything that he has done in the last ten to fifteen years was already present in some form or other in the work of his early years. Naiman believes that by about 1965 Brodsky had written everything he was going to write: 'If he had died then, disappeared from the scene, whatever, stopped writing, it would not matter, we would still have Brodsky.'[62] To Krivulin, it seems that Brodsky has remained down that metaphysical mineshaft where man is alone face-to-face with the Universe.[63] The vision of apocalypse is indeed one of his central themes. Despite all this, his poetic evolution is self-evident. The mature Brodsky is, as a matter of principle, obstinately unliterary. Brodsky's neutral 'mat' intonation goes hand in hand with an extremely heavily laden semantics and syntax, with rhythmical complexity, and a very diverse vocabulary. Krivulin noted the paradox of

59. Kulle, 'Tam gde oni konchili', p. 5.
60. L. Loseff, 'Poetics of faith', p. 200.
61. Brodsky in interview with David Bethea.
62. Naiman, *Iosif Brodksii razmerom podlinnika*, p. 150.
63. Krivulin, *Brodsky through the Eyes*, p. 184.

Brodsky's poetics when he remarked that 'the more dead and impassive the poems written in emigration, the more tangible the intimacy, the life and the torment in them'.[64] In the opinion of Mikhail Barash, 'Brodsky's poetics persistently resists analytical investigation because of the densely merged heterogeneous characteristics within it.'[65] Lev Loseff writes that, 'the essence of Brodsky's poetry is in its stylistic disharmoniousness: its thematic disproportion, intonational asymmetry, in the absence of a balance of ideas'.[66]

It is generally recognised that the most distinctive contribution made by Brodsky to Russian poetry stems from his fresh encounter with the European tradition. Brodsky has broken out of the constrictions which Russian poetry had placed about itself by grafting a Polish and an English vine on to the branch of Russian poetry. In Loseff's view, 'Brodsky superbly grasped the connection between twentieth-century modernism and seventeenth-century metaphysical verse.'[67] He was the first to inject wit and vigour, biting irony, pure baroque coarseness, the cult of the concept and grandiose moving statements about time and space into Russian poetry. New growth, genres, themes and forms then blossomed. His encounter with English poetry meant a meeting with the great themes (such as death) and the great forms of literature before the advent of realism. Sedakova feels that it is to European poetry that we owe this new image of the poet, since it is unknown in Russian poetry. Brodsky's lyrical self is no longer a hero of his own dramas: in his case the poet is impersonal, above all, a literary man. The rest recedes into the background. The *peripeteiae* of his life are his bricks and mortar.[68]

Talking of the influence of English poetry on Brodsky, Naiman explains that when the Russian poet encounters English poetry he realises 'what aspects of Russian prosody have to be adjusted, what constructions have to be brought in to find the same wide harmonic range in the Russian'.[69] Ufliand offers a similar view that it is by now clear that the process of mutual influence existing between various different literatures is both timely and irreversible. Brodsky gave the whole process a powerful impetus by setting in motion a convergence of the English and Russian poetic traditions, which can now already be seen as his own particular contribution to Russian poetry.[70] Kushner and Meilakh also consider that Brodsky's crossing of Russian with English poetry has

64. Krivulin, 'Slovo o nobeliate', p. iii.
65. Barash, 'Mramor rechi'.
66. L. Loseff, 'Angliiskii Brodskii', p. 57.
67. L. Loseff, 'Poetics/Politics', p. 35.
68. Sedakova, *Brodsky through the Eyes*, pp. 247–8.
69. Naiman, ibid., p. 18.
70. Ufliand, ibid., p. 151.

resulted in a fertile hybrid. Parshchikov compares Brodsky to Zhukovskii, who in his view gave the Russians German Romanticism. It is through Brodsky that Anglo-American and Russian literatures communicate.[71] The Latin poets inspired Brodsky as much as they inspired the English.

Many poets are in no doubt that Brodsky has widened the linguistic range of Russian poetry very considerably by transplanting to Russian soil many of the qualities of English poetics, first and foremost the especial suggestiveness and weight of each individual word. What appears 'colourless' and 'tiresome' to Mikhail Aizenberg,[72] Kushner describes as great sophistication, expressivity and energy, while his complex syntactical constructions are virtuoso, if, at the same time, infuriating.[73] Elena Shvarts is also ready to concede that Brodsky brought a completely new musicality, and even a new form of thought to Russian poetry, something quite different from conventional expectations.[74] Rein places emphasis on two particular qualities in Brodsky's poetry. First, he brings to bear the full force of his intellectual powers in order to somehow resolve everything anew, offering new answers to old questions. Secondly, his extremely remarkable powers of observation are of a very special kind, sometimes taking in whole continents, sometimes a fleeing cat. These qualities in Rein's view are prosaic in nature. Brodsky has a prosaic kind of talent which has in fact permitted him to become the last great innovator in Russian poetry.[75] Rein describes Brodsky as a poet who has given 'to thought and vision, sound and feeling, a new, henceforth eternal form'.[76]

Such considerations lead naturally to consideration of the universality of Brodsky's poetry. 'Ultimately, that is the really important question', remarks Naiman.

> Rightly or wrongly, we were able to see Akhmatova, Pasternak, Tsvetaeva, Maiakovskii etc. as all on the same level, but who can we place alongside Brodsky? There is nobody. On the one hand this reveals his standing in the poetic hierarchy, but on the other, it is an unhealthy situation because a poet cannot be expected to synthesise. Quite the contrary, the narrower the furrow he ploughs the greater the poet. To this there is but one exception: that is, when, like Pushkin, he is a universal poet.[77]

71. Parshchikov, ibid., p. 272.
72. Aizenberg, 'Nekotorye drugie ...', p. 110.
73. Kushner, *Brodsky through the Eyes*, p. 107.
74. Shvarts, ibid., p. 222.
75. Rein, ibid., pp. 65–6.
76. Rein, paper to the International Conference.
77. Naiman, *Brodsky through the Eyes*, pp. 21–2.

Ol′ga Sedakova stresses Brodsky's tendency towards the universal and the monumental, towards grasping the whole of life from its zenith to its nadir, from one end of the horizon to the other – 'the view of the planet from the moon'.[78] Kublanovskii virtually echoes her when he says that 'Brodsky is by nature a monumentalist in verse, and there has been little monumentalism in Russian poetry in the twentieth century.' The source of this monumentalism lay, he feels, in Latin culture.[79] Rein recalls Brodsky's own answer to this question. In one of their conversations he had said that the scale of lyrical poetry is almost always dependent upon the scale of the poet, that the scale ought to be greater, that it ought to be on the scale of a country, a continent, some philosophical idea whether religious or sociological.[80]

Is it justified to compare Brodsky with Pushkin? In Naiman's view, they share the same epigrammatic ease in their reaction to events as they happen.[81] Gorbanevskaia makes a different kind of comparison when she observes that in the last ten years Brodsky has acquired a number of enemies. Emergent poets have stopped paying him his dues, just as they did to Pushkin. This is simply because in order to understand him, one has to move at the same speed as he does.[82] Kublanovskii, by contrast, argues that Pushkin grew ever closer to a populist ('pochvennicheskii') standpoint, thereby developing in a direction diametrically opposed to Brodsky's.[83] Loseff, on the other hand, whose judgements on Brodsky are, as a rule, the most sound, noted the principal affinity between the two when he commented that

> … the model of Brodsky's poetic thinking is constructed along Pushkinian lines, that is to say, on the lines of a dialogue between Russian and European man. This is an astoundingly Russian trait. It is what Pushkin and his Pléiade did with French poetics; it is what Russian lyric poets of the mid-nineteenth century did with Heine and German poetics. Brodsky has done the same thing exactly with his transplantation of the great tree of English poetics to the Russian wilds.[84]

If Brodsky can be said to have made a stand for anything in our world, it is, Naiman feels, that he is holding the fort against vulgarity, chaos and those who seek to bring the lofty walls of the cultural and spiritual castle tumbling down. These are not, perhaps, the towers upon

78. Sedakova, ibid., p. 249.
79. Kublanovskii, ibid., p. 204.
80. Rein, ibid., p. 66.
81. Naiman, *Brodsky through the Eyes*, p. 21.
82. Gorbanevskaia, ibid., p. 88.
83. Kublanovskii, ibid., p. 204.
84. Loseff, ibid., p. 129.

which Brodsky takes his own stand, but he knows who dwells there and he takes some pressure off the defenders; his gaze is directed towards the ideals symbolised by those high towers. That essentially is his mission.[85] Kushner is convinced that no one has reflected our times as completely as Brodsky.[86]

Viktor Kulle feels that Brodsky's poetry has become a linguistic reality in which he, and all poets in their twenties, must and do exist today. Brodsky influences them not with the authority of his Nobel Prize, but primarily because he possesses an unbelievable technical mastery. He seems now, especially for young poets, to be in the very air they breathe, and his poetry is seen as a stage in the evolution of the Russian language. Kulle explains that Brodsky not only altered the language poets use, but cleansed Soviet Newspeak of its dross, elevating it to the rank of a literary language.[87] This alone has earned him comparison with Pushkin. No Russian poet could ask for more.

Translated by Andrea Sillis

Bibliography of Russian Poets Talking and Writing about Brodsky

Akhmadulina, Bella, interviewed by V. Polukhina, *Brodsky's Poetics and Aesthetics*, eds L. Loseff and V. Polukhina, London, 1990, pp. 194–204

Akhmatova, Anna, in Anatolii Naiman, *Rasskazy o Anne Akhmatovoi*, Moskva, 1989, pp. 10, 124, 137–42, 171, 210–11 (covering the period 1961–6)

—— 'Dialog poetov (Tri pis´ma Akhmatovoi k Brodskomu)', letters from 1964–5 published by Iakov Gordin, *Akhmatovskii sbornik*, eds S. Deduline and G. Superfin, Paris, 1989, pp. 221–4

Aizenberg, Mikhail, 'Nekotorye drugie ... Variant khroniki: pervaia versiia', *Teatr*, no. 4, 1991, pp. 98–118

Barash, Mikhail, '*K Uranii*: O novoi knige stikhov Iosifa Brodskogo', *Russkaia mysl´*, 6 Nov. 1987, p. 10

—— 'Mramor rechi', 1988, unpublished

Bek, Tat´iana, interviewed by E. Gradova, *Literaturnaia gazeta*, 13 May 1993, p. 3

Bershin, Efim, 'Prorok? Eretic? Dezertir?', in conversation with other writers, *Literaturnaia gazeta*, 7 Apr. 1993, p. 3

85. Naiman, ibid., p. 17.
86. Kushner, ibid., p. 105.
87. Kulle, 'The Linguistic Reality', pp. 81–3.

Betaki, Vasilii, 'Ostanovis´ mgnoven´e', *Kontinent*, no. 35, 1982, pp. 384–8

Bobyshev, Dmitrii, 'Akhmatovskie siroty', *Russkaia mysl´*, 8 Mar. 1984, pp. 8–9

Chinnov, Igor´, interviewed by Ol´ga Chernova, *Ogonek*, 1992, no. 9, p. 14

Chizhova, Elena, 'Liubov´ sil´nei razluki', preface to Iosif Brodskii, *Pis´ma rimskomu drugu*, Leningrad, 1991, pp. 3–14

——— '"Evterpa, ty?" Liubovnaia lirika Brodskogo', *Russian Literature*, issue dedicated to Brodsky, forthcoming in 1994

Gorbanevskaia, Natal´ia, 'Iz Stokgol´ma – s liubov´iu', *Russkaia mysl´*, 18 Dec. 1987, p. 16

——— Interviewed by V. Polukhina, *Brodsky Through the Eyes of his Contemporaries*, Basingstoke/New York, 1992, pp. 74–93

——— 'Tri polovinki karmannoi lukovitsy', a review of Brodsky's *Primechaniia paporotnika, Russkaia mysl´*, 25 Jan. 1991, p. 14

——— 'Iosif Brodskii – razmerom podlinnika', a review of *Iosif Brodskii razmerom podlinnika*, ed. G. Komarov, Tallinn, 1990, in *Russkaia mysl´*, 29 Mar. 1991, p. 13

——— 'Neskol´ko strannoi kazhetsia mne...', *Russkaia mysl´*, 16 Oct. 1992, p. 9

Gorbovskii, Gleb, *Ostyvshie sledy*, Leningrad, 1991, pp. 217, 279–81

Gordin, Iakov, 'Delo Brodskogo', *Neva*, no. 2, 1989, pp. 134–66

——— Interviewed by V. Polukhina, *Brodsky Through the Eyes of his Contemporaries*, ibid., pp. 29–73

——— 'Poet tragicheskii, no chelovek veselyi', *Chas pik*, 12 Nov. 1990, p. 7; reprinted under the title 'Drugoi Brodskii', in *Iosif Brodskii razmerom podlinnika*, pp. 215–21

——— 'Strannik', introduction to Iosif Brodskii, *Izbrannoe*, Moscow, 1993, pp. 5–18

Gozias, Solomon, *The Blue Lagoon Anthology of Modern Russian Poetry*, eds K. Kuz´minskii and G. Kovalev, Newtonville, Mass., 1986, vol. 2B, pp. 183–7

Gul´, Roman, 'O neprilichiiakh i oglobliakh', *Novyi zhurnal*, vol. 131, 1978, p. 285

Iakimchuk, Nikolai, *Kak sudili poeta (delo I. Brodskogo)*, Leningrad, 1990

Karabchievskii, Yurii, *Voskresenie Maiakovskogo*, Munich, 1985, pp. 272–9

Kolker, Yurii, 'Epigramma', *Izrail´skii dnevnik*, Feb. 1988, p. 20

——— 'Neskol´ko nabliudenii (o stikhakh Iosifa Brodskogo)', *Grani*, vol. 162, 1991, pp. 93–152

Kreps, Mikhail, *O poezii Iosifa Brodskogo*, Ann Arbor, Michigan, 1984

——— A parody in verse 'Tsarevna-liagushka', *Novyi zhurnal*, vol. 179, 1990, pp. 25–9

Krivulin, Viktor, (under the pseudonym of Kalomirov) 'Iosif Brodskii (mesto)', *Vestnik russkogo khristianskogo dvizheniia*, vol. 123, 1977, pp. 140–51; reprinted in *Poetika Brodskogo*, ed. Lev Loseff, Tenafly, NJ, 1986, pp. 219–29

—— 'Dvadtsat´ let noveishei russkoi poezii', *Literaturnoe prilozhenie k Russkoi mysli*, 27 Dec. 1985, pp. vi–viii

—— 'Slovo o nobeliate Iosifa Brodskogo', *Literary supplement to Russkaia mysl´*, 11 Nov. 1988, pp. ii–iii

—— 'Russkii poet – amerikanskii grazhdanin na frantsuzskom ekrane', *Russkaia mysl´*, 3 Mar. 1989, p. 13

—— 'Problema knigi v tvorchestve I. Brodskogo', a paper to the International Conference: *Poeziia Brodskogo, kul'tura Rossii i Zapada*, Leningrad, 7–9 Jan. 1990 (unpublished)

—— Interviewed by V. Polukhina, *Brodsky Through the Eyes of his Contemporaries*, pp. 176–99

—— 'Teatr Iosifa Brodskogo', *Sovremennaia dramaturgia*, no. 3, 1991, pp. 15–17

Kublanovskii, Iurii, 'Na predele lirisma', *Russkaia mysl´*, 11 Aug. 1983, p. 10

—— 'Poeziia novogo izmereniia', *Vestnik russkogo khristianskogo dvizhenia*, vol. 151, no. 3, 1987, pp. 91–3; revised version reprinted in *Novyi mir*, no. 2, 1991, pp. 242–6

—— Interviewed by V. Polukhina, *Brodsky Through the Eyes of his Contemporaries*, pp. 200–14

—— 'On postoianno vedet s Tvortsom svoego roda tiazhbu', *Literaturnaia gazeta*, 16 May 1990, p. 6

—— 'Poeziia novogo izmereniia', *Novyi mir*, no. 2, 1991, pp. 242–6

Kulle, Viktor, 'Struktura avtorskogo "Ia" v stikhotvorenii Brodskogo "Niotkuda s liubov´iu"', *Novyi zhurnal*, no. 180, 1990, pp. 159–72

—— 'Obretshii rechi dar v glukhonemoi vselennoi (Nabroski ob estetike Iosifa Brodskogo)', *Rodnik,* no. 3, 1990, pp. 77–80

—— 'Tam, gde oni konchili, ty nachinaesh´', Introduction to Iosif Brodskii, *Bog sokhraniaet vse*, ed. V. Kulle, Moskva, 1992, pp. 5–6

—— 'The Linguistic Reality in which we all live', interviewed by V. Polukhina, *Essays in Poetics*, vol. 17, no. 2, 1992, pp. 72–83

—— 'Iosif Brodskii: paradoksy vospriiatiia', *Structure and Tradition in Russian Society*, Slavica Helsingiensia, forthcoming in 1994

—— Review of V. Polukhina, *Brodsky Through the Eyes of his Contemporaries*, in *Grani*, no. 167, 1993, pp. 297–302

Kushner, Alexandr, 'O Brodskom', 'Zametki na poliakh', 'Protivostoianie', in *Apollon v snegu*, Leningrad, 1991, pp. 392–6, 441–4, 500–1 respectively

—— 'Neskol´ko slov', *Iosif Brodskii razmerom podlinnika*, pp. 234–41

—— 'Tsikl stikhotovorenii', *Iosif Brodskii razmerom podlinnika*, pp. 234–9

—— 'Poet bezuteshnoi mysli', *Literaturnaia gazeta*, 16 May 1990, p. 6

—— Interviewed by V. Polukhina, *Brodsky Through the Eyes of his Contemporaries*, ibid., pp. 100–12

Kuz´min, Dmitrii, 'K voprosu o simvole v rannem tvorchestve Iosifa Brodskogo', a paper given to *Pervye Vsesoiuznye Brodskie chteniia*, May 1990, Moskva, unpublished

—— 'Privkhodiashchie obstoiatel´stva', *Nezavisimaia gazeta*, 17 Mar. 1993, p. 7

Kuz´minskii, Konstantin, *The Blue Lagoon Anthology of Modern Russian Poetry*, eds K. Kuz´minskii and G. Kovalev, vol. 1, Newtonville, Mass., 1980, pp. 24–39, *passim*; vol 2A, 1983, pp. 106, 111, *passim*; vol. 2B, 1986, pp. 177, 180, 182–91, 264, 267, 272, 282, *passim*; vol 3A, 1986, *passim*; vol. 3B, 1986, 'Zdravstvuite Brodskii', pp. 754–8, *passim*; vol 4A, 1983, *passim*; vol. 4B, 1983, *passim*, vol. 5A, 1986, *passim*; vol. 5B, 1986, *passim*

—— 'Laureat "Eriki"', *Russkaia mysl´*, 30 Oct. 1987, pp. 11, 14

Len, Stanislav, 'Gusenitsa Vladimira Nabokova', *Chelovek i priroda*, no. 11, 1989, pp. 65–75

—— 'Brodskii i bronzovyi vek russkogo stikha', paper given to the International Conference: *Poeziia Brodskogo, kul´tura Rossii i Zapada*, Leningrad, 7–9 Jan. 1990, unpublished

Limonov, Eduard, 'Poet-bukhgalter', *Muleta. Seneinyi al´bom, A-1984*, Paris, 1984, pp. 132–5

—— 'Limonov o Brodskom', *Alma Mater*, Sept. 1990, p. 6

Loseff, Aleksei (pseudonym of Aleksei Lifshutz), 'Niotkuda s liubov´iu... (Zametki o stikhakh Iosifa Brodskogo)', *Kontinent*, no. 14, 1977, pp. 307–31

—— 'Iosif Brodskii: posviashchaetsia logike', *Vestnik russkogo khristianskogo dvizheniia*, vol. 127, 1978, pp. 124–30

—— 'Iosif Brodskii. Predislovie', *Ekho*, no. 1, 1980, pp. 23–30

—— 'Angliiskii Brodskii', *Chast´ rechi. Al´manakh*, no 1, 1980, pp. 53–60

—— 'Pervyi liricheskii tsykl Iosifa Brodskogo', *Chast´ rechi. Al´manakh*, no. 2/3, 1981, pp. 63–8

Loseff, Lev (pseudonym of Aleksei Lifschutz), 'Poka narod zhiv, zhiva i poeziia...', interviewed by Iurii Kublanovskii, *Russkaia mysl´*, 28 July 1983, p. 9

—— 'Ironicheskii monument: p´esa Iosifa Brodskogo *Mramor*', *Russkaia mysl´*, 14 June 1984, p. 10

—— Review of B. Ezerskaia, *Mastera, Russian Review*, vol. 44, no. 2, 1985, pp. 198–9

—— 'Brodskii: ot mifa k poetu,' introduction to *Poetika Brodskogo*, pp. 7–15

—— 'Chekhovskii lirism u Brodskogo', *Poetika Brodskogo*, pp. 185–97

—— 'Prazdnik spravedlivosti', *Russkaia mysl´*, 30 Oct. 1987, p. 9

—— 'Moi drug idiot po lesu ...', *Russkaia mysl´*, 16 June 1989, pp. 8–9

—— 'Poetics of Faith', *Aspects of Modern Russian and Czech Literature*, ed. A. McMillin, Columbus, Ohio, 1989, pp. 188–201

—— 'Poetics/Politics', in Loseff, L. and Polukhina, V., eds, *Brodsky's Poetics and Aesthetics*, pp. 34–55

—— Interviewed by V. Polukhina, *Brodsky through the Eyes of his Contemporaries*, pp. 113–39

—— 'Joseph Brodskii', *Gels et Dégels*, Paris, 1990, pp. 725–40

—— 'Home and Abroad in the Works of Brodsky', *Under Eastern Eyes: The West as Reflected in Recent Russian Emigré Writings*, ed. A. McMillin, Basingstoke, 1991, pp. 25–41

Loseff, L. and Polukhina, V., eds, *Brodsky's Poetics and Aesthetics*, London, 1990

Meilakh, Mikhail, interviewed by V. Polukhina, *Brodsky through the Eyes of his Contemporaries*, pp. 158–75

—— 'Zametki o poezii Brodskogo', paper given to the International Conference: *Poeziia Iosifa Brodskogo, kul´tura Rossii i Zapada*, Leningrad, 7–9 Jan. 1990, unpublished

Naiman, Anatolii, 'Zametki dlia pamiati', in Brodskii, *Ostanovka v pustyne*, New York, 1970, pp. 7–15

—— Interviewed by V. Polukhina in 1989, in *Iosif Brodskii razmerom podlinnika*, pp. 127–53; English version in V. Polukhina, *Brodsky through the Eyes of his Contemporaries*, ibid., pp. 1–28

—— 'Velichie poeticheskogo zamysla', *Russkaia mysl´*, Special supplement, 25 May 1990, pp. ii–iii

—— 'Printsip ravenstva slov i ego razvitie', a paper to the panel on Brodsky at the Fourth World Congress for Soviet and East European Studies, Harrogate, England, July 1990

—— 'Prostranstvo Uranii. 50 let Iosifu Brodskomu', *Oktiabr´*, 1990, no. 9, pp. 193–8

—— 'Bukvy, prostupaiushchie na stene', *Literaturnaia gazeta*, 21 Apr. 1993, p. 6

Nekrasov, Vsevolod, *Stikhi iz zhurnala*, Moscow, 1989, pp. 6, 8, 38

Ozerov, Lev, 'Nu, kak tam Flavii', a parody on Brodsky, *Literaturnaia gazeta*, 3 June 1992, p. 16

Parshchikov, Aleksei, interviewed by V. Polukhina, *Brodsky through the Eyes of his Contemporaries*, pp. 261–75

Polukhina, V., *Brodsky Through the Eyes of his Contemporaries*, Basingstoke/New York, 1992

Prigov, Dmitrii, interviewed by V. Voznesenskii, *Knizhnoe obozrenie*, 3 July 1992, pp. 8–9

Rein, Evgenii, interviewed by V. Polukhina, *Brodsky through the Eyes of his Contemporaries*, pp. 53–73

—— Opening remarks to the International Conference: *Poeziia Brodskogo, kul´tura Rossii i Zapada*, Leningrad, 7–9 Jan. 1990, unpublished

—— 'Na izliote romantizma', in interview with Tat´iana Rasskazova, *Literaturnaia gazeta*, 26 Aug. 1992, p. 5

Rozhdestvenskii, Vsevolod, 'Iosif Brodskii – Zimniaia pochta – sbornik stikhov', *Russkaia mysl´*, Literary supplement, 11 Nov. 1988, p. iv. (Material relating to 1965)

Savitskii, Dmitrii, 'Poche du mois', *Magazine Littéraire*, May 1987, p. 97

—— 'Un parasite chez les Nobel', *Libération*, 23 Oct. 1987, pp. 38–9

—— 'Et la Neva va ...', *Libération*, 9 Dec. 1987, p. 42

—— 'Brodski, c'est Byzance', *Libération*, 6 Oct. 1988, p. ix

—— 'Brodski: du Goulag au Nobel', *Emois*, Lausanne, no. 10, 1988, 58–63

Sedakova, Ol´ga, interviewed by V. Polukhina, *Brodsky through the Eyes of his Contemporaries*, pp. 237–60

Shcherbina, Tat´iana, 'Brodskii: Zhidkie kristally', *Ural*, no. 1, 1990

Shefner, Vadim, 'O rukopisi Iosifa Brodskogo "Zimniaia pochta"', *Russkaia mysl´*, Literary supplement, 11 Nov. 1988, p. v

Shvarts, Elena, interviewed by V. Polukhina, *Brodsky through the Eyes of his Contemporaries*, pp. 215–36

Soprovskii, Aleksandr, 'Konets prekrasnoi epokhi', *Kontinent*, no. 32, 1982, pp. 335–54

—— 'Poety – vid. A vovse ne poroda', *Smena*, 26 Apr. 1991, p. 4

Ufliand, Vladimir, 'Intelligentsiia. Nekotorye soobrazheniia terminologii', *Russkaia mysl´*, 6 Jan. 1989, p. 11

—— Interviewed by V. Polukhina, *Brodsky through the Eyes of his Contemporaries*, pp. 140–57

—— 'Ot poeta k mifu', *Russkaia mysl´*, 16 June 1989, p. 8, reprinted in *Iosif Brodskii razmerom podlinnika*, pp. 163–4 and also in *Avrora*, no. 5, 1990, pp. 58–9

—— Preface to Iosif Brodskii, *Osennii krik iastreba*, Leningrad, 1990, pp. 3–4

—— 'Moguchaia piterskaia khvor´', *Zvezda*, no. 1, 1990, pp. 179–84

—— 'Kak stat´ znamenitym', *Iskorka*, no. 5, 1990, pp. 44–5

—— 'Belyi Peterburgskii vecher 25 maia', *Avrora*, no 12, 1990, pp. 129–35

—— 'Shest´desiat minut demokratii', *Russkaia mysl´*, 19 July 1991, p. 13

Ushakova, Elena, interviewed by V. Polukhina, *Brodsky through the Eyes of his Contemporaries*, pp. 94–9

Vanshenkin, K., review of *Sochineniia Iosifa Brodskogo*, in *Literaturnaia gazeta*, 14 July 1993, p. 4

–12–

Trifonov on Dostoevskii

David Gillespie

Iurii Valentinovich Trifonov (1925–81) is one of the foremost Soviet writers active during the 'stagnation' years of the 1960s and 1970s, and, indeed, his major fiction was written and published during the Brezhnev period. The time is now ripe for a retrospective appraisal of these years, and the individuals who resisted the pressures to conform. Indeed, in recent years both Russian and Western critics have become particularly interested in the work of Trifonov, for here is a writer who published regularly when other writers were repressed or exiled abroad, yet who was one of the few 'official' writers to maintain integrity and the respect of the reading public by providing as truthful a picture of his society as the times would allow.[1]

In particular, Trifonov described the moral choices forced upon individuals by the rigours of Soviet society, hard choices that are the result of the temptation to 'exchange' ideals or values for material betterment or status. In Trifonov's Moscow stories, such as 'The Exchange' (1969), 'Preliminary Stocktaking' (1970), 'The Long Farewell' (1971) and 'Another Life' (1975), there are few individuals who get through the trials of everyday life with their principles and integrity intact. Either Trifonov's central characters abandon the ideals they or their families once held dear, or the struggle to maintain them proves too much and they die young.[2]

---

1. A version of this paper was read at the British Association of Slavonic and East European Studies' Twentieth Century Literature Conference at Mansfield College, Oxford, September 1992. I am indebted to fellow participants for their helpful comments, subsequently incorporated into the final version.

Trifonov has been particularly well served by Western critics: recent studies include Nina Kolesnikoff, *Yury Trifonov: A Critical Study*, Ann Arbor, Michigan, 1991, and Josephine Woll, *Invented Truth: Soviet Reality and the Literary Imagination of Iurii Trifonov*, Durham and London, 1991.

2. Here, as elsewhere, reference will be to the original date and place of publication (Moscow unless stated otherwise): 'Obmen', *Novyi mir*, no. 12, 1969, pp. 29–65; 'Predvaritel´nye itogi', *Novyi mir*, no. 10, 1970, pp. 52–82; 'Dolgoe proshchanie', *Novyi mir*, no. 8, 1971, pp. 53–107; 'Drugaia zhizn´´', *Novyi mir*, no. 8, 1975, pp. 7–99.

David Gillespie

Furthermore, Trifonov gives his modern world historical depth by juxtaposing past and present, as if seeking the roots of the contemporary malaise in the past. Whereas most of his plots are set in the present, he has also devoted many pages to the Stalin years, as in *The House on the Embankment* (1976), *Time and Place* (1981) and *Disappearance*, published only in 1987. Similarly, he writes about the Civil War of 1918–21, as in the non-fictional *The Glow of the Campfire* (1965–6), and the novel *The Old Man* (1978). The political terrorism of the 'People's Will' organisation in the 1870s–1880s is the subject of his historical novel *Impatience* (1973).[3] All of these works, in various ways, revolve around the struggle of freedom and tyranny, concepts that dominate Russia's historical destiny. In Trifonov's works, as in Russian history, tyranny usually wins out. Furthermore, these concepts fight it out within the individual soul, so that the tension thus created lies at the heart of both his Moscow stories of moral decay and individual betrayal, and his more overtly historical studies. His interest in Dostoevskii can be related to the development of this theme.

With his sharp eye for individual foibles, his use of the salient detail, and his unwillingness to judge or condemn the actions of his characters, Trifonov has often been likened to Anton Chekhov.[4] Trifonov was himself very much aware of the traditions of Russian literature, and wrote appreciatively on such writers as Chekhov himself, Maksim Gor´kii, Lev Tolstoi, Konstantin Paustovskii, Ivan Bunin and Dostoevskii.[5] Furthermore, in his fiction he often conducts a dialogue with other writers: his novel *The Old Man* is in many ways a reworking, fifty years on, of *And Quiet Flows the Don*, with its emphasis on the brutality of the Civil War, where atrocities are carried out by both Reds and Whites, and its account of the fate of the Don Cossacks (Trifonov's father was himself born a Don Cossack).[6] The last major works to be written, *Time and*

3. 'Dom na naberezhnoi', *Druzhba narodov*, no. 1, 1976, pp. 83–167; 'Vremia i mesto', *Druzhba narodov*, no. 9, 1981, pp. 72–148, no. 10, pp. 22–108; 'Ischeznovenie', *Druzhba narodov*, no. 1, 1987, pp. 6–95; 'Otblesk kostra', *Znamia*, no. 2, 1965, pp. 142–60, no. 3, pp. 152–77; subsequently enlarged in book form, Moscow, 1966; 'Starik', *Druzhba narodov*, no. 3, 1978, pp. 27–153; 'Neterpenie', *Novyi mir*, no. 3, 1973, pp. 44–116, no. 4, pp. 35–112, no. 5, pp. 8–90.

4. See, for instance, Andrew Durkin, 'Trifonov's "Taking Stock": The Role of Čexovian Subtext', *Slavic and East European Journal*, vol. 28, no. 1, 1984, pp. 32–41; Richard Lourie, 'Tales of a Soviet Chekhov', *The New York Times Book Review*, 18 Mar. 1984, p. 7; Carolina De Maegd-Soëp, *Trifonov and the Drama of the Russian Intelligentsia*, Ghent, 1990.

5. See the articles 'Truth and Beauty', 'A. M. Gor´kii', 'Tolstoi Lev Nikolaevich', 'Lessons of a Master', 'I. A. Bunin' and 'Nechaev, Verkhovenskii and others', in the collection of his non-fictional writings entitled *How Our Word Resounds*, Moscow, 1985.

6. On the two novels, see Herman Ermolaev, 'Proshloe i nastoiashchee v "Starike" Iuriia Trifonova', *Russian Language Journal*, vol. 128, 1983, pp. 131–45.

Place and the cycle of short stories *The Overturned House*, are attempts at a synthesis of life and art, where life reproduces art and where art and literature themselves become a form of reality.[7] Trifonov's study of Dostoevskii, however, is particularly revealing, because it relates to his own overriding historical theme: the tension between ends and means, and the historical, political and moral consequences.

Dostoevskii's name crops up in many of Trifonov's works, often merely incidentally. Even in his first novel, the Stalin Prize-winning *Students* (1950), the politically unsound Professor Kozel´skii is noted as the author of a book on Dostoevskii. Kozel´skii is a professor of classical literature, and therefore it is hardly surprising that he should have made a study of this particular writer. However, it is entirely in the spirit of the times – the constant search for enemies real and imaginary, and the ideological intolerance that characterise Stalin's last years – that such an obviously backward-looking character as Kozel´skii should study a writer who, in the eyes of orthodox Marxist-Leninist critics, is a political reactionary. Trifonov substantially rewrote this novel in 1976 as *The House on the Embankment*, a work which gives a stark portrayal of the fear, envy, arrests and denunciations commonplace during the Stalin years. Moreover, in this latter work Dostoevskii occupies a central place, for the actions of the central character as he betrays his academic supervisor are likened to the actions of Raskol´nikov in killing the old money-lender in *Crime and Punishment*.

The ambitious but vacuous postgraduate student Vadim Glebov visits his supervisor Professor Ganchuk, who has just been publicly denounced and dismissed from his post – with Glebov's own connivance. It is the late 1940s, and the institute in which Glebov studies is shaken by a campaign to root out 'bourgeois intellectuals'. Ganchuk is an authority on Gor´kii, and greets Glebov thus:

> Ganchuk said that he had underestimated Gor´kii, that Aleksei Maksimych was wrong and that a new understanding was needed ... He said something like: what had tormented Dostoevskii – everything was permitted if there was nothing but a dark room with spiders – exists today, only in a mediocre and mundane form ... Today's Raskol´nikovs don't axe old moneylenders to death, but still suffer anguish at the thought of crossing the same frontier. And after all, what was the essential difference between killing someone with an axe or something else? Between killing, or simply giving them a shove to clear a space for yourself?[8]

7. See my article on the latter work, 'Unity through Disparity: Trifonov's *The Overturned House*', *Australian Slavonic and East European Studies*, vol. 5, no. 1, 1991, pp. 45–58.

8. Iu. Trifonov, *Sobranie sochinenii v chetyrekh tomakh*, Moscow, 1985–7, vol. 2, 1986, p. 488.

Ganchuk comes to realise that the conflict of good and evil goes deep into man's inner being, that Gor´kii, the father of Soviet literature and founder of Socialist Realism, depicts only the surface details of this conflict. Gor´kii's positivism, and the whole subsequent tradition of Soviet literature based on the Marxist precept of 'being determines consciousness', are at best inadequate, at worst a lie. In this work Trifonov indicates the profound relevance of Dostoevskii's vision for an understanding of the Soviet experience.[9]

Trifonov's novel *Impatience*, about the 'People's Will', is also to a large extent *The Devils* revisited, with the ideas and methods of Sergei Nechaev a central part (Dostoevskii himself appears as an incidental character, writing to the writer and publisher Aleksei Suvorin with his reflections on the terrorists' acts and thinking up a revolutionary's martyrdom for Alesha Karamazov). However, the Dostoevskii connection is not reduced to Trifonov simply redressing the nineteenth-century writer in modern garb.

Trifonov's interest in Dostoevskii stems from the contemporary relevance he saw in the work of the nineteenth-century writer. He admits as much when he states that Dostoevskii, in his view, 'was able to look more profoundly than other nineteenth-century writers into the present century and generally into what is called the human soul, that well that is sometimes bottomless'.[10] Towards the end of his life Trifonov wrote an article entitled 'The Enigma and Foresight of Dostoevskii', subsequently changed to 'Nechaev, Verkhovenskii and others', in which he dwells in detail on the contemporary significance of Dostoevskii's works, in particular *The Devils* (the article itself was published posthumously). *The Devils* is the name given by Dostoevskii to a group of radicals led by Petr Verkhovenskii who try to impose, with devastating consequences, their rationalist and utilitarian vision of the future on a provincial Russian town. For Trifonov, these 'devils' are not restricted to the nineteenth century.

Trifonov begins his article by asking 'Where does the enigma of Dostoevskii lie?'[11] He observes that Dostoevskii's works are not blessed with ornate or lyrical nature description or imagery, metaphors or vivid figures of speech. Instead, the reader is treated to an array of feelings, emotions and ideas that lay bare the human soul, the 'inner essence of people ('vnutrenniaia sut´ liudei')', revealing hidden secrets and motives. In order to penetrate into his characters' souls, Dostoevskii,

9. On further links between Trifonov's and Dostoevskii's novels, see Sigrid McLaughlin, 'Iurii Trifonov's *Dom na naberezhnoi* and Dostoevskii's *Prestuplenie i nakazanie*', *Canadian Slavonic Papers*, vol. 25, no. 2, June 1983, pp. 275–83.

10. Iu. Trifonov, 'A Novel with History', in *How our Word Resounds*, p. 329.

11. Ibid., p. 38.

writes Trifonov, places them in an 'an extreme situation ('ekstremal´naia situatsiia')', not one requiring physical adroitness or strength, but associated with torments of the soul caused by murder, poverty, humiliation, love. 'For Dostoevskii life was an extreme situation', concludes Trifonov.[12]

Trifonov, though, is not really interested in the characterisation or emotional power of Dostoevskii's works, and quickly moves on to the central issue: the truth of Dostoevskii's writings with regard to the twentieth century. Trifonov recounts the story of the murder of the student Ivanov in Moscow in 1869 by Sergei Nechaev and four confederates, remarking: 'for Russian history this murder is no less fateful than, say, the Populists' murder of Tsar Alexander II'.[13] Dostoevskii was to reproduce the murder and even its minute details in *The Devils*. For Trifonov, the murder's lasting significance lies in the character and ideals of Nechaev, its chief perpetrator.

Nechaev was a schoolteacher turned revolutionary who embraced a particularly ruthless usage of political terror to attain his ends. Trifonov notes that he 'charmed' the exiled radicals Bakunin and Ogarev when on the run abroad, getting a large sum of money out of the latter, and attempted to seduce Herzen's daughter. He was eventually caught, extradited from Switzerland in 1872 and sentenced. He spent his remaining years in the Peter and Paul Fortress in St Petersburg. His strength of will made him legendary: he spent two years in chains, and almost persuaded his guards to help him escape. His aims are outlined in his *Catechism of a Revolutionary*, which Trifonov in his article quotes at length: wholesale destruction, for the sake of which all human emotion and feeling are subordinated. 'All that is moral for him is that which furthers the triumph of the revolution.'[14] For Nechaev, a revolutionary is one who denies his own interests, feelings and property, and who devotes himself wholeheartedly to the cause of destruction: 'He knows only one science: destruction.'[15] Nechaev divides the population into certain categories, into which fall people according to their status and position. Some are under sentence of death, others to be used as slaves. But Nechaev refrains from stating what he would replace the existing structures with; all plans and theories for the future he regards as 'fruitless'. His cause is destruction for destruction's sake; terror becomes the end, and not simply the means towards it. Nechaev died in prison in 1882, thirteen years to the day after the murder of Ivanov.

12. Ibid., pp. 39–40.
13. Ibid., p. 41.
14. Ibid., p. 42. There are also extensive quotations from *Catechism of a revolutionary* in *Impatience*; see Trifonov, *Sobranie sochinenii*, vol. 3, 1986, pp. 347–9.
15. Trifonov, *How Our Word Resounds*, p. 42.

David Gillespie

In *The Devils* Nechaev becomes Petr Verkhovenskii, another archi-
tect of terror and murder. Verkhovenskii and his confederate Shigalev
talk of restructuring society by cutting off a hundred million heads, by
encouraging licentiousness of all kinds and the denigration of all moral
authority; in short, by levelling all of society to the lowest common
denominator. However, Dostoevskii portrays Verkhovenskii as both
awkard and even comic, as well as a maniacal, demonic figure. Trifonov
is himself impressed with Dostoevskii's treatment of Verkhovenskii not
only as a pathological prophet of violence, but as a somewhat rounded
and complex character.

The difference Trifonov sees between Nechaev and the Populists is
that the latter did not renounce Christian feelings of kindness, love,
comradeship, and were aghast at the possibility of innocent bystanders'
being caught up with their violence. Nechaev represented to them the
boundary between humanity and inhumanity beyond which they would
not go. In *Impatience* Trifonov brings together Andrei Zheliabov and
Nechaev for a short clandestine meeting (their confrontation is not historically documented) in order to show how far from Nechaev's thought
and methods are the Populists. Yet innocent people are killed by the
Populists, and in Trifonov's novel Zheliabov admits that circumstances
have forced the Populists closer to Nechaev's *Catechism*.

Trifonov is undoubtedly sympathetic towards the Populists, and portrays them in his novel as dedicated and idealistic young people at war
with an antiquated and repressive system of government. They are self-
less and totally dedicated. Indeed, he admits that he could have called
the novel *Selflessness*.[16] He does not condemn outright their acts of murder or terrorism, but merely bemoans the disillusionment of Russia's
bright young hopes and the tragedies of Russian history.[17] Likewise, as
the son of Valentin Trifonov, an Old Bolshevik executed in 1937, he
admires the devotion and selflessness of the generation that brought
about and fought for the October Revolution. In his Moscow stories, and
also in *The Old Man*, Trifonov shows how their idealism is subsequently betrayed and corrupted by their successors. Significantly, in *The Old
Man* Shigontsev, one of the bloodthirsty and pitiless Bolshevik com-
manders, is likened to Nechaev, and even advocates his self-abnegation:
'mankind will perish unless it changes its psychological make-up,
unless it rejects feelings and emotions'.[18]

Trifonov concludes his article with references to modern terrorists
and their methods, such as the mysterious Carlos, the Italian Red

16. 'The Present is an Alloy of History and the Future', in ibid., p. 235.
17. Trifonov writes elsewhere that the Populists he portrays 'were, as a rule, the most
genuine idealists... they had an inherent humanistic consciousness and ethic'. Ibid., p. 345.
18. 'The Old Man', in Trifonov, *Sobranie sochinenii*, vol. 3, 1986, p. 454.

Brigade and the West German Baader-Meinhof group. Trifonov obviously has an eye for the continuities as well as the disruptions of history: he has no doubt that the cataclysm of 1917–21 wrenched Russia away from Western Europe; he also sees similarities between the ruthlessness of those today who will blow up an airliner, with the loss of hundreds of lives, and the calculating coldness of Nechaev/Verkhovenskii. 'Modern terrorism, all those Baader gangs and Red Brigades – they're all Verkhovenskiis and Shigalevs', he writes elsewhere.[19] The 'devils' are still alive and causing havoc. The terrorists today, with unlimited access to millions through the media, have become 'cinema heroes'.

For Trifonov, the world is interconnected through a multitude of links, in this case its experience of terrorism in all its forms. Dostoevskii pointed to this by showing the rationalisation of terror, the denial and suppression of morality in the name of a cause. Furthermore, Dostoevskii's *The Devils* contains the essence of future conflicts in the twentieth century, with rationalists and atheists hellbent on reshaping the world according to their dogma. Trifonov writes that *The Devils* 'has a more contemporary resonance than the works of many contemporary writers', because 'the theme of devils has proved to be unusually disturbing – both dramatic and painful for the world'.[20] The fundamental link that Trifonov makes between the terrorists of now and those of hundred years ago is an internal one, as he states: 'Sooner or later the devil must kill the saint. Initially within himself.'[21] For Trifonov, Dostoevskii's legacy is the truth this insight has bestowed upon the twentieth century.

The purpose of this essay is not to compare the two writers, or suggest that Trifonov's services to Russian literature are commensurate with those of Dostoevskii. Indeed, Trifonov is not interested in characters as such, unlike Dostoevskii, and creates types that are instantly recognisable to Soviet readers. Trifonov is an altogether different writer, working in an entirely different time and under a repressive ideology. Trifonov's works are unlikely to maintain their hold on the world's reading public in a hundred years' time, like those of the great nineteenth-century writer.

Still, it is not enough to say that Trifonov merely pays homage to Dostoevskii in both his fiction and his publicism. Undoubtedly, Trifonov acknowledges the nineteenth-century writer's relevance and importance for an understanding of today's world, but he is also conducting his own dialogue with the great writer. He is, in a way, adapting Dostoevskii for modern usage. Trifonov's significance lies in his depic-

19. 'Writing on the edge of the possible', in *How our Word Resounds*, p. 338.
20. Ibid., p. 337.
21. 'Nechaev, Verkhovenskii and others', ibid., p. 51.

tion of the erosion or destruction of ideals and idealism, be it in modern-day Moscow, the terrible years of the Civil War, or the reign of Tsar Alexander II. However, he also shows how the modern world is moulded by those who, like Nechaev and Verkhovenskii, can impose their will on others, accept suffering for the good of the cause, and cut themselves off from the world of humanity. Thus, there is little essential difference between purveyors of terror, whether they be terrorists protesting against a political order, or men who make a revolution and fight to build a new world.

Zinov´ev on Chekhov

Michael Kirkwood

It is likely that the reader is more familiar with the work of Chekhov than with the work of Zinov´ev. Chekhov's niche in literature is secure, whereas it is still not clear whether what Zinov´ev writes can be called 'literature'. On the one hand he has been ranked with writers such as Apuleius, Rabelais, Sterne, Swift, Saltykov-Shchedrin; one article, written by a distinguished American professor is entitled: 'Zinoviev, Aleshkovsky, Rabelais, Sorrentino, possibly Pynchon, maybe James Joyce, and certainly *Tristram Shandy*: a comparative study of a satirical mode'.[1] On the other hand, most of his works do not easily fit any particular literary genre.

In the case of Zinov´ev, a man whose careers ranged from fighter-bomber pilot to logician and sociologist before his becoming a writer in 1976, a sketch of his life and views on literature may usefully precede a consideration of his attitude to Chekhov.

Aleksandr Aleksandrovich Zinov´ev was born on 29 October 1922 in a village 600 kilometres north-east of Moscow, the sixth of eleven siblings. In common with several Chekhov characters, notably Van´ka, Zinov´ev was sent away from the village to go to school. In Zinov´ev's case the destination was Moscow, where he arrived in 1933 to occupy the space under the window of the damp basement occupied by his father and grandfather, later to be joined by his elder brother and elder brother's wife and child, plus another elder brother, plus a sister. He left school with a gold medal, spent a year on the run after trouble with the authorities, volunteered for military service in October 1940 (he was still too young to be called up), and became a much-decorated fighter-bomber pilot, and after demobilisation, a student of philosophy at Moscow University. By 1974 he was Professor of Logic, specialising in the structure of scientific language, with an international academic

---

1. Edward J. Brown, in *Stanford Slavic Studies*, vol. 1, 1987, pp. 307–25.

reputation. His particular field was 'many-valued logic', a field that was highly mathematical and ideologically suspect.

He himself was ideologically suspect, and in fact his refusal to write in the spirit of Marxism-Leninism together with his inability to mask his view of the nature of Soviet society caused him to be a marked man, so that when he refused to turn down an invitation to become a member of the Finnish Academy of Sciences, measures were taken to dismiss him from his post. An immediate consequence of his dismissal (apart from material hardship) was an abundance of spare time, time which he used to write what for convenience we will term a 'novel', *The Yawning Heights*. On its publication in the West in 1976 this allegorical anatomy of Communist society was hailed by the literary establishment as a sensational – something or other, since it was not clear that it was, in fact, a work of literature. Indeed in many ways it was not a work of literature.

The book won many literary awards and its author became famous overnight. He promptly published another two books, and then, nearly as promptly, another four. The number of books he has written since 1974 is somewhere in the region of thirty. He has also published countless numbers of articles in a wide range of the world's press, recently including that of his native land.

Given that his works are unconventional as regards their literary form, it is not surprising to discover that Zinov´ev's views on such matters as the form and content of literature, the role of the writer in society and the relationship of literature to society are likewise unconventional.

Zinov´ev has expressed his views on literary matters in a series of interviews, articles and chapters in two of his three autobiographies, as well as via the pronouncements of various characters in his works.[2]

On the subject of his own taste in literature he has this to say:

Something kept preventing me from embracing literature wholeheartedly. What it was exactly is difficult to explain. However one reason is plain: my dislike of traditional and accepted literary norms. Of course, I read constantly. But very little of what I read was to my taste. I could not understand how

2. See, for instance, 'O *Ziiaiushchikh vysotakh, Bez illiuzii*, Lausanne, 1979, pp. 7–17; 'O tak nazyvaemoi nauchnoi fantastike', ibid., pp. 19–24; 'O pravdivosti i adekvatnosti literatury', ibid., pp. 115–16; 'God na zapade', ibid., pp. 117–23; 'Zametki o literature', *My i zapad*, Lausanne, 1981, pp. 79–85; 'O kommunizme, zapade, Rossii, literature', ibid., pp. 95–8; 'O *Zheltom dome*', ibid., pp. 99–102; 'Muki tvorchestva', *Zapiski nochnogo storozha*, Lausanne, 1979, pp. 30–1; 'Ob iskusstve', ibid., p. 59; 'Smekhotvornost´ tragedii', *V preddverii raia*, Lausanne, 1979, p. 251; 'O prirode, o fol´klore', *Zheltyi dom*, Lausanne, 1980, vol. 2, pp. 149–50; 'Ispoved´ pisatelia', *Gomo sovetikus*, Lausanne, 1982, p. 127; 'Russkii plach', *Moi dom – moia chuzhbina*, Lausanne, 1982, pp. 104–8; 'Ideologiia i literatura', *Ni svobody ni ravenstva ni bratstva*, Lausanne, 1983, pp. 48–55; *Mon Tchékhov*, Brussels, 1989, pp. 151–81; *Confessions d'un homme en trop*, Paris, 1990, pp. 370–3, 388–9, 438–40.

ordinary people who were not professional literary experts or bureaucrats of some other type in the arts field could be interested in Shakespeare, Dante, Tolstoi, Turgenev, Gor´kii ... I struggled through *The Brothers Karamazov* because it happened to be the only book in a room I had occasion to rent. One of my favourite writers was Knut Hamsun. As a rule I only liked particular books or bits of books. For instance, I only like the historical essay in Tolstoi's *War and Peace*, or the bit out of *Master and Margarita* which relates to Christ and Pilate. As for contemporary Russian literature I give pride of place to Vladimov's *Faithful Ruslan* and Erofeev's *Moskva-Petushki*. As you see, my taste in literature is far from exemplary.[3]

On the subject of the concerns of literature he is no less forthright:

The textbook explanation of what literature is about is quite clear. Literature is supposed to describe Ivan, Petr, Matrena, dogs, butterflies, flowers, etc. It should describe Ivan's eyes, who sleeps with Matrena, how the butterfly flutters and the flower smells.[4]

Nor does he spare the practitioners: 'Nowadays the reader has need of much that professional writers are not capable of providing (for example, a scientific analysis of his everyday life).'[5] On the other hand, the reader is capable of doing much for himself or herself which was formerly the business of the writer:

... new ways and means of reflecting reality (cinema, television, photography, journalism, popular-scientific literature, applied arts) have had an enormous effect on the way people interpret the world. Nowadays even the most average reader is capable of doing for himself what was previously considered the business of professional writers (for example, describing the outward appearance of people and the beauties of nature).[6]

Zinov´ev thus questions the nature and purpose of 'traditional' literature and 'conventional' writers in the context of the modern, complex world. There is here an echo of Trigorin:

I see that life and science are moving on while I fall further and further behind, like a peasant who has missed a train, and in fact I feel that I am only good for describing nature. In every other respect I am a fraud – to the marrow of my bones.[7]

3. *Bez illiuzii*, pp. 9–10.
4. Ibid., p. 10.
5. *My i zapad*, p. 79.
6. Ibid., p. 79
7. Chekhov, A. P., *Polnoe sobranie sochinenii i pisem v 30 tomakh*, 1974–83, Moscow, vol. 13, 1978, pp. 30–1.

In short, 'traditional' literature for Zinov´ev is an inadequate means of depicting the complex phenomena of modern reality. That is a task beyond the competence of 'conventional' writers. There are two criteria by which it is 'useful' to judge contemporary works of literature:

> When evaluating a contemporary work of literature it is useful to distinguish between two concepts which are very closely related and often confused – namely veracity and adequacy. The first of these relates to how truthfully, completely and thoroughly particular facts of life are described in a given work of literature. The second has to do with the question of how far that work corresponds to the spirit of the times, how closely it reflects the mode of thought of that part of the population which most clearly understands what is going on and experiences it most keenly.[8]

Linked with Zinov´ev's views on 'adequacy' in literature is his insistence on its importance as sociology. Zinov´ev describes works such as *The Yawning Heights* and *On the Threshold of Paradise* as 'sociological' novels, in which the science of sociology underlies the 'artistic' (if it may be so described) description of his world. He maintains that this approach has determined the shape of his works, a shape which changes from work to work mainly along the parameter of length. A Zinov´ev work consists of a greater or smaller number of individual texts, each with a title, strung together like links on a chain. The links may vary stylistically (and in his larger works they vary greatly, taking in virtually every known literary genre from poem to pastiche), giving his works (or so Zinov´ev maintains) a 'symphonic' structure, a structure which the reader can only discern if he or she tries to see the links between all 600 texts in, for example, *The Yawning Heights*, or the 824 texts in *The Madhouse*, simultaneously. The structural complexity derives from the sociological complexity of modern society, and just as society is maintained by the daily repetition of countless millions of different actions across the whole spectrum of human activity, the structure of a Zinov´ev work is to be seen as a concatenation of events which happen simultaneously. The linear order imposed by the need to write one word after another is to be subverted by reading the book virtually in any order the reader likes, and as many times as the reader has the stamina for the task.

On the other hand, although a scientific awareness of contemporary reality is an essential prerequisite for a writer of contemporary literature, a scientific description of contemporary reality is itself deficient in important respects. First, scientific progress is rarely to be achieved by an individual. In the modern age scientific discovery is much more often

8. *Bez illiuzii*, pp. 115–16.

a matter of teamwork. Secondly, much of importance falls outside the scientific domain and cannot be treated according to scientific principles. Progress can be made, however, if the principles of literature and science are combined.[9] Zinov´ev's training as a scientist allows him to imagine events and scenes which are logically possible, using the laws of probability as a stimulus to inspiration. These situations can be presented in (quasi-)artistic form and reveal something important about the nature of Communist society. Such situations are not scientifically acceptable, since they are imagined, but are artistically 'adequate', since they have their origin in scientific inspiration. Science thus enhances literature and vice versa.

Zinov´ev's creative work is thus a product of the marriage of science and art. But the world Zinov´ev describes is an abstract one of the laws which underlie human, social behaviour, the laws of logic and anti-logic, the effects of the dialectic. It is an ephemeral, complex world, the external trappings of which reduce to a few barren urban settings (most typically a derelict building site) and human beings who, at the depth of focus employed by Zinov´ev, are important only as tokens, not as individuals, and who, therefore, bear either the same name (for example Iban Ibanovich Ibanov in *The Yawning Heights)*, or a label denoting a social status such as Teacher, Party Member, Sociologist, Poet, etc. The settings and people are unimportant, for what Zinov´ev does, with the economy of the skilled cartoonist (he has drawn thousands of cartoons in the course of his life for a variety of wall and army newspapers), is depict a pitiless, barren, man-induced wilderness in which the protagonists are the immutable laws underlying human behaviour:

> I decided to make the laws of existence themselves the characters of my book and to depict them not as those mystical, noble, sometimes cruel, sometimes good, sometimes terrible, but always outstanding creatures as depicted by the official ideology and so-called social science, but as the usual miserable nonentities which they undoubtedly are.[10]

Caricature as an artistic device is not used by Zinov´ev gratuitously. An aesthetic problem to which he devotes much thought concerns the concept of 'Communist art', defined not as an ideological means of depicting reality (for example Socialist Realism) but as an artistically adequate means of depicting the reality of Communism.[11] Here it should be remembered that, for Zinov´ev, Soviet reality was, in the organisational sense, literally Communism in practice. What is required for the

9. See, for instance, 'O tak nazyvaemoi nauchnoi fantastike', ibid., pp. 19–24.
10. Ibid., p. 11.
11. See, for example, Chatterer's 'notes' on the subject of Communist art in *Ziiaiushchie vysoty*.

artistic interpretation of Communist reality is a 'grammar' which allows
one to gain a sufficiently 'adequate' perception of the nature of that
society. As the narrator in *Notes of a Nightwatchman* puts it:

> Have a go, for example, at depicting within the parameters of conventional
> poetry a meeting, an office, a queue, informers, etc. The result will be boring
> and false. An accurate description has to be laconic, grotesque, an apparent
> caricature. But not a caricature of something good. Rather, a good portrait of
> grotesque reality.[12]

Caricature, therefore, is a realistic way of depicting Communist reality.
Conventional ways of analysing that society (whether in the field of science or art) will of necessity produce a warped picture.

These remarks on Zinov´ev's view of literature, while not exhaustive
of his literary philosophy, are sufficient for a consideration of his
approach to Chekhov.

Zinov´ev writing about Chekhov reveals more about Zinov´ev than
Chekhov. Certainly he denies any intention of contributing to what he
calls 'Chekhovology'. The main repository of his thoughts on Chekhov
is his book on the writer, available to date only in French. Of the issues
raised by the book, we shall be examining in particular his claim to be
the sole inheritor in Russian letters of Chekhov's mantle – a claim
which, however fantastic it might at first appear, is not totally without
foundation.

We should begin by noting Zinov´ev's early interest in Chekhov. His
situation as a child was not unlike Van´ka's, and his first literary effort
was apparently a semi-autobiographical, Soviet version of Van´ka
which was highly praised, yet regarded as slightly suspect.[13] He was
also from an early age aware that he was living in the future which so
many of Chekhov's characters talk about or yearn for, a future which
differed somewhat from their imagined one, to put it mildly, although it
was arguably not so different from Chekhov's own view of it.

Zinov´ev's early interest was not, then, aesthetic. Rather it grew out
of his own experience. Chekhov wrote about Zinov´ev's own 'class',
about peasant life shorn of its Tolstoyian romanticism, about poverty
and misery, about life in damp, overcrowded basements, about Russian
servility and an over-developed respect for authority, about a life, in
short, which the October Revolution was supposed to sweep away. Yet
here was the young Zinov´ev, sharp-witted and underprivileged, experi-
encing with his whole being precisely the sort of pre-Revolutionary sit-

12. *Zapiski nochnogo storozha*, Lausanne, 1979, p. 59.
13. 'Alexander Zinoviev', *Contemporary Author Autobiography Series*, vol. 10,
Detroit, 1989, p. 324.

uation that officially no longer obtained. Moreover, Chekhov's work was infused by a type of humour very close to Zinov'ev's own. This is particularly true of Chekhov's early tales, but it is precisely tales like 'The Death of a Civil Servant', 'The Mask, 'Surgery', 'Triumph of the Victor', 'The Malefactor' that Zinov'ev as a boy particularly enjoyed.

Chekhov has continued to figure in Zinov'ev's (short) list of favourite writers; but not surprisingly, the reasons changed and developed as Zinov'ev himself grew older and more experienced. Zinov'ev's appreciation of Chekhov derives from his view that Chekhov in his writing captured many of the features of pre-Revolutionary Russian life which were of major sociological importance. Chekhov, for Zinov'ev, is both writer and sociologist, but more the former than the latter: 'Bien que l'on puisse inscrire Tchékhov dans la catégorie du réalisme sociologique, c'était un écrivain plutôt qu'un sociologue.'[14]

Zinov'ev, of course, is arguably more sociologist than writer, but Chekhov, from Zinov'ev's point of view as an analyst of Soviet society, is of great importance, and his relevance for an understanding of the Soviet Union is one of two aspects on which Zinov'ev concentrates. The other aspect concerns the links which Zinov'ev perceives between his own work and Chekhov's.

Zinov'ev explicitly deals with the first point in two sections of *Mon Tchékhov,* namely the sections entitled 'Tchékhov en Russie soviétique' and 'L'Héritage de l'histoire'.[15]

According to Zinov'ev, Chekhov's importance in the milieu of post-Revolutionary Russian culture is hard to overestimate. In the context of Soviet ideology his work, although not written from a Marxist perspective, was nonetheless of inestimable value as a description of pre-Revolutionary tsarism, feudalism and capitalism. Zinov'ev argues that, although writers like Zoshchenko, Olesha and Il'f and Petrov wrote in the manner of Chekhov, the people they described and their milieu were presented as belonging to the past. No one seemed to have realised (says Zinov'ev) that a Chekhovian approach was absolutely perfect for the post-Revolutionary period, during which the foundations of future Soviet society were being laid – by people who were the prototypes of the future, not merely representatives of the past. Everywhere one could meet Sergeant Prishibeev, or a Chameleon, or Man in a Case, and these were not a dying breed, but, if anything, a growing one. So Chekhov was a double-edged weapon in the armoury of the ideologist. On the one hand, Chekhov was useful as a critic of tsarist Russia. On the other, his types provided the Soviet citizenry with a handy means of recognising

14. *Mon Tchékhov,* p. 73.
15. Ibid., pp. 13–16, 46–51.

their Soviet equivalents, and therefore with a means of sharpening their critical awareness of the defects of the new system.

But not only was Chekhov a double-edged weapon as regards his human types, which were supposed to give way to the 'new Soviet Man'; the themes and problems with which he dealt in his work were destined to become, in the Soviet context, 'fundamental'. They include abstract themes such as 'the future', 'work', 'the meaning of life', as well as the more specific ones such as the growth of bureaucracy and the despoliation of the environment. Some of these will be considered later in this essay.

It is Chekhov's plays which are of primary importance for Zinov'ev, seen from the point of view of their 'sociological realism', to use Zinov'ev's own borrowing from the lexicon of historical literary criticism.

Zinov'ev emphasises the distinction between 'external action' ('action extérieure') and 'internal action' ('action intérieure') in relation to drama, quoting as an exponent of the former Aleksandr Ostrovskii, and of the latter, Anton Chekhov. Zinov'ev means by 'external action' the events and actions actually depicted on the stage, the latter motivated, explained or organised by what the characters themselves say. In the case of Chekhov the position is reversed. Action in the 'external' sense is subordinated to the working of intelligence: 'Chez Tchékhov ... ce qui fait évènement et spectacle est subordonné au travail de l'intelligence et à la discussion.'[16]

We have here rather an interesting parallel with Zinov'ev's view of history and his distinction between the external event and the unseen process, the former being regarded by him as 'froth', the latter as the underlying, deep current of the historical process. What, for Zinov'ev, is important in a Chekhov play is not that problems are solved (they are not), not that a 'slice of life' is shown, but that problems are discussed without answers being found, that life is realistically presented as an intelligent exploration of its complexity. Even a cursory examination of Zinov'ev's work will reveal that his characters are just as Chekhovian as Chekhov's in their ability to sit around and discuss the meaning of life endlessly, the difference being mainly that Chekhov's characters do their discussing in the genteel surroundings of the landed gentry, whereas Zinov'ev's tend to do theirs sitting in rubbish dumps or lying under a fence.

One aspect of Chekhov's world to which Zinov'ev draws special attention is that of the petty bureaucrat in the context of a growing bureaucracy:

16. Ibid., p. 62.

Ce qui me semble particulièrement important dans son œuvre, c'est la déscription de la tendance à la bureaucratisation de l'ensemble de la société russe, à la transformation d'une masse de gens, que l'on ne peut pas considérer formellement comme des fonctionnaires, en des êtres façonées à l'image de ceux-ci.[17]

But Chekhov does more than just describe this tendency in quantitative terms. He explores the relations between bureaucrats, and demonstrates how a petty bureaucrat can be a tyrant one day and servile the next, depending on the circumstances. In general Zinov'ev believes that Chekhov is unequalled in Russian literature in his ability to show how the social position of an individual determines all the other aspects of that individual's life.

Zinov'ev has some interesting things to say about Chekhov in relation to Russian attitudes to liberty and enserfment. Whereas the concept of Russian servility can be traced back to at least Lermontov via Chernyshevskii according to Zinov'ev, Chekhov by contrast sensed that there was a voluntary aspect to it which continued to exist after the emancipation of the serfs in 1861 and which did not disappear after the October Revolution. Chekhov's Sergeant Prishibeev and Belikov fulfil the role of what we might call servile activists. That is, they both voluntarily engage in activity designed to deprive them of liberty 'in case anything untoward were to happen' ('kak by chego ne vyshlo') in Belikov's famous phrase.

Zinov'ev notes that Soviet critics accuse Chekhov of having failed to discern the latent readiness in the Russian people to throw off their chains by way of revolution, but goes on to observe that Chekhov discerned something else – namely that at the level of society to which he penetrated, freedom was no longer a political question, but a sociological one. In other words, the question arises as to why millions of people accept their lack of freedom. Zinov'ev's view is that subjugation by force may work in relation to a small population for a limited period but cannot be the explanation why generation after generation accepts a situation of domination. The question of why people are oppressed is replaced by the question of why people prefer to be oppressed.

The voluntary nature of oppression, already detected by Chekhov, was intensified after the Revolution as a consequence of the proliferation of the Soviet politico-administrative system. Many more people than before the Revolution became participants in the administration of power. The distribution of power, like the distribution of goods and services, was related to one's social position. Soviet enserfment is of a particular type in which submission on the part of the individual is compensated for by that individual's exercise of authority over those

17. Ibid., p. 77.

around him. Thus an *ersatz* liberty is offered: not the aspiration to be free, but the aspiration to deprive another of his or her desire for liberty.

One stratum of the population which is of particular interest to Zinov´ev is the intelligentsia and it is not surprising, therefore, that he pays particular attention to Chekhov's treatment of it. According to Zinov´ev, Chekhov regarded it from two points of view, firstly as a social group alongside bureaucrats, landowners, workers, peasants, etc., but secondly as a group of people whose function was to permit society to know itself, to think about the situation in the country, to pose questions and seek answers. These two aspects were fused together, of course, and Zinov´ev considers that the main theme in Chekhov's work of his mature period was the examination of socio-political problems in the form in which they were expressed in the thoughts, feelings and conduct of the intelligentsia, considered, not as the conscience of society, but as the consciousness of society, that is, as its ego.

For Zinov´ev 'the intelligentsia' is a diffuse concept in the Soviet context. On the one hand its membership comprises a highly disparate range of professions and on the other the social hierarchy within any one profession is so vast that in real terms people belong to social categories which are so diverse as to remove any usefulness from the term 'intelligentsia'. In Chekhov's time this process of diversification was just beginning. As Chekhov showed, however, the intelligentsia even then was a milieu in which hypocrisy, selfishness, cynicism, fatuity and self-deception flourished. Chekhov's heroes apart, there were not all that many representatives of the intelligentsia of the time who thought that 'we can't go on living like this', that they should serve the people, or work for the common good and for the benefit of future generations.

We should remember, of course, that the Soviet intelligentsia is Zinov´ev's *bête noire*, and that he regards himself as an honourable exception. Chekhov, too, is granted that status. Zinov´ev's discussion of Chekhov's treatment of the intelligentsia is clearly aimed at establishing a link not only between the intelligentsia of Chekhov's time and the Soviet intelligentsia, but also between Chekhov and Zinov´ev *qua* writers.

A theme which recurs constantly in the work of Chekhov is the future and how it is perceived by his characters. Actually Zinov´ev is unimpressed by Chekhov's treatment of this theme:

> Bien-sûr ses personnages se prononcent sur le futur et ils en rêvent. Leurs commentaires sont assez discordant, parfois nettement opposés. D'autre part il est difficile de faire la part entre ce qu'ils affirment avec certitude et ce qui ressort de leurs simples désirs. Aussi est-il impossible de tirer de leurs propos une conception plus ou moins déterminées de l'avenir de Russie.[18]

18. Ibid., pp. 119–20.

Here Zinov´ev seems to be arguing against himself. Earlier (see p. 176) he praised Chekhov for his ability to represent reality as the discussion of problems without the necessary discovery of solutions. What could be more problematic than a discussion of the future? Also, does Zinov´ev really believe that Chekhov offered a range of 'alternative futures', so to speak, merely because he himself was not sure precisely what the future would look like? After all, he has made whole armies of his characters discuss the future, no two visions of which are identical.

Zinov´ev does not retract his criticism of Chekhov but implicitly tones it down by saying that: 'Le thème de l'avenir n'est chez lui qu'un prétexte pour parler du présent.'[19] He then goes on to note that he, too, in his own works treats the theme of the future 'à la manière de Tchékhov', yet again forging a link between Chekhov and himself.

If Zinov´ev accuses Chekhov of ducking the issue of what the future of Russia was going to be, he suspects that Chekhov may actually have believed in the virtue of working for the good of others, notably future generations. Certainly he acknowledges that many of Chekhov's characters so believe, but just in case Chekhov himself might have believed it, Zinov´ev states categorically: 'Le slogan de vivre pour les générations à venir est une illusion et une tromperie de ceux qui vivent actuellement.'[20]

On balance, however, Zinov´ev would probably agree that Chekhov's characters discuss the future and the virtue, indeed the therapeutic value, of work as a means of escape from the present and from their awareness of the excruciating boredom, emptiness and futility of their lives. Here again there is a clear parallel with his own work. His own characters, living in the future as predicted by, for example, Korolev in 'A Practical Example', feel just as frustrated, bored, useless and unhappy as Chekhov's did fifty or seventy years before. Just as Zinov´ev has created a whole range of stereotypes which parallel those which appear in Chekhov's early tales, he has another set which parallel the 'superfluous people' that populate Chekhov's world of genteel irrelevance. The great tragedy is that, whereas Chekhov's educated, genteel young ladies and gentlemen are linked with Russia's past, representing the bottom end, as it were, of the privileged castes whose income did not derive from their labour, Zinov´ev's characters feel equally useless in a world in which to be unemployed is illegal.

A discussion of the futility of life and the irrelevance of labour or work as a source of happiness leads naturally to a discussion of the meaning of life itself. Here Zinov´ev is clear and unambiguous: the meaning of life is rebellion – rebellion, if necessary, against the universe.

19. Ibid., p. 124.
20. Ibid., p. 121.

It is interesting to read his reaction to *Uncle Vania*. He quotes Sonia's advice to her uncle that they should labour selflessly for the rest of their lives in the service of others, without hope of reward, save for peace in the next world, and then says: '*L'Oncle Vania* (et, partiellement, ses autres pièces) n'a pas seulement éveillé en moi la révolte, mais aussi la fureur.'[21]

One can well imagine Zinov´ev's rage at the submissiveness of people like Sonia. Zinov´ev is constitutionally absolutely incapable of accepting the meek submission of an individual to his or her fate. His whole biography is a history of rebellion, of going his own way, of speaking his mind. Sonia and he could not be further apart. Zinov´ev's solution, both in real life and in his books, has been to work out an ideological and psychological self-defence mechanism for use by citizens in the Soviet leviathan who are powerless to effect any change in the social order. A description of it is to be found in such works as *Go to Golgotha*, *Live!*, and (at inordinate length) in *Confessions d'un homme en trop*. It includes such commandments as 'do not turn the other cheek'.

The Chekhov work in Zinov´ev's treatise to which he refers more than to any other is 'Ward No. 6'. This is not surprising. First, the theme of the institution for the mentally disadvantaged is a major one in Zinov´ev's own work. There is, for example, *On the Threshold of Paradise*, or his two-volume *The Madhouse*, the chief protagonist of which actually works with mental patients (as did Zinov´ev himself in his days as a junior research fellow at the Institute of Philosophy in Moscow). Secondly, there is the whole question in the Soviet context of psychiatry as punishment and infringement of liberty. Thirdly, there is the question of how madness, or mental illness, generally, is to be defined. Yet another link between Chekhov and Zinov´ev is thus established.

A discussion of the clinical aspects of mental illness is, of course, beyond the scope of this essay. However, the aspect which Zinov´ev emphasises is the socio-political, rather than the medical definition of 'normality'. That is to say, it is perfectly possible to argue that the discrepancy between Chekhov's moral view of how the world ought to be and how he saw it in reality allows him to represent 'normal Russia' in the microcosm of Ward No. 6. In the Soviet context, argues Zinov´ev, morally upright behaviour, including criticism and the exercise of the right to free speech can be, almost literally, described as a pathological condition.

21. Ibid., p. 133.

Zinov´ev himself goes one further than Chekhov in his own description of a mental hospital in Partgrad, the provincial Russian town undergoing *perestroika* as described in Zinov´ev's novella *Katastroika*:

A new type of mental patient, of specifically *perestroika* bent, began to arrive at the hospital. They were the Gorbachevs, El´tsins, Sakharovs, Solzhenitsyns, Trotskiis, Bukharins, Tukhachevskiis, Vlasovs, Nikolais, Anastasias, Stolypins and other impersonators of individuals who were formerly held to be exploiters, reactionaries, enemies of the people, traitors, and who are now incorporated into the ranks of the innocent victims of the Stalin terror, ideological opponents of Stalinism and geniuses who anticipated Gorbachev´s *perestroika* ... [They] began to demand the privatisation of all the means of production, liquidation of the party and the KGB, opening the borders, disbanding the army, dividing the country into a plethora of independent states and much more that even the most enthusiastic supporters of *perestroika* and Westerners did not want ...

It was these *perestroika* nutcases and enthusiasts who brought news of *perestroika* to the psychiatric hospital. Things began to happen which, in Krutov's words, you wouldn't find going on in a madhouse. The new-style nutcases demanded self-government, the non-interference of doctors in the healing process and the transfer of the hospital to a system of self-cure (by analogy with self-financing) and the freedom to go round the bend as an inalienable human right. Old-style nutcases declared all this to be counter-revolutionary and demanded the transfer of the hospital onto a war-time footing. They began to be released. The streets of the town filled up with Napoleons, Lenins, Stalins, Robespierres, Khomeinis, Mao-tse-Tungs, Dzerzhinskiis, Hitlers, Mussolinis and other representatives of a bygone era. They created havoc wherever they went, purloined everything in sight and put on such a performance that many citizens began to seek entrance to the hospital where, according to rumour, genuine democracy had begun to reign.[22]

This is an appropriate point at which to examine Zinov´ev's attitude towards 'objectivity' in literature. His main thesis (which again links his own work with Chekhov's) is that there exists a certain type of reality that can only be described 'objectively' via humour and satire. As he says himself:

Il faut distinguer l'humeur et la satire en tant que moyens littéraires destinés à provoquer le rire du lecteur et, d'autre part, en tant que moyens de connaissance et d'exposition destinés à réfléter l'essence objective des phénomènes de la vie. Tchékhov était un humoriste dans cette seconde acceptation.[23]

22. *Katastroika. Povest´ o perestroike v Partgrade*, Lausanne, 1990, pp. 115–16.
23. *Mon Tchékhov*, p. 153.

Here, of course, he is referring to the later Chekhov. Zinov´ev states uncontroversially that Chekhov's humour in his early work is aimed chiefly at diverting the reader, but that he soon elevates it to the status of what Zinov´ev calls 'cognitive humour' and 'sociological satire'. At this point it ceases to be amusing. The works of Gogol´ and Saltykov-Shchedrin provoke an intellectual type of laughter and must be judged by aesthetic criteria. The same is true of Chekhov's work. There is perhaps nothing particularly novel in Zinov´ev's observations. Whether Chekhov's plays are comedies or not is one of the oldest questions in 'Chekhovology'. On the other hand, the idea that satire and humour are the most objective ways of describing a certain type of reality seem new. With regard to his own work, he states that he tried out every literary means at his disposal (which is incontrovertibly true) and became convinced that a non-satirical description of Soviet reality would be anodyne, false, or biased in its favour. Anecdotes, he argues, give a much more objective description of Soviet reality than 'hundreds of tons of official literature', including the production of officially sanctioned 'critics' like Evtushenko, Voznesenskii and Aitmatov. In this sense, the work of Venedikt Erofeev, Galich and Vysotskii represents the acme of objectivity in 'la poésie'.

Another question which interests Zinov´ev is Chekhov's attitude to happiness. Zinov´ev's view is that Chekhov's formula for happiness is the belief that things could be even worse than they are, a formula which has even more relevance in Soviet circumstances. Chekhov's view of Russia's destiny was that of a patient with an incurable disease, and that his attitude was that of doctor to patient. Zinov´ev's point is that Chekhov demonstrated in his work his awareness that the root of all evil lay in the social relations which obtained in the Russia of his time. The crucial moral question, however, is this: since the laws governing the social behaviour of large groups are immutable, how is man to resist them, given that the behaviour they engender does not correspond to our moral ideas of 'goodness', 'happiness' and 'equality'? For Chekhov that was an impasse, according to Zinov´ev. How could he reconcile the contradiction between reality and moral ideals? Either by making reality conform to the ideal or by renouncing the ideal. Chekhov, deep down, feared to resolve the contradiction in that manner, whence, according to Zinov´ev, his nostalgic yearning for the ideal and his despair as regards the future. His attitude, thus, was more that of the doctor who feels a sense of helplessness in the presence of a dying patient than that of the priest who has faith in the life beyond.

This brief analysis of Zinov´ev's views on Chekhov has established a number of links between the two writers, links which Zinov´ev himself was eager to reveal. We shall review these briefly and evaluate Zinov´ev's claim to be Chekhov's successor in Russian letters.

At first sight comparison seems ridiculous. Some of Zinov´ev's works run to 700 pages. Chekhov's longest prose work (excluding *Sakhalin Island*) is 'Steppe', containing some eighty pages or so. Zinov´ev's works are, however, concatenations of short texts with titles, and in this respect they are comparable with Chekhov's. Indeed, Chekhov's tales are probably, on average, longer than the average length of an individual Zinov´ev text.

Closer inspection reveals that there are affinities between Chekhov's early tales and Zinov´ev's anecdotes and episodes. It might be amusing, for instance, to compare Chekhov's 'Eclipse of the Moon' with Zinov´ev's Soviet equivalent 'In the Light of the Eclipse'. Both writers have a similar, well-developed sense of humour. For every Chekhovian 'official', 'chameleon' and 'Sergeant Prishibeev' one can find a Zinov´evan 'careerist', 'bloke-on-the-make' or 'pensioner'.

In terms of their world-view they are not dissimilar. Chekhov's exploration of pre-Revolutionary Russian society has its counterpart in Zinov´ev's exploration of post-Revolutionary Soviet society. The former is the embryo of the latter. Both writers display their characters as living their lives out in a hopeless quest for solutions to life's great problems, without finding them. Neither writer is prepared to provide them. Their attitude to God and the world beyond the grave is similar. Neither exists, alas. Life exists only on this earth and man has a duty to live it like a human being.

Let us, however, not exaggerate the similarities between the two writers. Chekhov, as Zinov´ev notes, is more writer than sociologist. Zinov´ev is probably more sociologist than writer. The area of overlap is the short *rasskaz* or anecdote. In Chekhov's case his early tales are the outcome of his apprenticeship as a writer of *belles lettres*. In Zinov´ev's case, they interweave with his more serious socio-political writing. Their concerns only partly interconnect. Chekhov's works fall securely within the parameters of 'conventional literature'. Zinov´ev's do not. To that extent, attempts to compare their works are exposed to the danger of appearing to compare literary apples with sociological oranges.

Zinov´ev, as he admits himself, is interested in Chekhov primarily as a sociologist. His appreciation of Chekhov's humour apart, he has little, if anything, to say about Chekhov's aesthetics. By emphasising the sociological aspect of Chekhov's work, Zinov´ev underscores what the two writers have in common. By neglecting the aesthetic aspect, he automatically excludes comparison in conventional literary-critical terms. His claim to inherit Chekhov's mantle, however, although based on what he claims to be their respective contributions to the sociology of Russia, also rests at least partly on strictly literary criteria:

Dans le livre *Les Vivants*, que j'écrivis en 1982, mais qui est resté inédit jusqu'à présent pour toute une série de raisons,[24] mes personnages se heurtent au problème de la vie en tant que problème de l'auto-défence idéologique et psychologique dans des conditions où ils sont impuissants à transformer l'ordre social. Ils me semblent être, de ce point de vue, les héritiers des personnages tchékhoviens.[25]

Finally we should say a few words about the subtext of Zinov´ev's analysis of Chekhov. We might, for instance, wonder why it was not until 1989 that Zinov´ev published a book on an author who has fascinated him since his childhood. Probably the answer is that he had too many other things to do. On the other hand, one might argue that the timing of its publication is in tune with the process of 'revisionism' which Zinov´ev embarked upon some time after the rise of Gorbachev to a position of supreme power.

Before the advent of *glasnost´*, *perestroika*, the dismantling of old, monolithic structures and the construction of new, arguably pluralistic institutions, Zinov´ev's model of Communism stressed its stability, a stability which derived from an all-pervasive politico-administrative system, legitimised by an equally all-pervasive ideology which created a kind of force-field, within which the Soviet citizenry was trapped and by which its thought processes and behaviour were constantly influenced. Moreover, in his early work Zinov´ev was wont to stress that the Communist system arose largely out of the ruins of the collapse of the old order and that the structures which developed owed little to Stalin and a lot to the need to administer a large population in a large territory in a context in which the State, having taken everything into 'public ownership', had become responsible for everything.

Since 1986, however, we notice a gradual process of readjustment. Whereas he had never paid any attention to national issues before, asserting that Communism was a social system which made national issues irrelevant,[26] he now asserts that Communism was never likely to be as successful in the Baltic states as in the rest of the Soviet Union, for historical reasons.[27] Likewise he increasingly notes the influence of Russia's past on the formation of the Soviet state in the 1920s and

24. It was, in fact, published in the same year as *Mon Tchékhov: Zhivi!*, Lausanne, 1989.

25. *Mon Tchékhov*, p. 135.

26. For instance, in his major work of theory (*Kommunizm kak real´nost´*, Lausanne, 1981), he devotes less than one half-page to a discussion of the 'national question', noting that (p. 163): 'as Soviet experience shows, the Communist system handles nationality issues successfully'.

27. *Il Superpotere in URSS*, Milan, 1990, p. 21; *Perestroïka et contre-perestroïka*, Paris, 1991, p. 17.

1930s, an influence he had played down in the past. Russian history and Russian culture are recognised as having played an important role in the development of Soviet institutions.[28] In this context, therefore, Zinov´ev's book on Chekhov, with its emphasis on the links not only between Zinov´ev and Chekhov but equally between the world of Chekhov and post-Revolutionary Russia, can be seen as part of this process of readjustment.

28. *Il Superpotere in URSS*, pp. 20–2; *Perestroïka et contre-perestroïka*, pp. 17–21.

Index

Academy of Sciences
in St Petersburg, 2, 5
Acmeism, 64–5
Acmeist, 78, 88, 88–30, 88–31
see also Akhmatova, A.
Adamovich, Georgii, 91–2, 94
aesthetics, 31
debate over, xv, 15–17, 19, 21
see also Fet, A.
Gumilev and Ivanov on, 52–1
Aizlewood, Robin, xv
Akhmatova, Anna, xiii, 70, 75–9, 146
Amedeo Modigliani, 110, 116
Brodsky and, 139–47 *passim*, 151
death of, 111
Evening, 76
Gumilev and, ix, 53–4, 64
'Komarovskie nabroski', 110–116
passim
Mandel'shtam, Pasternak, Tsvetaeva
and, 99–116 *passim*
'Nas chetvero', 105, 116
on Mandel'shtam, 102, 107, 114–15
on Pasternak, 102, 113
on Tsvetaeva, 100–4, 120
Pages from a Diary, 110, 114–16
Poem without a Hero, 100–11 *passim*,
115–16
Requiem, 102, 107
The Rosary, 76
see also Parnok, S., Tsvetaeva, M.
America(n), 71, 119, 131–2, 145, 151
Annenkov, Pavel, 15–16
Apollo, 14, 25, 97
Apollon, 54–5, 60, 65
art
social relevance, 20, 28–30
Auden, Wystan Hugh, 119, 145
Austen, Jane, 67–1, 69
d'Auteroche, Chappe
Voyage en Sibérie, 12
autobiography, x, 32, 43, 73, 170
autobiographical, 81, 110, 174

Baader-Meinhof, 167

Bakhtin, Mikhail, 44
Bakunin, Mikhail, 165
Bakunina, Ekaterina, 71
Bal'mont, Konstantin, 83, 89
Baltic states, 184
Barash, Mikhail, 148, 150
Barney, Natalie, 71
Baroque, 143, 150
Barthes, Roland, xv
Bashkirtseva, Mariia, 70
Baudelaire, Charles-Pierre, 32
Beckett, Samuel, 126
Beethoven, Ludwig van, 20–16
Belinskii, Vissarion, 17, 67
Berdiaev, Nikolai, 64
Berlin, 131
Bethea, David, 144–5
Blok, Aleksandr, 56, 64, 76, 83, 86–23,
88–30
Bloom, Harold, xv
Boileau, Nicolas, 6–8
Bolshevik, 166
Botkin, Vasilii, 16, 18
Boyd, Brian, 132–3
Boym, Svetlana, 84–11, 90
Brentano, Bettina, 71
Brezhnev, Leonid, 161
Briusov, Valerii, xiii, 60, 64–33, 70–1,
78, 83
Gumilev and, 52, 54, 54–9, 56
see also Symbolism, Tsvetaeva, M.
Brodsky, Joseph
A Part of Speech, 148
'Catastrophes in the Air', 123
Less Than One, 119, 146
myth of, xvi, 139–53
Nobel Prize, 142, 146, 153
on Tsvetaeva, 97, 117–30
'Preface', in *Modern Russian Poets on
Poetry*, xv, 25
Stikhotvoreniia i poemy, 140
'The Poet and Prose', 118, 120, 123
see also Dostoevskii, F., Krivulin, V.,
Kushner, A.,
Sedakova, O.

Brontë, Charlotte, 69
Buhks, Nora, xi
Bukhshtab, B. Ia., 18
Bulgakov, Mikhail
    Master and Margarita, 171
Bunin, Ivan, 162
Buslaev, Peter, 13
Byron, George Gordon
    Pushkin and, ix

Calvinism, 123
Camus, Albert, 49
capitalism, xivn 6, 175
    see also Lukács, G.
Catherine the Great, 14
censorship, 28, 48
    censors, 118
Chekhov, Anton, 162
    'A Dreary Story', 32, 41–5 *passim*
    Chekhovian hero(es), 42, 45, 47, 178
    death of, 40,
    In the Twilight, 27
    Ivanov, 41–5 *passim*
    Merezhkovskii and, xii, xvi, 27–37
    Shestov on, xvi, 39–50
    Stories, 27
    'The Betrothed', 42
    'The Black Monk', 41, 46
    'The Duel', 41–2, 45
    'The Lady with the Pet Dog', 42
    'The Name-Day Party', 31
    The Reed Pipe, 37
    The Seagull, 39, 42, 46
    'The Steppe', 29, 34, 183
    'The Teacher of Literature', 45
    The Wood Demon, 31
    Three Sisters, 37
    Uncle Vania, 39, 41, 46, 180
    'Ward No. 6', 41, 45, 180
    Zinov'ev and, xiii
        see also Zinov'ev, A.
    see also Kuz'min, V., Meister, C.,
        Pleshcheev, A.,
        Severnyi vestnik, Suvorin, A.
Chernyshevskii, Nikolai, 22, 177
    *The Aesthetic Relations of Art to
        Reality*, 15
Chulkov, Mikhail, 4
Chukovskii, Kornei, 67
Churilin, T., 83
Civil War, 162, 168
Cixous, Hélène, xv, 85–18
Coleridge, Samuel Taylor, 119
Communism, 184
    Communist, 170, 173–4
Cossacks, Don, 162

creative process, xiv–v, 51
    critics and, 18–19, 21
        see also Fet, A.
    reader and, 92
critic(s)
    poet and, 19, 21, 77, 81, 93, 95, 97
        see also poet
    utilitarian, 94
    women writers as, 67–79
    writer and, xiv–v, 17, 20, 51, 63, 94
        see also Fet, A., Gumilev, N.
    writer as, ix–xvi *passim*, 17
    see also Grigor'ev, A., Soviet,
        Tsvetaeva, M.
criticism, x–xiii
    gender identity, xiv
    genre of, 74, 90
    ideological, 51
    prose-poetry as, xv
    of critics, 82, 93, 97
    relation to creativity, xiv–v
    see also émigré

Dante, Alighieri, xiii, 105, 115, 120–1, 171
    Dantesque, 104
    The Divine Comedy, 115
Davidson, Pamela, xii
Derrida, Jacques, xv
Diagilev, Serge, 36, 39
Dobroliubov, Nikolai, 17, 22
    Fet and, 15–2
    'What is Oblomovism?', 15
Dostoevskii, Fedor, xiii–xiv, 17, 36, 69,
        91–44, 96
    Brodsky on, 123
    Crime and Punishment, 44, 135, 137, 163
    death of, xi
    demystification of, 137
    Merezhkovskii and, 32, 35
    Mikhailovskii on, 47
    Notes from Underground, 44, 47–16
    Shestov and, 43, 48
    Tolstoi and, ix
    The Brothers Karamazov, 137, 171
    The Devils, 164–7
    The Double, 135
    The Gambler, 136
    The Possessed, 137
    see also Nabokov, V., Trifonov, I.
Druzhinin, Aleksandr
    Fet and, 16

Eagleton, Terry, xiv–6, xvi
East, the
    Eastern verse, 62
écriture féminine, 85

Efron, Sergei, 120
Elagin, Ivan, 13
  *Epistle from Mr Elagin to Mr
    Sumarokov*, 7–9
elegy, 119–20
Eliot, George, 69
Eliot, Thomas Stearns, xii
  'The Function of Criticism', xiv
emigration, x, 150
  Nabokov and, xiii
  Tsvetaeva and, 107
  Russian, 72, 121
émigré(s), xiin4, 83, 93, 131–2, 145
  criticism and critics, 82, 134, 134–9
  Paris, 83–5, 118
England, 107–6, 128
  English
    language, 142
    poetry, 150–2
    poet(s), 123–4
    women, 68–9
enjambment, 122
epic poem/poet, 34, 96
Erofeev, Venedikt, 171, 182
Esenin, Sergei, 83, 141
Europe, 62, 134, 150, 152, 167
  literature, 40
Evtushenko, Evgenii, 147, 182
existentialism, 49, 144
  existential(ist), 39, 42, 125–6, 141
  see also Shestov, L.
experimentation
  with style, 3
  experimental novel, 35

feminine, the, 71
  body, 84
  creativity, 78
  language, 84–9 *passim*
  personality, 70
  see also gender, identity
femininity, 72, 75, 78, 85
feminist
  critics, 68–9
  literary historians, 67
  work, 78
Fet, Afanasii, 29
  aesthetics, 16, 20–3
  Dobroliubov and, 15–2
  Grigor'ev and, 19–21
  influence of Nekrasov on, xv, 18
  influence of Turgenev on, xv, 18–21
    passim, 24
  musicality, 16, 18, 24
  'On the poetry of F. Tiutchev', 15, 17,
    19, 25

on critic and writer, 20–1
on Tiutchev, xii, xv, 15–25
on writer as critic, 17
polemic, 16, 19, 20
  Reminiscences, 19
Schopenhauer and, 17
  Sovremennik and, 16, 18
    see also Sovremennik
  see also Bukhshtab, B. Ia., Nekrasov,
    N., Turgenev, I.
feudalism, 175
Field, Andrew, 132
fin de siècle, 48
Finland
  Finnish, 170
Flaubert, Gustave, 136
Fleming, Stephen le, xvi
Fofanov, Konstantin, 35
folk, 95, 97, 107–6, 115
  hero, 8
    see also Lomonosov, M.
  poetry, 121
  tale, 73, 77
Formalist(s), 88, 95, 95–65
Forrester, Sibelan, xi, xv
Foucault, Michel, xvi
France, 117
  French, 71, 174
    classicism, xii, 6–8
    existentialist thought, 49
  see also Paris
Freud, Sigmund, 144
Frost, Robert, 123–4
Futurism
  Futurist(s), 84
  Cubo-futurist, 78

Gabriack, Cherubina de, 71, 78, 83
Garshin, Vsevolod, 34–5
Gaskell, Elizabeth, 69
gender, 70, 74–5, 81, 83–4, 87–90 *passim*
  identity, xiv
  -marked, 72, 96
  gendered voice, 78
genre
  dissolution of, xi
  of writer on writer, x
  see also autobiography, criticism,
    elegy, epic, literary
    essay,love poetry, memoirs, para-
    ble, parody, satire
Germany, 3
  German, 117, 119, 126–7
  romanticism, 62, 71, 83, 151
  see also Berlin, Leipzig
Gertsyk, Adelaida, 71–2, 76, 78, 83

Index

Gifford, Henry, xv
Gillespie, David, xvi
Gippius, Zinaida, 68, 71–2, 78, 83
   Merezhkovskii and, 32–3
Goethe, Johann Wolfgang von, 20, 24, 83
   Goethian, 33
Gogol', Nikolai, 131, 182
Goncharov, Ivan, 17, 45, 47
   'Better late than never', 17
Goncharova, Natal'ia, 71
Gorbachev, Mikhail, 181, 184
Gorbanevskaia, Natal'ia, 144, 148, 152
Gordin, Iakov, 142–3
Gor'kii, Maksim, 162–4, 171
   Chekhov and, 36–7
   Palace of Culture, 140
Gothic
   novels, 133
Grigor'ev, Apollon, 20–1
   as critic and poet, 19
   on Fet, 19
Gumilev, Nikolai, 83, 109, 141
   Akhmatova and, ix
   on Ivanov, xii, 51–65
   Pearls, 57–8
   Romanticheskie tsvety, 57
   Zhemchuga, 54
   see also Acmeism, Akhmatova, A.,
      Briusov, V., Ivanov, V.,
      symbolism
Gurevich, Liubov', 68, 73

Hegel, Georg Wilhelm Friedrich, 50
Heine, Heinrich, 20–16, 152
Heldt, Barbara, 67–2, 83–8, 89
Holy Synod, 2

idealism, 34–5, 43–7, 168
   idealist(s) 166–17
identity, 77, 81, 89, 90–41, 92, 97, 144
   change of, xiv
   female, 72, 79
   gender, xiv
impressionism
   impressionist(s), 35
Ivanov, Viacheslav, 78, 84–11, 88–30
   Cor Ardens, 51–8 *passim*, 62, 65
   Gumilev on, xii, 51–65
   influence on Gumilev, 53–7 *passim*,
      63–4
   Tender Mystery, 65
   'tower', x, 53, 53–6
   Transparency, 57–8
   see also Berdiaev, N., Gumilev, N.,
      mysticism, theosophy

Jackson, Robert, 41–2
   see also Chekhov, A., Shestov, L.
James, Henry, ix
Jew(s), 145–6
Jones, Gareth, xvi
Jones, Malcolm, xvi

Kantemir, Antiokh, 1–2, 6, 11, 13
Kaplan, Cora, 68, 73
Karamzin, Nikolai, x, 12
   Pantheon of Russian Writers, 10–13
   What is Necessary for an Author?, 10
Karlinsky, Simon, 82–3, 89, 94–58, 118,
      120, 125
Keats, John, 124
Kelly, Catriona, xiv
KGB, 181
Kheraskov, Mikhail, 11, 13
   Discourse on Russian Poetry, 9
Kheraskova, Elizaveta, 13
Khlebnikov, Velimir, 59
Khodasevich, Vladislav, 83–7, 96–66, 113
Kierkegaard, Soren Aaby, 49, 139
Kiev, 39, 115
Kirkwood, Mike, xiii
Komarovo, 111–13
Kozitskii, Georgii, 13
Kozlovskii, Fedor, 13
Kremlin, 103
Krivulin, Viktor, 140–1, 143, 149
Krolik, Feofil, 2, 13
Kublanovskii, Iurii, 146, 148, 152
Kulle, Viktor, 140, 149, 153
Kushner, Alexander, 139, 142, 146–7,
      150–1, 153
Kuz'min, V., 31
Kuzmin, Mikhail, 60
Kuz'mina-Karavaeva, Elizaveta, 70, 78

Lawrence, David Herbert, 47, 123
   Sons and Lovers, ix
'Learned Watch', 2, 4, 5, 13
Leipzig, 13
Lenin, Vladimir, 113
   see also Marx, K.
Leningrad, 111, 144
Lermontov, Mikhail, 30, 56, 56–14, 63,
      141, 177
literary essay, x–xii, 39, 68
Lomonosov, Mikhail, xvi, 2, 12
   as mythical/folk hero, 8–10
   death of, 3
   drunkenness, 5, 8
   *Letter on the Rules of Russian
      Versification*, 3

Sumarokov, Trediakovskii and, 2–13
  passim
Loseff, Lev, 141, 146, 149–52 *passim*
Lotman, Iurii, 10
love poetry, 74–5, 77
Lukács, Georg, xivn6
Lukin, Vladimir, 13
L'vova, Nadezhda, 70, 75–8

Maiakovskii, Vladimir, 83, 84–11, 86,
  89, 141, 151
Maikov, Vasilii, 13
Mandel'shtam, Nadezhda, 146
  memoirs, x, 114
Mandel'shtam, Osip, xi, xiii, 113, 122,
  127, 141, 147, 149
  Akhmatova, Pasternak, Tsvetaeva and,
    99–116
  as critic, 84–11
  Conversations about Dante, xiii, 121
  on Akhmatova, 115
  Sturm und Drang, 115
  The Egyptian Stamp, and Noise of
    Time, 113
  Verses on the Unknown Soldier, 102, 114
  see also Akhmatova, A., Tsvetaeva, M.
Marx, Karl, 144
  Marxism(-Leninism), 170
  Marxist(-Leninist), 163–4, 175
materialism, 34–5, 46–7
  materialist(ic), 33, 45
Maupassant, Guy de, 44
Meister, Charles, 40–1, 47
  see also Chekhov, A., Shestov, L.
memoirs, x, 70, 73–4, 81, 108
  see also Bashkirtseva, M.,
    Mandel'shtam, N.
Merezhkovskii, Dmitrii
  'An old question apropos of a new
    talent', 27
  Chekhov and, xii, xvi, 27–37
  On the Reasons for Decline and on
    New Trends in Contemporary
    Russian Literature, 33, 36
  Religious-Philosophical Society, 35
  reviewers and, 28
  Symbols, 32
  The Approaching Vandal, 36
  wife, 32–3
  see also Gippius, Z.
  see also Fofanov, K., Kuz'min, V.,
    Mikhailovskii, N., Pleshcheev, A.,
    Protopopov, M., Skabichevskii,
    symbolism, A., Uspenskii, G.
Mikhailovskii, Nikolai, 29, 31–2, 35, 47

Milosz, Czeslaw, 126
Miroliubov, Viktor, 36
modernism, 150
  modernist, 74, 79
  modernity, 84–12
Molière, 6, 8
  Les Femmes savantes, 7
Moscow, 33, 39, 161–2, 165–9 *passim*,
  180
  Academy, 6
  heart of Russia, 63
Munch, Edvard, 43
music, 30, 34, 37, 114, 124, 139, 141,
  151
  modern art and, 28
  Tsvetaeva and, 90
  see also Fet, A.
mysticism, 53
  mystic(al), 29, 33, 35, 37, 55, 57,
    59–60, 97, 173
myth, 96
  of Brodsky, 139–153
  mythological spirit, 9–10, 14

Nabokov, Vladimir, 149
  Despair, 131, 133, 135
  Dostoevskii and, xi, 131–7
  Invitation to a Beheading, 136
  Lectures on Russian Literature, 131
  Lolita, 136
  Look at the Harlequins!, 131
  reviews written in emigration, xiii
  The Defence, 136
  The Enchanter, 137
  The Eye, 135
  The Gift, 131, 135
  see also Boyd, B., Field, A.
Naiman, Anatolii, xiii, 140, 143, 145,
  149–52
nationalism
  national spirit, 33
  Russianness, 148
  Slav soul, 62–3
  'unrussianness', 134
naturalism, 34
  naturalistic, 57
Nechaev, Sergei, 164–8
  Catechism of a Revolutionary, 165–6
Nekrasov, Nikolai, xiii, 67
  Fet and, xv, 16, 18, 22, 23
New Testament, the, 49
New York, 115, 146
Nietzsche, Friedrich Wilhelm, 43–4, 55
nihilism, 47
Novikov, Nikolai, 12–13

Index

Essay at an Historical Dictionary of Russian Writers, 11
The Painter, 10

occultism, 53–7, 62
Old Testament
    Ecclesiastes, 143
    Proverbs, 105
Ostrovskii, Alexander, 176

parable, xi, 133
Paris, 71, 83–5, 101, 120
Parnok, Sofiia, 70, 72, 77–9, 83
    on Akhmatova, 74–5
parody, xi, 132, 135–7, 139
Pasternak, Boris, xiii, 141, 145, 151
    Aerial Ways, 105, 113, 115–16
    Akhmatova, Mandel'shtam, Tsvetaeva
        and, 99–116
    Doctor Zhivago, 113
    My Sister Life, 82, 85–6, 91
    Nobel Prize, 113
    Safe Conduct, 113
    see also Rilke, R. M., Stalin, I.,
        Tsvetaeva, M.
Paustovskii, Konstantin, 162
Pavlova, Karolina, 69, 71, 76, 83, 88–31
Pavlovskii, Aleksei, 90
'People's Will', 162, 164
perestroika, 181, 184
Peter the Great, 9
    first wife, 111–8
    Petrine values, 1
    post-Petrine reaction, 14
    pre-Petrine Russia, 2
    reforms, 1, 9
Petrov, Vasilii, 4, 13, 175
Pisarev, Dmitrii, 16–17, 67
Pisemskii, Aleksei, 17
Platonov, Andrei, 123
Pleshcheev, Anton, 27, 31, 33
Poe, Edgar Allan, 32
poet(s)
    -critic, 77, 83–4, 95
    nature, 22–3, 29
    poetic process, 82, 88
    prose of, xiii, 25
    reader and, 87, 92, 94
poetry
    as verse-criticism, xv
    philosophical, 55, 57
    practice of, 3
Poland
    Polish, 150
Polonskii, Iakov, 19

Polukhina, Valentina, xvi
populism
    populist(s), 32, 152, 165–6
positivism, 43–4, 164
    positivist(ic), 32, 34, 45–7
Prigov, Dmitrii, 147
Prokopovich, Feofan, 1–2, 6, 13
Protopopov, M., 27, 29
Pushkin, Aleksandr, xiii, 15, 56, 63, 71,
        76, 82–3, 95, 141, 144
    age of, the, xn2
    Brodsky and, 139, 143, 147, 151–3
    Byron and, ix
    Evgenii Onegin, xi
    Fet and, 20, 24
    mythologising of, xvi
    Tiutchev and, 21, 23

reader, the
    as writer, x, xv
    writer and, xiv–xv
    see also critic(s), poet(s), writer(s)
realism, 28, 34–5, 72–3, 123, 126, 150,
        176
    realist(s), 49, 69
    realistic, 122
Red Brigade, the, 166–7
Rein, Evgenii, 145–8 *passim*, 151–2
Rembrandt, Harmensz van Rijn, 20–16
revolution, the, 86, 122, 166, 174, 177
    post-, 83–8, 175, 183, 185
    pre-, 174–5, 183
    revolutionary, 49
Reyfman, Irina, 8–9, 12
Rilke, Rainer Maria, 83, 117
    Duineser Elegien, 117
    Pasternak and, 117, 125
    Sonette an Orpheus, 117
    Tsvetaeva and, 100–1, 117–30
Romanov, Konstantin, 19
romanticism, 54, 58, 174
    romantic, 76, 85, 137, 142
    see also Germany
Rostopchina, Evdokiia, 69, 76
Rozanov, Vasilii, xvi
Różewicz, Tadeusz, 126
Ruban, Vasilii, 4
Russia
    modern theatre, 13
    intelligentsia, 37, 139, 178
Russian Orthodox Church, 2, 101, 120,
        129
    see also Holy Synod
Russkoe slovo, 15, 19, 36
Russo-Japanese war, 49

Index

St Petersburg, 2, 32, 34, 36, 99, 165
Saltykov-Shchedrin, Mikhail, 169, 182
samizdat, 139
Sand, George, 69
Sartre, Jean-Paul, 145
satire, 1–8 *passim*, 118, 169, 181–2
Schiller, Johann Christoph Friedrich von,
   20, 24
Schopenhauer, Arthur, 17
Sedakova, Ol'ga, 142–3, 150
Severianin, Igor', 70, 78
Severnyi vestnik, 27, 31
Shakespeare, William, 76, 100, 104, 171
Shelgunov, Nikolai, 17–18
Shestov, Lev
   Apotheosis of Groundlessness, 39, 47
   Dostoevskii and Nietzsche: the
      Philosophy of Tragedy, 43
   on Chekhov, xvi, 39–50
   The Good in the Teaching of Tolstoi
      and Nietzsche: Philosophy
      and Preaching, 43
   Tsvetaeva and, 120, 123
   see also Diagilev, S., Dostoevskii, F.,
      existentialism, Jackson, R.,
      Meister, C., Nietzsche, F.,
      Tolstoi, L., *Voprosy zhizni*
Shostakovich, Dmitrii, 145
Shuvalov, Ivan, 4
Shvarts, Elena, 148, 151
Silver Age, the, x, 75, 83, 88–30
Skabichevskii, Aleksandr, 29
Socialist Realism, 164, 173
Solov'ev, Vladimir, 19
Soviet, 86, 95, 118, 153, 161, 174–80
   passim, 184–5
   critics, 90, 177
   literature, 164
   readers, 167
   reality, 173, 182
   society, 170, 175, 183
Sovremennik, 15–23 *passim*
   see also Fet, A.
Spasovich, Vladimir, 35
Stalin, Iosif, 162–3, 181, 184
   Pasternak and, 113
   post-Stalin, 142
Steiner, George, ix
Strakhov, Nikolai, 19
Sumarokov, Aleksandr
   Elegy to Mr Dmitrevskii on the Death
      of Mr Volkov, 13
   Epistles, 6, 13
   Lomonosov, Trediakovskii and, 3–13
      passim

nervous tic, 4, 11
'On Bad Rhymesters', 4
The Busy Bee, 3–4
Tresotinius, 7
Suvorin, Aleksei, 30–5 *passim*, 164
Switzerland, 165
   Swiss, 117
Symbolism, 32, 60–4 *passim*
   anti-Symbolist, 64
   post-Symbolist, 60, 71–2, 78–9
   Symbol(s) 34–5
   symbolist(s) 49, 52, 65, 68, 71–2,
      76–9, 82, 88–30, 89, 107–6
   symbolic, 57
   see also Ivanov, V., Merezhkovskii, D.

theosophy, 53, 53–7, 62
Tiutchev, Fedor
   as nature poet, 22–3
   Fet on, xii, xv, 15–25
   'poet of thought', 17, 22–4
   see also Pushkin, A.
Todorov, Tzvetan, xvi
Tolstoi, Lev, 33, 162, 171, 174
   Anna Karenina, 45
   Confession, 32
   'Death of Ivan Il'ich', 44
   Dostoevskii and, ix
   Fet and, 19
   Merezhkovskii and, 35
   Nietzsche and, 43
   philosophy of history, 49
   Shestov and, 44, 47
   War and Peace, 42, 45, 171
Trediakovskii, Vasilii, 2
   A Novel and Short Method for the
      Composition of Russian Verses, 3
   as anti-hero, 8–11
   as pedant, 12
   death of, 3
   Lomonosov, Sumarokov and, 3–13
      passim
   The Warmth of Spring, 5
Trifonov, Iurii
   And Quiet Flows the Don, 162
   Impatience, 162, 164, 166
   on Dostoevskii, 161–8
   Students, 163
   The Glow of the Campfire, 162
   The House on the Embankment, 162–3
   The Old Man, 162, 166
   The Overturned House, 163
   Time and Place, 162–3
Trudy i dni, 60
Tsar Alexander II, 165, 168

Index

tsarism, 175
Tsarskoe Selo, 112
Tsebrikova, Mariia, 69
Tsvetaeva, Marina, xiii, 69, 71, 74, 78,
    139, 141, 147, 151
    Akhmatova, Mandel'shtam, Pasternak
        and, 99–116, 117–18, 127–8
    'A Poet about Criticism/the Critic', 82,
        85, 92–8 *passim*
    as critic, 81–98
    autobiographical prose, 81
    critical essays, xi
    death of, 103, 105
    'Downpour of Light', 82, 86–7, 90–1
    Essay of a Room, 118
    From the Sea, 118
    'Hero of Labour', 82, 91
    Kirillovnas, 112
    musicality, 90, 129
    'Novogodnee', 100, 104, 106, 118–29
        passim
    on Akhmatova, 83, 108
    on Briusov, 70, 82–6 *passim*, 89, 92,
    on Mandel'shtam, 83
    on Pasternak, 83, 85–91, 99
    Pages from Tarusa, 112
    Poem of Air, 100–7 *passim*
    Poem of the End, 117–18
    Poem of the Staircase, 118, 128
    Poets, 121
    The Poet and Time, 122
    The Ratcatcher, 118
    The Swain, 73
    Verses to Akhmatova, 108–9
    view of reading, xv
    see also Brodsky, J., Maiakovskii, V.,
        Rilke, R. M., Shestov, L.,
        Symbolism
Turgenev, Ivan, 17, 22–3, 33, 35, 171
    Chekhov and 39
    Fet and, xv, 16, 18–19, 21, 21–17
    Henry James and, ix
Tvardovskii, Aleksandr, xiii

Ufliand, Vladimir, 141, 146, 150
Uspenskii, Gleb, 32

Veinberg, P., 35
Vladimov, Georgii, 171
Volkov, Fedor, 13
Voloshin, Maksimilian, 71, 78, 83, 84–10

Voprosy zhizni, 39
Voznesenskii, Andrei, 147, 182

Wellek, Réné, 84–11, 88, 90
West, the, 130, 134, 142, 145, 149, 170
    Western
        critics, 43, 79, 161
        culture, 86
        philosophy, 47
        readers, 49
    Westerners, 181
Wollstonecraft, Mary, 69
women writers, Russian, xiv, 93
    as critics of women writers, 67–79
    see also Akhmatova, A., L'vova, N.,
        Parnok, S., Tsvetaeva, M.
women's writing, 70, 74, 76
    development of, 79
    history of, 67
    status, 68
    literary tradition, 67
writer(s)
    as critic, ix–xvi *passim*, 17, 68, 73–4,
        79, 95, 175
        see also critic(s)
    as political force, 1–2
    as reader, x, xv
    as teacher, x, 133
    attacking writer, xi, 4, 6–7
    critic/reader and, xiv–xv, 17, 20, 51,
        63, 90, 94, 98
        see also Fet, A., Gumilev, N.
    on writer, x–xvii *passim*, 51
    privileged status of, xiv
    prominence in society, 1, 95
writing 'profession', the, x–xiii, 68

Yalta, 39
Yeats, William Butler, xiii

Zhadovskaia, Iuliia, 76
Zinov'ev, Aleksandr Aleksandrovich
    Confessions d'un homme en trop, 180
    Katastroika, 181
    Notes of a Nightwatchman, 174
    on Chekhov, xiii, 169–85
    On the Threshold of Paradise, 172,
        180
    The Madhouse, 172, 180
    The Yawning Heights, 170, 172–3